SOLIDARITY IN
BIOMEDICINE AND BEYOND

In times of global economic and political crises, the notion of solidarity is gaining new currency. This book argues that a solidarity-based perspective can help us to find new ways to address pressing problems. Exemplified by three cases studies from the field of biomedicine: databases for health and disease research, personalised healthcare and organ donation, it explores how solidarity can make a difference in how we frame problems, and in the policy solutions that we can offer.

BARBARA PRAINSACK is Professor of Sociology at the Department of Global Health & Social Medicine at King's College London. Her work looks at social, ethical and regulatory aspects of bioscience and biomedicine, often giving a voice to alternative or marginalised perspectives. She is a member of the National Bioethics Council in Austria, and the Ethics Group at the UK National DNA Database.

ALENA BUYX is Professor of Biomedical Ethics and Co-Director of the Institute of Experimental Medicine, Christian-Albrechts-Universität zu Kiel, Germany. She directs several bioethics research projects; provides local, national and international research and clinical ethics advisory; and publishes and lectures widely. Alena is member of the German Ethics Council and the National Ethics Commission of the German Medical Association.

CAMBRIDGE BIOETHICS AND LAW

This series of books was founded by Cambridge University Press with Alexander McCall Smith as its first editor in 2003. It focuses on the law's complex and troubled relationship with medicine across both the developed and the developing world. Since the early 1990s, we have seen in many countries increasing resort to the courts by dissatisfied patients and a growing use of the courts to attempt to resolve intractable ethical dilemmas. At the same time, legislatures across the world have struggled to address the questions posed by both the successes and the failures of modern medicine, while international organisations such as the WHO and UNESCO now regularly address issues of medical law.

It follows that we would expect ethical and policy questions to be integral to the analysis of the legal issues discussed in this series. This series responds to the high profile of medical law in universities, in legal and medical practice, as well as in public and political affairs. We seek to reflect the evidence that many major health-related policy debates in the United Kingdom, Europe and the international community involve a strong medical law dimension. With that in mind, we seek to address how legal analysis might have a trans-jurisdictional and international relevance. Organ retention, embryonic stem-cell research, physician-assisted suicide and the allocation of resources to fund healthcare are but a few examples among many. The emphasis of this series is thus on matters of public concern and/or practical significance. We look for books that could make a difference to the development of medical law and enhance the role of medico-legal debate in policy circles. That is not to say that we lack interest in the important theoretical dimensions of the subject, but we aim to ensure that theoretical debate is grounded in the realities of how the law does and should interact with medicine and healthcare.

Series Editors
Professor Margaret Brazier, *University of Manchester*
Professor Graeme Laurie, *University of Edinburgh*
Professor Richard Ashcroft, *Queen Mary, University of London*
Professor Eric M. Meslin, *Indiana University*

SOLIDARITY IN BIOMEDICINE AND BEYOND

BARBARA PRAINSACK

King's College London, UK

ALENA BUYX

University of Kiel, Germany

CAMBRIDGE
UNIVERSITY PRESS

CAMBRIDGE
UNIVERSITY PRESS

University Printing House, Cambridge CB2 8BS, United Kingdom

One Liberty Plaza, 20th Floor, New York, NY 10006, USA

477 Williamstown Road, Port Melbourne, VIC 3207, Australia

314-321, 3rd Floor, Plot 3, Splendor Forum, Jasola District Centre, New Delhi - 110025, India

79 Anson Road, #06-04/06, Singapore 079906

Cambridge University Press is part of the University of Cambridge.

It furthers the University's mission by disseminating knowledge in the pursuit of education, learning and research at the highest international levels of excellence.

www.cambridge.org
Information on this title: www.cambridge.org/9781107424784
DOI: 10.1017/9781139696593

First published 2017
First paperback edition 2018

A catalogue record for this publication is available from the British Library

Library of Congress Cataloging in Publication data
Names: Prainsack, Barbara, author. | Buyx, Alena, author.
Title: Solidarity in biomedicine and beyond / Barbara Prainsack, Alena Buyx.
Description: Cambridge, United Kingdom ; New York, NY, USA : Cambridge
    University Press, 2017. | Includes bibliographical references and index.
Identifiers: LCCN 2016032816 | ISBN 9781107074248 (hardback)
Subjects: | MESH: Biomedical Research | Cooperative Behavior | Group Processes
Classification: LCC R850 | NLM W 20.5 | DDC 610.72/4—dc23 LC record
available at https://lccn.loc.gov/2016032816

ISBN 978-1-107-07424-8 Hardback
ISBN 978-1-107-42478-4 Paperback

CONTENTS

FOREWORD

For many of us – those of us of a certain age, at least – our first meaning-ful encounter with the term *solidarity* was in the early 1980s, with the rapid emergence of the Polish trade union, *Solidarność*. From our per-spective in the United Kingdom, it seemed almost ironic that one of the most prominent resistance movements in Eastern Europe should take *solidarity* as its banner in opposing a government which, one would have thought, should have itself been rooted in solidaristic ideals. Instead, in many communist countries, references to solidarity were abused to sup-port grave injustices.

Of course, solidarity has a much longer, broader and even more complex history than this, as Alena Buyx and Barbara Prainsack make clear. But the upshot of its use in the context of the Eastern European upheaval was that solidarity was a term that belonged mainly to political philosophy and principally to politics of the left at a time when UK politics – along with the politics of much of the West – was beginning its long drift to the right.

Speaking from a UK perspective, even though we had in the NHS and the welfare state institutions that were arguably among the most solidar-istic anywhere in the world, we became rather confused as to whether appeals to solidarity had moved beyond the bounds of respectable public discourse. It was a term that could be used in localised, interpersonal contexts, but there was some unease with its use at a societal level, given some of the practices that some political regimes had used it to justify. We did, nevertheless, look to other parts of Europe and admire the way with which *solidarité* seemed to permeate at all levels and signify fights *against* oppression and inequality, and *for* social justice. Or maybe that was just me.

In the meantime, *bioethics* was a youth, finding its way in a world that was losing many of its old certainties. We were no longer so confident that we should simply do what our doctor said. We were no longer sure that science would deliver progress that was an unqualified good. And we were no longer sure (if ever, indeed, we had been) that our interests as individuals and as communities and societies were adequately protected by those in authority. But what had emerged in bioethics up until then had largely been based on an individualistic approach to ethics, whether through a human rights base in Europe, or an autonomy-based approach in the United States.

But increasingly, the idea that bioethics could and should engage a more public perspective took hold – a question of public good that is distinct from the protection of, or negotiation between, individual interests. The Nuffield Council on Bioethics (the UK's *de facto* national ethics council and one of the oldest such institutions), whilst never having committed itself to a particular approach or set of principles (rather, constructing an ethical framework for each case at hand) found itself in precisely this place – where individual and societal interests are both engaged – when it published its report on Public Health (2007).

Given the backdrop of solidarity as a concept used mainly in a political context, it should be no surprise, perhaps, that it was in the discussion of the underlying political philosophy that the Council first called on solidarity in support of its bioethical analysis. Actually it settled on the term 'the value of community' as expressing what it saw as the extended role of the classic liberal state: '... some speak of "fraternity," others of "solidarity." We prefer the term "community" which is the value of belonging to a society in which each person's welfare, and that of the whole community, matters to everyone.'

Having moved in that direction, we then continued on the path. In subsequent reports – notably Dementia (2009), Medical Profiling and Online Medicine (2010), Biofuels (2011) and Human Bodies (2011) – solidarity was referred to and employed more specifically and directly.

So it was that in 2010 the Council felt that if we were to use solidarity as a core value and principle in our work, we should try to find it a more comfortable home in the wider lexicon of contemporary bioethics. We should try to find, or at least help to find, a more settled understanding of it, and not just at a conceptual level, but also in its practical application in bioethics. That is, to bring together its political meaning and its use as a matter of practical ethics, not least because ethics is intrinsically a political activity.

So we engaged Buyx and Prainsack in their respective roles – Buyx as the project lead on solidarity within the Council and Prainsack as a research fellow. Working in this way, and on a cross-cutting concept rather than a scientific or technological development, was a new departure for the Council. But it has been an extremely positive one – and we have since repeated it in a similar fashion in looking at 'naturalness', another concept with a long history but an uncertain use in bioethics.

Their early work on solidarity, with an initial report for the Council in November 2011 and subsequent papers, contributed the first examination of the meaning of solidarity and how it can and should be used in concrete contexts. As Prainsack and Buyx themselves put it back then – uncovering its descriptive use(s) and its prescriptive role. The report generated a lot of debate and the Council was very pleased to see its international impact – academic citations, papers and conferences devoted to the report's solidarity framework and, increasingly and probably most importantly, references in the policy world.

That Prainsack and Buyx have achieved all that is very much to their credit, as is the fact they have persisted in their work – listening, engaging, responding and adapting. Here, in this important new book, they have extended the theoretical analysis of solidarity in its descriptive and normative/prescriptive aspects, and have also extended the debate to new fields of application – health databases, personalised healthcare and transplantation/donation. So in addition to further refining their theoretical solidarity framework, their case studies highlight the potential of solidarity to be applied – usefully, and concretely – to pressing issues in biomedicine, both classical and emerging ones.

This book is a significant step in their work and in the contribution it makes to the wider academic and policy debates. The authors usefully show both what solidarity is, and what it does or can do, exploring complex issues of ethics and policy making in accessible language and always with a view to the real world. This is particularly striking with a term like solidarity, one with such a colourful history, and that has so often been (mis-)used for partisan political ends, or in vaguely idealistic ways. Giving solidarity firm meaning and divesting it of many of its past connotations enables academics, practitioners and policy makers to usefully work with the term in many different contexts. The case studies in the book offer clear examples, but there is still much further to go, more ways and places in which it can be employed. Indeed, the greatest achievement of Prainsack and Buyx's work is perhaps to have broadened and also 'restored' the applicability of the concept of solidarity so as to give it purchase globally, and far beyond the realm of biomedicine.

I feel privileged to have played some small part in this, and pleased to have been associated with the work at its early stages before it developed into something with such real-world application. Which just about enables me to contrive a conclusion in the form of a quote from Lech Walesa, the leader of *Solidarność*, and later President of Poland: 'The supply of words in the world market is plentiful but the demand is falling. Let deeds follow words now.' Well, this is a book, and so it is inevitably full of words, but it is notable that this important contribution extends from what the word solidarity *means* to what it *signifies*, whilst inviting a much more practical look at what it *does*.

Hugh Whittall
Nuffield Council on Bioethics, UK

Solidarity: A Brief History
of A Concept and A Project

1.1   Introduction

Solidarity is gaining currency at the moment. Against the background of global economic crises, climate change and environmental disasters, and armed conflicts, we hear calls for solidarity with increasing frequency. Global solidarity, national solidarity, or solidarity with refugees are causes that are becoming more prominent in public discourse after solidarity seems to have worked silently in the background for the last decades: as a principle guiding the design of health and social care systems in Europe and beyond, as a value that informs resource allocation or as a societal ideal.

The background assumption of this book is that in times of global crises we do indeed need more, and not less, solidarity. This is particularly true in the case of medicine, healthcare and the biomedical sciences. In these areas, mutual assistance and support in the face of human vulnerability play central roles. People helping each other in times of need, supporting disease research or organising communal healthcare, to name but a few examples, have all been described as practices of solidarity.

But what *is* solidarity? Within the wide literature on solidarity, it is used in different contexts, to support different goals and with many different meanings. Most authors treat solidarity as a prosocial notion. But beyond this small denominator, there is no unity. Some authors see solidarity as an emotion, others as a moral ideal, a 'natural' characteristic of groups or societies, a political idea or a regulatory concept – and some criticise it as an empty label. The meaning of solidarity seems difficult to pin down. Like with some of the fundamental concepts in our lives, such as love or friendship, most people have an intuitive understanding of what they mean, and yet they would struggle to define them. To some extent, this 'vagueness' is productive: Because love and friendship – and, as we will argue, solidarity – matter to everyone, these words must be open enough to accommodate a wide range of experiences, feelings and practices. Yet at the same time they need to be specific and firm enough, as concepts,

to serve as points of reference to justify or explain actions. This is particularly important in connection to solidarity: while love and friendship
denote explicitly personal and 'private' relations, solidarity is frequently
invoked in regulatory and policy-making contexts, e.g. in the organisation of social care, healthcare or research. Here, leaving the meaning of
solidarity under-determined limits the utility of the concept for policy and
practice considerably.

1.2   A Concise Overview of the History of Solidarity

One possible reason for the under-determination of the notion of solidarity in most of the literature is that the concept itself has a very patterned history in Western thought, without the continuity of debate and
development that other terms have had, such as justice, responsibility,
freedom or liberty. While solidarity appeared as a concept in Roman law[1]
and subsequently influenced legal codes in several European countries, an
understanding of the term that resembles contemporary, more political
iterations, does not appear until the early eighteenth century (and then
soon shows its versatility and affinity to influence many different disciplines and contexts). Often, articles or books addressing solidarity begin
to recount its history by referring to the increasing use and currency of the
term *solidarité* during the French Revolution. As Norwegian social policy
scholar Steinar Stern pointed out, the meaning and use of the concept of
solidarité was extended into the political realm by revolutionary leaders
and thinkers of the later eighteenth century (Stern 2005).

In 1842, French journalist and utopian socialist Hippolyte Renaud published a pamphlet titled *Solidarité* in which he criticised the manner in
which exponents of opposing ideologies posed their arguments. Drawing
upon the work of the socialist thinker Charles Fourier, he argued that both
sides were overlooking that many of their goals were in fact aligned, and
that all humans were connected in their pursuit of well-being. Renaud's
book helped to spread the idea of solidarity beyond the borders of France,
especially into Germany and England, where it was taken up by socialist
and workers' movements. The idea of solidarity underpinned early trade
union developments and has played an important role in Marxist and

[1] Etymologically, the term solidarity stems from the Roman law concept of *in solidum*, which
signified that a contract was joint between two or several creditors or debtors, see Bayertz
(1999: 3).

socialist rhetoric, often with the distinguishing feature of a disregard for national borders, to achieve mutual support among all workers.[2]

The French 'father of sociology', Auguste Comte, with his book *System of Positive Polity* (1875 [1851]) greatly increased the visibility of the term solidarity and cemented its importance in the wider field of the social sciences. Comte saw solidarity as a remedy for the increasing individualisation and atomisation of society, which he considered detrimental to the well-being of the collective. Comte's work on solidarity has influenced most of the scholarship on solidarity after him, including Emile Durkheim's distinction between mechanical and organic solidarity, which he developed in *The Division of Labour in Society* (1893). People in early societies, prior to the division of labour, Durkheim argued, were bound together by the feeling of sameness; they did the same work, were part of the same family or fought against the same natural threats. This situation he termed 'mechanical solidarity'. The increasing specialisation of work, however, which went hand-in-hand with changes in how and where people lived, altered the nature of ties between people. Durkheim referred to this latter situation as 'organic solidarity', to signify that people were bonded together by being dependent on each other. Durkheim in turn influenced the understandings of solidarity by many others in the emerging discipline of the social sciences (see Chapter 2).

Another important field contributing to the early development of solidaristic ideas and uses of the term was Christian thought. The Catholic notion of solidarity, for example, with its strong roots in Thomas Aquinas' work, stressing community and fellowship between all human beings, was meant to be a normative principle for the organisation of communal life. As writers such as German Catholic ethicist and economist Heinrich Pesch pointed out in his *Teaching Guide to Economics* (1905–23, vol. 5), solidarity reflected the deep interconnectedness of all of creation, and the individual's God-given orientation towards and need of community and social life. The fellowship of friars in Catholic orders, whose fates were tied to one another in very immediate ways, served as an ideal for how people sharing a particular situation should feel connected to each other, and assist each other. This type of solidarity thus captured an important element that persists in contemporary understandings of solidarity, namely the idea of

---

[2] A continuation of the Marxist and socialist traditions of solidarity among all members of a 'class' with no regard for national borders can be found, for example, in transnational movements opposing global capitalism (see for example Notes from Nowhere 2003; Renaud 2010).

fellowship of people who recognise important similarities between each other. This stands in contrast to the asymmetrical relationship that underpins the idea of charity, for example. There are different nuances to the specific meaning of solidarity in different Christian traditions, and many more in other than Christian faiths (see e.g. Kliksberg 2003; Leff 2006; Moses 2006; Schwarz 2009). However, in most, if not all, religious traditions, the notion of solidarity is connected to discussions of social justice, the fellowship of all beings (or all believers) created in the image of God and assistance to those in need. In other words, within these traditions, solidarity assumes the role of a religious-moral imperative to assist others in their quests for social justice, and more generally, for leading a good life.

This very short historical overview highlights several important elements of the meaning of solidarity that appear, in different guises, in many different contexts and traditions. These elements are also still relevant today. They are: a sense of being 'bound together', e.g. by sharing similar objectives or circumstances; mutual assistance and help, particularly in situations of hardships; symmetric relationships between those engaged in solidary practices at the moment of enacting solidarity (i.e. despite other parts of their lives not being equal or even similar) and a link to both individual and collective well-being. We will pick up some aspects of the history of solidarity again in the next three chapters, where we discuss scholarship on solidarity in the twentieth century. In these chapters, we also sketch debates in the social and political sciences and in philosophy that have influenced this scholarship. Due to the Western etymology of the notion of solidarity, this book focuses largely on Western thought and writing. Within this tradition we cite primarily the English-speaking literature. We thereby exclude rich areas of inquiry, for example the literature on the solidarity economy from Latin America and other non-English-speaking regions.

1.3   Why Solidarity? Our Previous Work on Solidarity for the Nuffield Council on Bioethics

The increasing use of solidarity in public and policy-relevant debates at the beginning of our century, particularly in the field of health and medicine, did not remain unnoticed by policy makers and civil society organisations. Nor did the peculiar fact that while references to solidarity kept popping up in public and academic discourse, there was a distinct lack of clarity about what it meant – and more importantly, what it should 'do' in the field of biomedicine and health. In 2010, the Nuffield Council on

Bioethics (NCoB) – Britain's *de facto* national ethics council, and one of the oldest and best-known bioethics councils in the world – decided to respond to the growing visibility of the term by commissioning a working paper on solidarity in bioethics. The Council had been using solidarity in several of its previous reports, including the report on Public Health in 2007, the report on Dementia in 2009 and the report on Biofuels in 2011. Reflecting the heterogeneity of uses in many other fields, however, there was no consistency in how the term was used, nor was it entirely clear how it had influenced policy recommendations in the reports. Under the leadership of its Chair at the time, Albert Weale, and its Director, Hugh Whittall, the Council took the view that there was likely significant potential for the term to inform important ethical and policy debates in biomedicine and health, but that this potential had not yet been fully explored. While there was awareness of the small yet distinguished literature in biomedical ethics that had devoted specific attention to solidarity in health policy, medical ethics and related areas, this had not, it was felt, influenced to a sufficient extent discussions at the intersection of ethical analysis and policy development. For these reasons, the intended working paper on solidarity was supposed to provide an overview of how solidarity had so far permeated recent bioethical writings, as well as relevant scholarship in related fields. The Council also hoped that it should help distinguish the concept of solidarity from other such terms, including 'altruism', 'charity' etc. These clarifications would then pave the way for future uses of the concept of solidarity in Council reports.

With generous funding from the Nuffield Foundation and the UK Arts and Humanities Research Council (AHRC), a fellowship was instigated. One of us (AB) developed and oversaw the project as Assistant Director of the Council at the time, while the other (BP) became the Council's Solidarity Fellow for six months. We thus had the pleasure of working together on the solidarity working paper. Our enthusiasm for the project was such that it quickly outgrew the working paper format, resulting in the Report *Solidarity – reflections on an emerging concept in bioethics*,[3] published in 2011. This we put together fairly quickly, owing to the original timeline, while exceeding our brief significantly. In the following section, we present a short summary of some of the main findings from the literature review, which formed the first part of the Report (Prainsack and Buyx 2011).

---

[3] Hereafter any reference to Report (with a capital R) refers to our solidarity report from 2011.

1.4   Solidarity as an Emerging Concept
in Recent Bioethical Writing

We arrived at our findings in the Report via two routes: first, a systematic analysis of the literature,[4] and second, a wealth of verbal and written expert input from two large workshops; from Council members and staff and from many others who provided comments and peer review. Very broadly, to give a flavour of the results of our analyses, we found that despite the fact that the frequency of mentions of the term solidarity had indeed increased in public and academic discourse, in bioethical writings specifically, explicit references were relatively rare. This was particularly striking compared with other terms such as autonomy, justice, privacy, identity, which were all addressed prominently and explicitly. We hypothesised that with more explicit focus on solidarity and more analysis of what solidarity means and what it can do in bioethical discourse and policy making, its rise to prominence could be expected to continue further.

Our Report found that where solidarity was addressed explicitly, its meaning was heterogeneous and often unclear (note that we excluded from our analysis works that used solidarity only once, e.g. as a keyword or a programmatic 'flag' in the title, without ever returning to or discussing the term). Most explicit uses of solidarity fell into one of two categories: (i) descriptive: referring to the existence of social cohesion within a particular group; or (ii) prescriptive: calling for more social cohesion within a group. If the meaning of the term was taken to be descriptive, typically as describing an empirical fact – i.e. that particular people are tied together by bonds of mutual assistance, shared goals or other aspects of a situation that they share – then solidarity was often seen as a precondition for all social and political life. If the term was used in a prescriptive manner, for example in normative calls for mutual support within a specific group of people, or for more social cohesion in society as a whole, the assessment of the value and importance of solidarity typically took on a more explicitly political form (Prainsack and Buyx 2011, Chapter 3).

Similarly, we found that solidarity was taken to apply to a great variety of different instances and groups, ranging from solidarity within a family to solidarity with all people in the world, or even all living creatures.[5] At the same time, there was little scholarship within bioethics that discussed, either

---

[4] The methodology used is described in detail in Prainsack and Buyx (2011).
[5] Attention to the latter has grown further since the publication of our Report, also in the context of the One Health movement (see e.g. Rock and Degeling 2015; Zinsstag et al. 2011).

empirically or conceptually, how group identities and notions of belonging emerge. Where such discussions existed, explicit references to solidarity appeared mainly in four different contexts within the bioethical literature. The first context was public health, where solidarity was regularly used to justify the comparably strong interference of state authorities with the personal freedom of people, compared to other areas of medicine (e.g. mandatory vaccinations, restrictions on the freedom of movement in case of pandemics, etc.). The second context in which solidarity was often referred to explicitly comprises discussions about justice and equity of healthcare systems. Here, solidarity was typically seen as a value or principle that could justify certain rationales of resource allocation. Third, solidarity was also often invoked normatively in connection with providing assistance to poor countries and societies in the context of global health. Fourth and finally, we also found frequent discussions of solidarity as a European, as opposed to an American, value. This latter point cut across all other thematic domains: it became pertinent when authors contrasted European healthcare systems with US healthcare, or when the role of autonomy in bioethics was discussed (Table 1.1).

In our 2011 Report we also reflected on the fact that these four contexts in which discussions of solidarity were more prominent than in other fields are relatively young – or, as was the case with Public Health Ethics, at least recently strongly growing – areas of exploration in bioethics. To our minds, it was no coincidence that solidarity rose to greater prominence over the last decades, since this was exactly the time during which the four areas developed from smaller sidelines of bioethical scholarship into full-blown debates spanning the entire discipline and engaging academics, policy makers and the public in equal measure. All four areas invite invocations of solidarity because their central focus is not the individual patient but the health of societies or of all humankind.

We found that most of the authors writing about solidarity in the four contexts did so with a distinct aim of regarding solidarity's importance and use. They called for further attention to solidarity when discussing bioethical and social questions, or even for its protection against threats such as the increasing individualisation within modern (welfare) states (see e.g. Aarden et al. 2010; Ashcroft et al. 2000; Baylis et al. 2008; Calhoun 2002; Capaldi 1999; Coleman 1990; Gibbon and Novas 2007; Gunson 2009; Houtepen and Ter Meulen 2000a, Husted 1999; Putnam 1993, 1995, 2000; Rabinow 1992, 1996; Rippe 1998; Scholz 2008; Ter Meulen et al. 2010; UNESCO 2005). Others were more critical towards the use of the concept of solidarity, with the main critique often levelled not at the concept itself, but at its use in order to justify a particular goal or conduct

Table 1.1 *Four contexts in which discussions of solidarity play an important role in the bioethical and related literature (based on analysis in Prainsack and Buyx 2011)*

Context	Some Important Examples[a]
Context 1: Solidarity and public health ethics	Anand et al. (2004); Baylis et al. (2008); Bengtsson et al. 2011; Callahan (2003); Callahan and Jennings (2002); Childress et al. (2002); Churchill (2002); Coggon (2010); Craig (2011); Dean (1996); De Wachter (1998); Faden and Shebaya (2010); Holm (n.d.); Houtepen and ter Meulen (2000b); Institute of Medicine (1988); Jennings (2001, 2007); Kelsen (1967); NCoB (2007, 2009); O'Neill (2002, 2003); Petrini (2009, 2010a, 2010b); Petrini et al. (2010); Petrini and Gainotti (2008); Powers and Faden (2006); Roberts and Reich (2002); Rousseau (1988[1762]); Sen (1999); Shalev (2010); Sherwin (1998); Singer et al. (2003); Stirrat and Gill (2005); Tauber (2002); Widdows (2011); Young (1990)
Context 2: Solidarity and healthcare systems	Anand et al. (2004); Bonnie et al. (2010); Rose (1996, 1999, 2006); Schmidt (2008); Schuyt (1995); Ter Meulen et al. (2010); Tinghög et al. (2010); Trappenburg (2000); Van Hoyweghen and Horstman (2010); Van der Made et al. (2010); Wikler (2004)
Context 3: Solidarity and global health	Benatar et al. (2003); Aulisio (2006); Barry (2001); Brunkhorst (2005); Daniels (2008); Glasner and Rothman (2001); Gostin et al. (2010); Gould (2007, 2010); Gunson (2009); Harmon (2006); Hellsten (2008); Holm and William-Jones (2006); Verkerk and Lindemann (2010); Pensky (2007); Ruger (2006); Santoro (2009); Scholz (2008); UNESCO (2005); Verkerk and Lindemann (2010); Weale (1990); Widdows (2011)
Context 4: Solidarity as a European value	Beauchamp and Childress (2008); Boshammer and Kayß (1998); Castells (1996); Daniels (2006); Häyry (2003, 2004, 2005); Hermerén (2008); Hinrichs (1995); Holm (1995); O'Neill (2002); Sass (1992); Tomasini (2010)

[a]This table is meant to offer interested readers a quick overview of key publications in each context. It is not a comprehensive list of all relevant publications in the field.

(e.g. Aarden et al. 2010; Capaldi 1999; Husted 1999). Several authors criticised that solidarity was too vague to justify anything (e.g. Gunson 2009, also Rippe 1998). In addition, some objections to solidarity focused on its substantive content as such and marked it as inherently anti-individualistic (e.g. Capaldi 1999; Heyd 2007).

In addition to these findings, we observed that social, economic or natural crises seemed to lead to a greater prominence of reflections on solidarity and what it meant. Thus, attention to solidarity seemed to increase exactly at a time when solidarity itself was assumed to be in danger of disappearing (see Chapter 3). This, we found, was the case in public discourse, as well as in policy documents, and several authors remarked on the interplay of crises and solidarity (see e.g. Roemer 2009; Schuyt 1995; Van Hoyweghen 2010).

1.5 Looking Ahead: Our Working Definition of Solidarity and Three Case Studies

While engaging with the writings summarised earlier, we discovered that there was still some scope to add to the clarity of the debate around solidarity in biomedical ethics. We also felt that it was challenging to suggest a notion of solidarity for the Council's future ethical and policy-related work based on our analysis of existing literature, due to the heterogeneity of uses we had found in the field. This, then, led us to a departure from our original brief: we developed our own working definition of solidarity. Our aim in doing so was dual. We wanted to capture all the elements we felt were specific and unique to solidarity, and thus to improve the analytic clarity of the concept. In addition, in view of the Council's interest in utilising solidarity more in future reports, we also sought to arrive at a definition that could be applied directly and fruitfully to policy development in biomedicine and beyond.

With this in mind, we put together a definition of solidarity that was, of course, not 'made up from scratch'; this would not have done justice to the many rich accounts we encountered during our work on the Report. Instead, we brought together several central elements from other, earlier definitions, while putting emphasis on what we believed set solidarity apart, importantly, from related concepts. The understanding we sketched out we then applied to three case studies, in order to show the potential for solidarity – in our understanding – to add new perspectives to longstanding and complex bioethical debates and to help develop innovative policy solutions. We found the biggest potential for this in our first case study on research biobanks. Solidarity, we argued, captured the prosocial disposition and motivation of many participants in such research initiatives. There was also significant potential to apply solidarity to several major ethical and practical problems that the field of research biobanking had been grappling with. We proposed to include solidarity as an important principle in the governance of biobanking, and we suggested a number of practical changes that result from such a solidarity-based approach to biobank governance. We have continued our focus on this area, refined our thinking and expanded it towards including all health-related databases (see Prainsack and Buyx 2013; and Chapter 5).

In the second case study in the Report for the Council, we examined solidarity in connection with global pandemics. Here we found, due to the great differences in risks, benefits and costs over the relatively short time span of a pandemic, that the potential to mobilise solidarity was more limited. Solidarity can play an important role in the prevention and containment of pandemics at the interpersonal level, but for state intervention, particularly for binding norms, we argued that other concepts and arguments need to be referred to in order to justify these. This case study, with its conclusions that were surprising to some – certainly also to us initially – drew some criticism, which we have responded to in other publications (e.g. Prainsack and Buyx 2012b) and which we engage with in some detail in Chapters 3 and 4.

The third case study included in our Report examined the often-heard argument that those responsible for their own ill health, due to poor lifestyle choices or reckless behaviour, are harming publicly funded healthcare by imposing the costs of their self-imposed health issues on everyone else who is contributing to the system. We showed that this is a frequently misunderstood application of solidarity to the healthcare context, which rests on a flawed and narrow conception of the risks involved. We argued that an argument based on solidarity would come to an almost opposite conclusion, namely that a solidarity-based approach to lifestyle-related diseases would mandate that we foreground what people share in common, instead of what sets them apart. We concluded that stratification on the basis of alleged responsibility for lifestyle 'choice' has no place in a public healthcare system (Buyx and Prainsack 2012). Although we continue working on this topic, we did not include it as a dedicated chapter in this book. Our aim for this volume was to broaden the range of our case studies to show in what varied fields and contexts a solidarity-based approach can suggest new ways of framing problems, and show new solutions.

1.6   Overview of this Book: Solidarity, Theory and Practice

As we have summarised earlier, in our Report for the Nuffield Council, we discussed contemporary bioethical accounts of solidarity and then developed our own definition of solidarity, applying it to three practical case studies (Prainsack and Buyx 2011). Since our Report was based on merely one six-month long project, there were, inevitably, things that our initial project could not do: we did not, for example, situate our understanding of solidarity explicitly within the larger strands of thinking on the individual and the self; on society and community; on inclusion, exclusion and difference; on central concepts such as autonomy, or justice; or on political entities such as the welfare state. Neither did we explain in sufficient depth and detail the normativity of our account.

1.6.1   *Theory*

In this book, we attempt to close this gap. We do this in the following way: in the next chapter, we give a broad overview of prominent theories and accounts from the social sciences, philosophy and related fields, with a focus on the central themes, ideas and arguments that have contributed to understandings of solidarity generally, and to our own account specifically. By doing so we prepare the ground for our understanding of solidarity, and show how our understanding of solidarity builds upon and extends some prominent lines of thought that have played out in substantive and often controversial debates over the last 50 years. Not all of these accounts – in fact, few of these – focus on solidarity specifically. Even in those cases where authors do not address solidarity explicitly, however, they discuss the themes, ideas and concepts which are central to solidarity overall, and which we sought to integrate into our account.

Against this intellectual background, we then introduce our own account of solidarity (Chapter 3). Over the last few years, we have continued to develop our approach further, to deepen and refine our definition of solidarity, and to address some issues that were pointed out to us by our critics. We believe that this has improved our conception of solidarity, made it clearer, and also laid the ground for more in-depth policy application. In Chapter 3 we also take some time to respond to some of our critics.

The fourth chapter then provides a discussion of specifically normative accounts of solidarity. By this we mean accounts of solidarity that are normative in that they specify what solidarity should be about, or those that argue that solidarity is (always) a good thing. We discuss such accounts under three broad headings (deontic group solidarity; political solidarity and universal solidarity) and examine how they inform, and also how they contrast with our own approach. Several of the themes presented in Chapter 2 are picked up again at this point, and several authors that we mentioned previously are also discussed here, but with a particular view to normative versions of solidarity and the related arguments. This was missing from our earlier work and we gladly take the opportunity here to provide some in-depth engagement with this important aspect of the debate around solidarity.

Our own approach is thus bracketed by engagement with the 'social', more descriptive, and the moral-philosophical, more normative work by many influential thinkers. For example, from social and political scholarship on the individual and society we take our understanding of the embedded, relational self (Baylis et al. 2008; Mackenzie and Stoljar 2000; Nedelsky 2011). From postmodern, feminist and care ethics scholarship we learned a lot about the role that public understandings of similarity and difference play in fostering or limiting solidarity (see especially Dean 1996). And by those working on welfare state ethics and policy, we were inspired to distinguish between solidarity as a community value, where it needs to be voluntary, and solidarity as a system value, where it can be – and needs to be – enforceable by law (Ter Meulen et al. 2010), which led us to distinguish between three different tiers of solidarity. Chapters 2–4 thus not only reflect the many sources of our work we want to give due acknowledgement to in this book – in fact, we hope that we succeed in highlighting that our account of solidarity is both in line and inspired by broad and influential developments in the Western world. They are also an illustration of the fact that our understanding of solidarity bridges the descriptive and normative realms.

1.6.2   Practice

Chapters 2–4 form the theoretical part of the book, engaging with important lines of scholarship on solidarity, and detailing our own understanding of the term. In the second part of our book, comprising Chapters 5–7, we turn to practical application of our understanding, exemplified by three case studies. In the first case study (Chapter 5) we turn our attention to the ethics, practice and governance of the rapidly developing field of health databases, and show how solidarity can inform our thinking and practice. In addition to research biobanks our discussion now includes all kinds of databases that hold health-relevant data in any form. A solidarity-based governance approach abandons the idea that individual control at every step of the process is the overarching goal. Instead, when specific criteria are met, it replaces such focus on individual control with, to paraphrase Barbara Koenig, consent to a research mission and governance scheme (see Koenig 2014; cf. Laurie 2004). This approach has specific implications for practice, ranging from changes to the consent process to the creation of a 'harm mitigation fund'. The latter realises the commitment that, if we assume that solidaristic contributions of information to databases regularly entail that people accept certain risks, we need to ensure that if harm occurs, people are not left alone to mitigate or rectify that harm. In sum, we argue that solidarity-based database governance can overcome the unproductive dichotomy between personal and collective benefit, and that giving up this dichotomy moves different concerns to the foreground: instead of a focus on technical aspects such as informed consent or a conceptual focus on individual autonomy, a solidarity-based approach shifts our attention to shared societal benefit and shared societal responsibility, and approaches privacy and data protection as both collective and personal goods.

Chapter 6 discusses solidarity in the context of the vision that healthcare should be 'personalised' to better match individual characteristics; a development that is also referred to as 'precision medicine'. The trend towards personalised and precision medicine has received a lot of enthusiastic support, but it has also been criticised as marking the departure towards an individualistic and de-solidarising type of medicine where only those who can pay for the latest technologies will receive the best treatment. We share this latter concern and thus seek to outline ways in which a solidarity-based perspective can avoid this scenario. Doing so means that we cannot merely trust in the power of algorithms and big data to make medicine better and cheaper, and that we understand personalisation as pertaining to wider characteristics than merely genomic ones. The notion of solidarity can go a long way in helping us to reach this goal, again because of its departure from a dichotomous treatment of the personal and the population. The oscillation between the personal and the population level is also, we argue, a core feature of data-rich personalised medicine. In this sense, personalised medicine can bring the personal and collective level not farther apart, but closer together. Exemplified by measures at three different levels – patient access to individual raw data, the use of incentives for healthier lifestyle choices and the organisation of publicly funded healthcare – we look at some of the most important implications of a solidarity-based approach to personalised healthcare.

The third case study, in Chapter 7, looks at a more 'traditional' part of the medical ethics debate around practice and regulation, namely transplantation and organ donation. As a unique, 'gift-giving' practice of a healthy person donating her organ to a gravely ill one who would otherwise have a much poorer quality of life or even die, organ donation, both from live and from deceased donors, has been considered as a paradigmatic example of solidarity by some authors in the past. We discuss several different scenarios of organ donation, including non-directed living donation; so-called organ donation 'clubs' and other forms of giving priority to registered donors; and the debate around 'opt-out' versus 'opt-in' legislation for post-mortem organ donation, and examine how these practices map against our understanding of solidarity. We end by arguing that non-directed organ donation is currently incorrectly framed as an archetypical example of 'pure' altruism, and that this framing impedes the practice's uptake. We suggest that it should also be explicitly described and promoted as a solidaristic practice. Regarding donation 'clubs' and other forms of priority to registered donors (and their families), we correct the assumption that these are solidaristic practices; in some cases, they could even be harmful to solidaristic motivations. Finally, we find that the move from an opt-in system of organ donation to an opt-out system, if implemented step-wise and within a context of trustworthy institutions governed by the rule of law and ethics, can be understood as a solidaristic measure.

Chapter 8 brings together the main insights, themes and conclusions that have emerged from our discussions throughout this book. It also presents some unsolved issued and discusses some remaining open questions from our work, broadening the scope of our solidarity understanding beyond biomedicine. Finally, it suggests directions for future research and policy around solidarity. We do the latter because, while we believe we have covered quite some distance ever since we started our joint project on solidarity, we feel that there is still a lot to do.

Acknowledgements and Thanks

We would like to conclude this Introduction by acknowledging in a prominent place the help that we have received, in our thinking, writing and funding, from many people and organisations over the years. Albert Weale had the initial idea for the project and has remained a source of encouragement and wisdom to us ever since. The Secretariat of the Nuffield Council, notably Hugh Whittall, who wrote a wonderful foreword, supported the work in numerous ways. The Nuffield Foundation, the AHRC, the NCoB and the Economic and Social Research Council (ESRC) in the United Kingdom have all supported the Fellowship in 2011 that marked the beginning of our solidarity project. The Brocher Foundation in Hermance, Switzerland, generously hosted a symposium on our work on solidarity in 2012. Our work has also benefitted greatly from the insightful comments and constructive feedback from current and former members of the NCoB, in particular Roger Brownsword, Robin Gill, Søren Holm, Tim Lewens, Bronwyn Parry, Nikolas Rose, Dame Marilyn Strathern and Jonathan Wolff. Former Council member Graeme Laurie has been a champion of our work from the start. We thank him for including this book in the series he edits for Cambridge University Press and for his inspired words in the Afterword.

And we are indebted to the following people who have provided comments on various drafts, chapters and talks at various stages of development (the usual disclaimer applies): Misha Angrist, Gabriele Badano, Hagai Boas, Kathrin Braun, Silvia Camporesi, Ruth Chadwick, Luca Chiapperino, Angus Clarke, S.D. Noam Cook, Sean Cordell, Peter Dabrock, Angus Dawson, Lorenzo Del Savio, Edward (Ted) Dove, Kathryn Ehrich, Sarah Franklin, Carrie Friese, Marie Gaille, Roy Gilbar, Beth Greenhough, David Gurwitz, Yael Hashiloni-Dolev, Klaus Hoeyer, Ruth Horn, Ine van Hoyweghen, Angeliki Kerasidou, Hanna Kienzler, Martin Langanke, Federica Lucivero, Jeantine Lunshof, Michaela Mayrhofer, Jennifer Merchant, Ingrid Metzler, Christopher Newdick, Maartje Niezen, Gísli Pálsson, Andrew Papanikitas, Manuela Perrotta, Anne Phillips, Andreas Reis, David Reubi, Annette Rid, Benedict Rumboldt, Birgit Sauer, Harald Schmid, Carmel Shalev, Tamar Sharon, Gil Siegal, Kadri Simm, Tim Spector, Meike Srowig, Karl Ucakar, Martin Weiß, Peter West-Oram, Marcel Verweij and Hendrik Wagenaar.

We also thank Finola O'Sullivan, our wonderful editor at Cambridge University Press, for her enthusiasm and support. Mona Rudolph has been absolutely tireless and invaluable in helping us prepare the manuscript; we owe her a huge debt. Both Jona Röseler and Wiebke Herr provided important assistance.

Some of these people have helped us because they are our friends; others have helped us by critically engaging with our work in their own writing; most have helped without any expectation of a direct benefit. We thank all of them for their solidarity. Hendrik Wagenaar, Josef Lentsch, Jann Buyx Lentsch and Pieter Buyx Lentsch we thank for their love.

PART I

Theorising Solidarity

Solidarity: Intellectual Background and Important Themes

2.1 Introduction

In this chapter, we draw out some key themes, ideas and concepts from the social sciences, philosophy and other disciplines that have influenced our conceptualisation of solidarity. Our overview contains the most influential works related to solidarity in the English language, and it follows a roughly chronological structure. It does not aim to provide a comprehensive review of scholarship on solidarity in the social sciences and humanities (which can be found elsewhere: Jeffries 2014; Sternø 2005). Instead, it also includes works and debates that do not discuss solidarity explicitly and specifically, but that we found to have an important bearing on how solidarity should be conceptualised. This chapter thus lays the ground for the introduction of our own definition of solidarity, to which Chapter 3 will be devoted.

2.2 Some Early Sociological Work on Solidarity

We have introduced the etymological root of solidarity in the Roman law concept of *in solidum* in the previous chapter.[1] A similar notion existed in the law of classical Greece, where citizens within an *oikos* – i.e. a household that often included extended families – were sometimes jointly responsible for debts that any of them had occurred, or could jointly accept paybacks that any of the members of the *oikos* was entitled to receive (Smith and Sorrell 2014: 222). Solidarity entered the Western political domain in the late eighteenth century, fuelled by French revolutionaries who also used the closely related term *fraternité* to refer to 'a feeling of political community and the wish to emphasise what was held in common' (Sternø 2005: 27; see also Brunkhorst 2005). This feeling of political community was soon extended to larger groups for which the revolutionaries claimed to speak.

---

[1] *In solidum* referred to joint contractual debts or entitlements between several people.

The idea of mutual assistance among citizens had already played an important role in social contract theories of the sixteenth and seventeenth centuries. These sought to provide a political justification for the existence of state power, that is, for political communities in which people had given up their 'natural' liberties – e.g. to take anything they saw, to kill their enemies, to settle wherever they liked, etc. – and instituted civil liberties in return. Although the idea of mutual assistance played an important role in social contract theories, thinkers in these traditions were not concerned with the notion of solidarity in an explicit and specific manner. One of the first social theorists to do so was Emile Durkheim, whose distinction between mechanical and organic solidarity has been a major influence on scholarship on solidarity since then (we discussed it briefly in Chapter 1). Durkheim's work on solidarity not only reflects his idea of how people relate to each other, but also gives insight into his understanding of personhood and subjectivity[2] more generally. Like for many of his contemporaries, Durkheim saw the transition from traditional to modern societies as a major societal shift that needed to be understood and explained. For him, one of the main drivers of this shift was the increasing division of labour, which affected not only where and how people lived but also the social bonds between them. Before the division of labour, Durkheim thought, bonds between people were so strong that people's identities and interests were developed, perceived and articulated collectively. Such 'mechanical solidarity', as he called it, even preceded the emergence of individual subjectivity.

With the increasing division of labour, another division – namely that of the collective into individuals – became possible. And with the concept of individual subjectivity in modern societies came the idea that people 'autonomously' shaped their moral conduct, which meant that solidarity was no longer something to be taken for granted. Durkheim believed that solidarity could remain strong only if certain conditions were met (although a minimum of solidarity was necessary for any kind of social order; see Nisbet 1974). One of these conditions was justice: only a society free from grave social inequalities would give rise to solidarity. For Durkheim and many others after him, justice facilitates the forming and proliferation of moral and societal rules that bring about solidarity

---

[2] We use the terms personhood, subjectivity and individual identity as a cluster of concepts that all refer to processes and characteristics of the self-understanding of humans. Our focus on the overlaps between these terms should not be seen to imply that there are no differences in how these terms are used by particular authors.

at the level of individual and group practice. It is in this sense that solidarity is 'the reverse side of justice', as Jürgen Habermas famously called it (Habermas 1984, 1986).

Durkheim's understanding of 'mechanical' solidarity as something primordial – in the sense that it precedes individual subjectivity – differs from the approach of another great sociologist and contemporary of Durkheim, Max Weber. For Weber, individual subjectivity has always existed; it is ahistorical. Consequently, individuals can choose to be solidaristic with others or not, which gives solidarity a much weaker role in Weber's conception of social life than is the case with Durkheim. Moreover, while for Durkheim solidarity was a key concept through which he conceptualised personhood and social practice, Weber was not particularly interested in the notion of solidarity as such; for him, solidarity was a type of social relationship that people could choose to engage in if it suited them. Solidarity plays an important role only in Weber's distinction between affective communal and rationally motivated associative relationships in society (Weber 1964 [1922]). These two types of relationships, for which Weber marked different types of society in history, in turn drew upon the work of the German social theorist Ferdinand Tönnies (1855–1936), who had used the term *Gemeinschaft* (community) to describe the supposedly direct, intimate and personal ties that predominantly shaped social relations in the pre-capitalist era. He contrasted these immediate and thick bonds of community with the allegedly less immediate, often non-personal and more abstract ties that bind people together in a modern society (*Gesellschaft*) (Tönnies 1957 [1887]). Weber thought that the non-personal ties characterising modern societies required rational, deliberate action from individuals who decided to consciously commit to establishing or maintaining such ties. He argued that these *societal* ties, on the one hand, were clearly spelled out and 'visible', whereas the personal and intimate ties characterising *communities*, on the other hand, were embodied, affective and not explicitly articulated.

From the above, it could seem that Weber's differentiation between bonds within the *community* vs. *society* is largely congruent with Durkheim's distinction between mechanical and organic solidarity. This view, however, would be mistaken, as the ways in which Weber and Durkheim conceived the relationship between subjectivity and solidarity are incompatible. For Durkheim, the mechanical solidarity prevalent in traditional societies was a powerful force that shaped people's consciousness and identities. Consciousness and identities were collective before they became individual. Weber's thinking, in contrast, starts with the individual who then chooses her conduct, and decides with whom, if anyone, she wants to be solidaristic.[3] Thus, while Durkheim's concepts of mechanical and organic solidarity, and Tönnies' and Weber's conceptualisation of community and society speak to some of the same issues, their categories are not congruent with each other, neither in what they refer to nor in what they assume.

The subsequent development of the meaning and use of solidarity was influenced very strongly by the French Revolution, where it was also linked with the concept of *fraternité*, brotherhood. It was here that differences between solidarity and other prosocial practices and bonds that were based on sympathy and charity became more pronounced. The revolutionaries fought for general rights, not for immediate benefits; their battles were about the freedom and autonomy of citizens, not about assistance within families or security in the bosom of state or church. Their ideas about mutual assistance and solidarity were inseparably connected to fights for greater reciprocity and greater equality, and for a redistribution of power in democratic terms. This is what German political sociologist Hauke Brunkhorst means when he says that solidarity 'is nothing but the democratic realization of individual freedom' (Brunkhorst 2005: 3).

While we fully agree with Brunkhorst on the importance of seeing solidarity as connected to battles for power and reciprocity, we disagree with his emphasis on *individual* freedom. The French revolution, and civil rights movements afterwards, fought against the discrimination of certain groups and for equal rights for all citizens. However, these fights did not typically entail the idea that these goals could be achieved only by means of individual freedom (see also Smith and Sorrell 2014: 224). On the contrary, battles for civil rights were as much about groups and collectivities as they were about individuals. It is against this backdrop that we seek to conceptualise the notion of solidarity as one that includes both, the individual and the collective level, and argue that this is in fact one of the strengths of the concept that has not yet been made enough use of.

---

[3] Tönnies is closer to Weber but gives less weight to individual agency, with his understanding that the 'natural', intimate bonds between people within traditional communities are something that people cannot voluntarily choose, while the 'artificial' ties in modern societies are at the disposal of individuals.

2.3   Solidarity-Related Themes in Recent and Contemporary Social and Political Thought

In the twentieth century, solidarity has attracted new interest. In continental Europe outside of the former communist block, solidarity has played an important role in shaping state institutions and welfare state arrangements in the post-war period (Baldwin 1990; Silver 1994) (the origins of which date back to the nineteenth century, of course). Solidarity has been seen as part of the 'fabric' of these societies to such an extent that it has become taken for granted; in large parts of Europe, solidarity attracts most attention when it is perceived as disappearing (e.g. Baldwin 1990; ter Meulen 2015; ter Meulen et al. 2010). Towards the end of the twentieth century, when even social democratic movements all over Europe started to replace solidaristic with neoliberal values, this development was seen as evidence for the disappearance of solidarity as well (Streeck 2014; Streeck and Schäfer 2013). Indeed, the departure from a type of thinking and policy making that treats solidaristic societies as a necessary precondition for the well-being of its citizens meant, to some degree, giving up the idea that some principles ensuring or protecting solidarity needed to be upheld regardless of their cost, for example by providing specific support to the most vulnerable groups of societies, including ill, old or unemployed people, people with disabilities and also many immigrants. The political, economic and social changes in the late twentieth century led to a growing sense that people are to be held accountable for their contribution to society, and for the costs they incur, which are measured in monetary terms (Mirowski 2014; Streeck 2014; Streeck and Schäfer 2013).[4] Against this backdrop, even in areas of the world where solidarity used to be strong as a value that shapes social and political institutions, it has started to take on a defensive position.

In some parts of Europe, solidarity had already been much weaker than in others. In post-communist countries in particular, solidarity has had a different and rather tainted history. During the time of communist rule, it was used as a programmatic term to justify the often autocratic institutions and practices of communist rulers. In the name of solidarity, grave injustices, restrictions to personal freedom and crimes against humanity were committed. It is for this reason that the concept of solidarity, and the values that it is seen to stand for are not popular in many post-communist countries (Sutrop

---

[4] In its 2010 report on medical profiling and online medicine, the Nuffield Council on Bioethics described this phenomenon in the context of healthcare policy under the concept of 'responsibilisation' (NCoB 2010: chapter 2).

and Simm 2011). Despite the fact that one prominent movement that helped prepare the fall of the 'Eastern bloc' used solidarity in its name, Solidarność in Poland (Paczkowski 2015), solidarity still appears to be tainted by the communist usage. A more individualistic, neoliberal society has been seen by many as a viable antithesis of the communist rule of the past (Pickel 1995). Even those parts of post-communist societies that do not endorse neoliberal individualistic values typically stay clear of references to the concept of solidarity when sketching an alternative, more desirable society than the one they have now (Pickel 1995; however, see Buzek and Surdej 2012).

In Anglo-Saxon countries, solidarity has never had a foothold as strong as in continental Europe (see e.g. Ashcroft et al. 2000, ter Meulen 2015), possibly owing to its initial development on the continent, and the assumption that it is – or was – a distinctly European value (Häyry 2005; Hermerén 2008; Prainsack and Buyx 2011; Sternø 2005; see also Chapter 1). Although Talcott Parsons (1937) is often credited with having 'translated' Durkheim's ideas of solidarity for an American audience, he did not directly refer to solidarity; moreover, the question of social order and the bonds that connect people to each other were mostly of theoretical interest to him (see Smith and Sorrell 2014: 225). In the United States specifically, attention to solidarity is mostly confined to academia and smaller, often left-wing political organisations; solidarity does not play the role it (still, and again) does in public discourse in many European countries. Also in countries such as Canada or the United Kingdom, although some important social institutions (e.g. public healthcare) are underpinned by solidaristic principles, and although feminist movements have embraced some of its core tenets, solidarity has not become as strong an ingredient of the social fabric of society as it has in large parts of continental Europe. Many theorists and thinkers who do use the term are associated with communitarian ideologies, such as, for example, the philosopher and bioethicist Daniel Callahan (Callahan 2003; see also Etzioni 2011).

2.4   Individuals, Community and the Self: Solidarity and Communitarianism

Communitarianism – understood as a loose family of approaches[5] – dates back to the earliest days of political philosophy. In its contemporary iteration, communitarianism evolved mainly in response to American

---

[5] For ease of language, we will refer to the family of approaches as 'communitarianism' nonetheless. We present broad themes, not a detailed account of the many authors that

philosopher John Rawls's seminal contribution to the field of political philosophy *A Theory of Justice* (1971). Communitarianism is commonly seen to make three types of claims (Bell 1993; Caney 1992), which distinguish it from liberalism, and from other theories of political philosophy. The first type comprises claims about the importance of tradition and social context for moral and political reasoning. The second are ontological and metaphysical claims about the social nature of the self (e.g. MacIntyre 1981) and the third are normative claims about the importance and value of community. Many authors also regard communitarianism as a predominantly virtue- and character-focused approach (Roberts and Reich 2002). Overall, communitarianism propagates the need of societies to take the collective as an important, if not the most important, point of reference.

Because of this focus on the collective level, communitarianism is often taken to be related to utilitarianism. This is mistaken insofar as a crucial difference between the two lies in communitarianism not usually being strictly consequentialist; communitarianism requires that the means to achieve desirable goals must comply with particular moral or ethical norms. In the words of Alfred Tauber,

> In a communitarian ethic, the communal structure determines not only how choices are made, but more particularly what those choices might be as driven by concern for the community at large. These may be utilitarian, but they may also be driven by other goals or ideals. Whatever the communal ethic, the position of the individual is balanced within and against social needs.

> (Tauber 2002: 25)

Communitarianism cannot be understood without taking into account the understandings of self- and personhood that communitarian thinkers subscribe to. Many contemporary communitarians employ a conception of the self as a fluid entity that is socially embedded and importantly shaped by her social relations (e.g. Taylor 1989). This conception is also prominent in feminist and postmodernist theory and underpins our own understanding of solidarity (see Chapter 3). It is this very idea, namely that humans are also importantly constituted by their 'attachments'

---

could be subsumed under the communitarian label. Moreover, many of the authors regularly discussed as being 'communitarians' do not self-ascribe as such. As Bell puts it: 'These critics of liberal theory [Alasdair MacIntyre, Michael Sandel, Charles Taylor and Michael Walzer] never did identify themselves with the communitarian movement (the communitarian label was pinned on them by others, usually critics), much less offer a grand communitarian theory as a systematic alternative to liberalism' (Bell 2013).

(Mason 2000: 10), that has been one of the main objections of contemporary communitarian writers to liberal and libertarian works, most prominently those by John Rawls and fellow political philosopher Robert Nozick (1974).

To recapitulate, Rawls sought to develop a theory of justice that would not, as utilitarianism did, entail the willingness to sacrifice the well-being of some individuals for the sake of the many. Instead, he sought to formulate an approach that focused on the rights and liberties of individuals in a fair and equal society. To develop a theory of justice that would be fair to all citizens, Rawls famously used the idea of the 'veil of ignorance': good rules, he argued, are those that people could agree on if they imagined that they were not yet born, and that they did not know whether they would be born female or male, rich or poor, healthy or ill, into what family and what part of the world. This, Rawls thought, would prevent people from selecting principles and norms that benefitted themselves and disadvantaged others. He then proposed a number of principles for a just society that he argued people behind a veil of ignorance would inevitably choose, including basic liberties, the difference principle and the principle of equality of opportunity.

The premise of Rawls's experiment attracted criticism from many sides.[6] Many doubted that Rawls was correct to assume that people were able to detach from their deepest commitments even when putting themselves into the hypothetical shoes of someone in the original position, that is, behind the veil of ignorance. In other words, the veil of ignorance was an interesting idea in a thought experiment, but ill-fitted to devise principles for a just society in the real world. No matter how hard we try, so the argument went, and how good our intentions are, nobody can step out of their own lives and beliefs and turn into a wholly dispassionate and fully independent and self-sufficient deliberator. For others, including American philosopher Michael Sandel, the idea of a veil of ignorance was not only too far-fetched but also theoretically undesirable, because the very idea that people should or could be morally neutral was to be rejected (Sandel 1981). The good life for a person was made and determined by exactly those aspects that the veil was supposed to let fall away, namely people's embeddedness in their community, in their social environment,

---

[6] Indeed, Rawls is often credited with reviving the whole field of political philosophy in the twentieth century by providing so rich an account, which also lent itself to in-depth criticism from writers such as Charles Taylor, Michael Sandel, Michael Walzer, Alasdair MacIntyre, Amitai Etzioni and many others.

their family and friends, and the cultural traditions that they are part of. In Bell's words, '[m]oral and political judgment will depend on the language of reasons and the interpretive framework within which agents view their world, hence it makes no sense to begin the political enterprise by abstracting from the interpretive dimensions of human beliefs, practices, and institutions' (Bell 2013, see also Benhabib 1992; Taylor 1985b).

Another important strand of criticism, expressed prominently by Charles Taylor (1989) and Alasdair MacIntyre (1981), revolved around the foundation of liberal and in particular libertarian approaches which many saw as an outcome of an overly individualistic conception of the self. This criticism was developed also in response to the work of Robert Nozick (1974), one of the most prominent libertarian authors, who put great emphasis on the protection of individual freedom. His idea that individuals had natural rights entailed that unless there was a very strong reason to justify them, interferences with individual freedom had to be avoided. The famous Nozickean statement that '[i]ndividuals have rights, and there are things no person or group may do to them (without violating their rights)' (Nozick 1974: ix) is underpinned by an understanding of the individual who, as the bearer of these rights, stands alone and independently. Individual rights precede any social relation, social institution or social contract both ontologically as well as morally (Mack 2015). Charles Taylor prominently criticised such an understanding of the individual as an atomised, self-sufficient subject, devoid of any connection or relation with others, and able to live and choose outside of any society or 'polis' (Taylor 1985c: chapter 7; Taylor 1989). Similarly, MacIntyre, in his book *After Virtue* (1981), argued that the Enlightenment project had failed in the task of providing us with guidance why we should do good. One of the reasons for this failure, according to MacIntyre, was that Enlightenment rendered the individual the central bearer of moral agency, so that morality and ethics came to be seen and treated as individual enterprises, with little focus on community and common goods (MacIntyre 1981: 215–16).[7]

---

[7] MacIntyre's critique of a 'society where there is no longer a shared conception of the community's good' (MacIntyre 1981: 216) is embedded in a larger critique of liberal capitalism, where protest and resistance have become the characteristics of 'public debate'. For MacIntyre, ethics should be guided by virtues, which for him are not abstract norms derived from larger abstract principles. Instead, they are grounded in practice. In developing this notion, MacIntyre draws upon Aristotle's ethics (and in particular his concept of teleology; rules are based on virtues which are derived from the *telos*), as well as the work of Thomas Aquinas.

The latter strand of criticism is summarised by philosopher and historian of science Alfred Tauber (2002: 24–5), who develops three key theses for contemporary communitarianism: first, that communities cannot be reduced to individuals and their rights; second, that community values are not simply the extrapolated values of autonomous individuals, but that they must include the values of reciprocity, trust, solidarity and tradition and third, that individuals do not, and cannot, stand in a direct unmediated relationship with the state and society. There are, to be sure, degrees of individual choice and independence, but the notion of strict social, political or ethical autonomy is regarded by communitarians as not only an intellectual fallacy but also a distortion of social reality. 'Most importantly', Tauber argues, 'the moral relation of the individual and the state demands a reciprocity of responsibility that places those values sustaining the community as paramount' (Tauber 2002: 25). This is where solidarity comes in: many scholars, including Axel Honneth or Jürgen Habermas, see reciprocity as the core constituting ingredient of solidarity. While reciprocity can be enforced by law – as is the case in contractual obligations or welfare state arrangements – there is a need for a broader reciprocity going beyond the remit of legal norms, and that is the remit of solidarity.[8]

Jürgen Habermas's reasons for emphasising the value of solidarity embody some of the same non-individualistic spirit that communitarians espouse. When Habermas calls solidarity 'the reverse side of justice' (Habermas 1994; see also Habermas et al. 2000), he does not posit that solidarity is a 'better' or more important value than justice, or even that it goes beyond justice. What he means is that while the operationalisation of justice in contemporary theory and practice is focused on the well-being of individuals, solidarity is capable of protecting the intersubjective fabric of society, which, in turn, also contributes to individual well-being.

An influential communitarian author in the field of bioethics specifically is Daniel Callahan. Callahan (2003: 499) sees the need for a communitarian perspective as emerging from the prevailing perspective of liberal individualism in bioethics.[9] The distinctive characteristic of communitarianism, he argues, is that it does not only consider the effect that an action, measure or policy has on the flourishing of individual entities, but that it is also concerned with wider implications. These include effects on human

[8] We return to the issue of reciprocity and the role it plays in our understanding of solidarity at various places in this book; see in particular Chapters 4 and 7.

[9] See also Bellah et al. (1985), who describe individualism as America's 'first language' (Bellah et al. 1985: 20), or, as Stout (1988: 193) circumscribes it, as 'the moral vocabulary Americans share'.

nature, the relationship between the public and the private, the welfare of the whole, human rights, participation and the relationship between individual and common good. Callahan illustrates this with an analogy:

> The important question for ecologists when new species are introduced into an existing environment is not just how well they will flourish individually, but what they will do to the network of other species. Will they live in harmony with them, perhaps improving the whole ensemble, or will they prove destructive? Or will they perhaps do a little of both? The function of communitarianism is to force us to ask the ecology question, now brought into the realm of ethics.

(Callahan 2003: 503)

A communitarian perspective is further seen to entail that one does not 'avoid substantive analysis and judgement', but instead tackles 'the hardest and deepest questions about the right uses of medical knowledge and technology' (Callahan 2003: 505). Communitarianism does not offer a formula or a set of criteria to carry out such analyses; instead, it is best understood as a way of framing issues. We will return to Callahan's interpretation of group solidarity more specifically in the next chapter.

One of the rare works addressing explicitly the relationship between the 'communitarian turn' (Chadwick 1999; see also Sutrop and Simm 2011) in ethics on the one hand and solidarity on the other is Bartha Knoppers and Ruth Chadwick's (2005) article on emerging trends in the context of human genetic research. Communitarianism, these authors argue, has challenged the dominant hierarchy of values in bioethics. In particular, echoing the debate between liberal, libertarian and communitarian thinkers sketched earlier, it has questioned the overarching role of individual autonomy, and it has extended the range of values that serve as points of reference in bioethical reasoning. Reciprocity, mutuality, citizenry, universality and solidarity are now all such points of reference, so these authors argue. With regard to solidarity specifically, Knoppers and Chadwick distinguish between *communal solidarity*, understood as shared practices that already exist in specific groups or communities, and *constitutive solidarity*, where the bond of solidarity is a common interest shared by a group of people (for a slightly different distinction between two kinds of solidarity using the same terms, see Husted 1999).[10]

---

[10] While we consider Knoppers's and Chadwicks's discussion of the five new reference points in ethics as extremely informative, their distinction between communal and constitutive solidarity is less fruitful; existing shared practices can be linked to a common interest, and common interests can be embedded in existing shared practice.

2.5   Relational Subjectivity, the Ethics of Care
and the Role of Difference: Precursors of,
and Influences from Feminist and Postmodern Scholarship

Despite the dominance of the understanding of persons as ideally autonomous individuals in Western thought that communitarians and others have criticised, relational understandings have had a long history. This history is especially pronounced in regions outside of Europe and North America. East Asian philosophies and social theories, in contrast, are well known for emphasising the extent to which people are shaped by their social relations and their role in society, rather than understanding them as the individual shapers of their subjectivity, happiness and ideal destiny (De Craemer 1983). However, in Western philosophy, the relational understandings of personhood have also been discussed for a very long time, and increasingly so in the twentieth century. Martin Heidegger (1996 [1972]) is one well-known philosopher who rejected the idea of a subject as a fixed, bounded, atomistic entity, which he argued did not capture the meaning of human existence. Heidegger used the German term *Dasein*, an untranslatable notion of being in, of and with the world, to refer to 'a complex and open-ended interconnection with the world' (see also Sharon 2014: 140). *Dasein* takes seriously not only the role of other human beings in the shaping of people's subjectivity but also their non-human environment. Opposition to a linear understanding of personhood, and a deeply relational understanding of how individual subjectivity comes into being were also recurring themes in Hannah Arendt's work (see e.g. Arendt 1978). Other important philosophical precursors of postmodern understandings of personhood are Friedrich Nietzsche's deconstruction of the 'self, the "I", as a 'social construction and moral illusion' (Aylesworth 2013; Nietzsche 2011), Ludwig Wittgenstein with the important role that he gave to language in making the world (Pitkin 1993; see also Rorty 1989), Max Scheler's insistence on the inseparability of individual and collective subjectivities and responsibilities (Scheler 1970), Jacques Lacan's deconstruction of ego identity (Lacan and Fink 2002 [Lacan 1966]), Louis Althuser's emphasis of the role of ideology in the formation of self-conscious subjects (Althuser 2006) and of course Michel Foucault's early work in which he questioned the very concept of the modern individual; instead, individuals were the product of power configurations that he referred to as discourse (Foucault 1977; see also Paras 2006). The work of Gilles Deleuze and Félix Guattari (1977 [1972]) was also particularly influential in strengthening non-dualistic understandings of subjectivity in wider areas of theory and practice. Analysing how psychoanalytical understandings of consciousness are related to modern subject positions, they argued in favour of an understanding of subjectivity that is fluid and decentred, which also resonates very strongly with feminist scholarship (see e.g. Butler 1990; Chodorow 1980; Kristeva 1980; Meyers 1994; Oliver 1998).

All these strands of philosophy and social theory have contributed to an understanding of subjects as always in the process of becoming. Moreover, subjectivity is not exclusively human in the sense that what others would call non-human factors and 'environments' are in fact inseparable parts of them. An understanding of subjectivity that is hybrid, fluid and decentred underpins much of postmodern theory, which is characterised not only by the end of the grand narratives (Lyotard 1984), but also, as Tamar Sharon puts it, by 'a sense of new historical possibilities [and] a new capacity to think outside the framework of modern binaries and modern identities' (Sharon 2014: 162).

It is against this backdrop of exploring and conceptualising the extent to which human subjectivity and personhood are relational – in the sense of being shaped by, dependent on and often oriented towards people's human, natural and artefactual environments – that we argue the 'turn to care' should be seen,[11] which is another strand of scholarship and practice that has influenced our understanding of solidarity. By the 'turn to care', we mean the trend among many strands of feminist, ethical and also communitarian scholarship to broaden our attention to the question of how we enable good individual choices towards including how we achieve a good way of living together by caring for each other. One of the most influential writers within this strand of scholarship is Carol Gilligan (1982), who proposed a departure from a rights-based discourse towards an ethics of care that foregrounds personal relationships, human vulnerability and moral responsibilities within these relationships. Since then, care ethics has become a strand of scholarship in its own right, both as a moral theory (e.g. Held 2006; Kittay 1999; Kuhse 1997; Noddings 1982; Ruddick 1982) and as a relational approach to understanding value and personhood that has influenced other disciplines such as science and technology

---

[11] Another important factor that contributed to the 'turn to care' was the rejection of the separation between the private and the public/political domains by feminist theorists. Caring used to be seen as a female duty and practice that was a central feature of the private and domestic. By bringing care as an ideal practice and normative value into the public domain, feminist scholars did not only break down the artificial separation between public and private, but they also helped to politicise the previously private and intimate (see also Tronto 2001).

studies, anthropology, policy studies or geography (e.g. Benhabib 1985; de la Ballacasa 2011; Mol 2008; Stone 2000).

It is noteworthy that solidarity does not play an explicit role within the care approach, and there are relatively few scholars in postmodern and feminist traditions that pay specific attention to it. Political theorist Jodi Dean's (1996) notion of 'reflective solidarity' is a notable exception. Dean aims at combining solidarity with a positive approach to difference. Seeing differences between ourselves and others, for Dean, is inevitable; however, we should be conscious and critically reflective of how and why we separate others from ourselves. Although Dean is not very explicit with regard to what enactments of solidarity – as opposed to enactments of exclusion – can and should look like, it is apparent that Dean's vision of 'reflective solidarity' in society and politics would lead to the inclusion of greater groups of people (e.g. women) into 'notions of civil society' (Dean 1996: 75; see also Habermas 1998; Pensky 2007). This is the case, at the very minimum, merely because their exclusion cannot be politically justified. In other words, 'reflective solidarity' would lead to greater inclusion because it renders visible the criteria and scopes of exclusion, which opens them up for negotiation.

Although Dean does not discuss Hans-Georg Gadamer in her book, her approach resonates with his understanding of the role of solidarity. Like earlier writers such as Durkheim, Gadamer thought solidarity was threatened by the increasing heterogenisation and atomisation of modern society. In other words, he was concerned about a society in which differences were much more visible than similarities (Gadamer 1967). Gadamer did not see a solution in mitigating 'factual' difference, but instead in changing the way we see and treat others. As Walhof (2006: 572) argues, Gadamer 'begins from the premise that there already *are* solidarities that underlie civic life. In his view, the political task facing us is to "discover" and give voice to those things we have in common'. It is in this focus on recognising similarities with others and critically reflecting the boundaries we draw between us and the others, where Dean's work relies on the groundwork prepared by Gadamer, and we do too.

Another twentieth-century thinker whose focus on reflecting and embracing difference has influenced our own approach is Richard Rorty. Rorty did not see difference as something parochial that needs to be overcome, but as an inevitable fact of social life. The relation between solidarity and difference is that solidarity is a kind of 'coping mechanism' (our term) for differences in society. Solidarity helps to ensure that difference does not turn into inequality. This, however, requires political and affective work: solidarity, Rorty argues, needs to be achieved 'by imagination, the imaginative ability to see strange people as fellow sufferers. [. . .] It is created by increasing our sensitivity to the particular details of the pain and humiliation of other, unfamiliar sorts of people' (Rorty 1989: xvi). When he does not believe that solidarity entails 'recognition of one another's common humanity' in this general sense (Rorty 1989: 189–91), this is not because of the unspecific nature of this similarity. Instead, it is because Rorty does not believe that there is a core of humanness that is simply 'out there' for us to see; our shared humanness is something that we need to re-enact and reiterate continuously. Rorty thus emphasised the active work of imaging difference as an important part of practicing solidarity (Rorty 1989; see also Fraser and Olson 1999; Rorty 2000).

2.6 Solidarity and Rational Choice

Despite advanced conceptualisations of postmodern (and 'posthuman'; see Sharon 2014) personhood and subjectivity in theoretical scholarship, the modern idea of the self-interested, atomistic individual still dominates many public and political debates as well as legal and ethical instruments. The paradigm of the rational, self-interested actor remains influential today, which is why we will now take a look at the role that solidarity plays in the work of writers in the rational choice tradition.

Michael Hechter (1987, 2015) is one of the few scholars in the rational choice tradition who wrote explicitly about solidarity. For Hechter, a sociologist, groupness is the core property of solidarity. He endorses a very particular understanding of the term 'group', however, stemming from his long-standing interest in how individual behaviour can be accounted for: groupness, in Hechter's understanding, is 'the group's capacity to affect the member's behaviour. The more solidarity there is within a group, the greater the influence it casts upon its members' (Hechter 1987: 8). Hechter's approach to solidarity is based upon the assumption that people deliberately form or join groups 'in order to consume excludable jointly produced goods' (Hechter 1987: 10). Insofar as group members comply with group rules out of a sense of obligation (not fear of coercion), they act out of solidarity. Hechter proposes a formula for the assessment of the level of solidarity within a group:

> A group's solidarity is a function of two independent factors: first, the extensiveness of its corporate obligations, and, second, the degree to which individual members actually comply with these obligations. Together, these provide the defining elements of solidarity. *The greater the average proportion of each member's private resources contributed to collective ends, the greater the solidarity of the group.*
>
> (Hechter 1987: 18; original emphasis)

Hechter does not derive any substantive normative conclusions from his understanding of solidarity; instead, his approach serves the explicit goal of helping rational choice-oriented social scientists to operationalise solidarity, a notion which some social theorists and scientists, so Hechter, too often relegate 'to darker corners of their intellectual realms, or [ignore] altogether' (Hechter 1987: 168). Although Hechter considers the empirical evidence for the prevalence of group solidarity as 'far from conclusive', in his book he attempts to show 'how a small set of behavioral assumptions can elucidate macrosociological processes by taking both social structures and individual actors into account' (Hechter 1987: 168).

Following the publication of Hechter's influential book in 1987, a number of rational choice scholars have used the notion of solidarity in their own work, or explored it empirically (e.g. Berman and Laitin 2008; Shimizu 2011; Widegren 1997). The rational choice variant of solidarity, which posits that solidaristic behaviour only emerges when people benefit from solidarity, or when they internalise solidaristic norms, has however not become widely influential in the social sciences or even sociology as a whole – not surprising in view of the alternatives available in these fields, sketched earlier.

2.7   Inequalities, the Welfare State and Contractual Solidarity

The modern welfare state first arose in the German-speaking world during the period of industrialisation, out of an interest to keep workers healthy and provide them with the means that should they fall ill, they could recover quickly and return to the workplace (Hills et al. 1994; Sigerist 1943; in the United Kingdom, the modern welfare state came into existence mainly as a response to the suffering during the Second World War). From these early beginnings, conceptualisations of the welfare state have changed considerably, particularly in continental Europe. Throughout continental European states, solidarity has played a role as a value guiding the design of the system, and as a value that influenced the allocation of resources. Angelika Poferl (2006: 311) called solidarity the 'flagship term of welfare states'. What the diverse strands of scholarship on the role of solidarity in welfarism in different countries and contexts share in common is that solidarity always refers to 'the way in which a society perceives and addresses social inequalities' (ibid). At the same time, how societies frame and tackle issues of social inequality has an effect on forms and patterns of solidarity. The dynamics between such political, economic and social 'background conditions' that enable and foster solidarity on the one hand, and concrete expressions of solidarity at the level of social practice on the other, has remained largely unexplored within scholarship on solidarity, Poferl argues. This diagnosis, which we support, has been one of the reasons why we developed a model of solidarity that conceptualises this relationship (see Chapter 3).

Rob Houtepen and Ruud ter Meulen (2000a: 329) also underline the central role of solidarity in welfare states. These authors also point out that this 'form of solidarity embodied in the provision of care and access to care in European societies' has changed radically in the last decades; according to them, it has developed from spontaneous articulations of solidarity 'in reciprocal arrangements of support and care within well-defined groups' to complex systems of institutionalised and legally enforced solidarity. They call the latter kind of solidarity 'contractual solidarity'. In a recent contribution, ter Meulen (2015) reiterates this view and diagnoses a growing gap between justice and solidarity. The tendency in modern democracies to give primacy to justice over solidarity, ter Meulen writes, bears 'the risk of a diminishing of attention for the personal bonds and commitments on the level of care practices. This may result in an impoverishment of the relations in health care which are fundamentally based on benevolence and commitment to the well-being of the other' (ter Meulen 2015: 18).

Already at the end of the twentieth century, Kurt Bayertz made a similar point. He emphasised the importance of welfare states including enforceable legal entitlements of individuals, rather than being based merely on programmatic commitments to moral ideals (Bayertz 1999: 22), a point that Brunkhorst (2005) also highlighted in connection with the French revolutionaries' fights for rights and freedoms of individual citizens. Interestingly, it is exactly the point that solidaristic arrangements and practices should entail enforceable legal entitlements that some scholars consider incompatible with the spirit of solidarity. For example, some argue that the presence of contractual relationships precludes a practice or a relationship from being solidaristic (e.g. Baurmann 1999: 243; Wildt 1999: 217). In other words, if someone gives something to someone else – either directly in the form of payment or indirectly by contributing to transfer payments via paying one's tax – because the receiver has a right to the reception of the good or service, the giving is seen as not being based on solidarity. Other authors implicitly support the understanding that solidarity can never be based on contractual or legal duties. Jodi Dean, for example, insists that solidarity cannot be demanded but only appealed to (Dean 1996: 12). Surprisingly, ter Meulen and colleagues (2010: 7) also seem to support the view that 'contractual solidarity' is not genuine solidarity when they argue that 'solidarity connotes voluntary action'; however, they also introduce the very helpful distinction between solidarity as a community value as opposed to solidarity as a system value (ter Meulen et al. 2010: 11), whereby the latter can contain articulations of solidarity in formal/legal arrangements. We will return to the discussion around the structural role of solidarity and whether it is necessarily voluntary in Chapters 3 and 4.

Finally, in the context of welfare states and the role solidarity plays in them, Richard Titmuss's seminal work on the gift relationship must be mentioned. Titmuss (1970) famously compared systems of paid blood donation (such as in the United States) with systems based on 'altruistic', unpaid donation (such as in the United Kingdom). Titmuss's conclusion was that systems of altruistic donation were not only morally more desirable as they rejected 'the possessive egoism of the market place' (Titmuss 1970: 13), but also safer and more efficient. Importantly, Titmuss understood gifts as manifestations of relationships between people. Although the term solidarity is not prominent in his work, Waldby and Mitchell (2006) draw an explicit link between Titmuss's gift relationship and social solidarity when they analyse, for example, that '[g]iving blood to the troops was a way to express solidarity and improve morale in the anxious conditions of world war' (Waldby and Mitchell 2006: 3). They draw out parallels between Titmuss's argument for an altruism-based welfare state and such spontaneous solidaristic practices.

2.8   Nation States and Global Solidarity

We will discuss normative scholarship on solidarity[12] in Chapter 4, where we will distinguish between approaches (1) focusing on solidarity within predetermined groups, (2) perceiving solidarity as existing primarily at the level of the nation state and (3) seeking to overcome national and other borders and working towards universal or global solidarity. In this chapter, we sketch a few works highlighting the need for a global practice or notion of solidarity that have had an important impact on social science scholarship and related fields, and on our understanding of solidarity.

In his monograph on *Global Solidarity*, Lawrence Wilde distinguishes three waves of thinking on this topic (Wilde 2013: 2–5). The first wave of global solidarity, he argues, consists of the thought of Cynics and

---

[12] By this we mean accounts of solidarity that are normative in that they say what solidarity should be about, or those that argue that solidarity is (always) a good thing.

Stoics, whom Wilde sees as early 'anarchists', opposed to state authority and 'asserting the ability of wise men to live without the tutelage of
political power' (Wilde 2013: 3). By opposing state rule, these traditions in
Ancient Greek thinking were also opposed to parochialism or 'club men-
tality' of any kind, thus preparing the ground for global solidarity. Wilde
calls the second wave of thinking on global solidarity the cosmopolitan
phase. Thinkers in this tradition, he describes, draw largely on the work
of Immanuel Kant, and in particular, *Perpetual Peace* (1795) and *Idea for
a Universal History with a Cosmopolitan Purpose* (1784). Wilde sees Kant
as motivated by the attempt to think a world order into being that would
render wars obsolete, and to promote a federation of sovereign states that
live as a universal 'commonwealth' (it should be noted that Kant himself
does not use the term solidarity in this context). While Kant's work was
influenced by Stoic thinking, the third wave of work on global solidarity,
which Wilde terms 'new cosmopolitanism', is in turn rooted in Kant's
thought. This third wave shares with earlier phases of cosmopolitan thinking the 'commitment to the idea that we have a moral obligation to care for
all human beings, without preference to those who happen to be our fellow
nationals, co-religionists, or members of any "insider" group' (Wilde
2013: 4). Today's cosmopolitanism has however, Wilde asserts, more or
less given up on the idea that a federation of sovereign states would be able
to prevent conflict and violence. Instead, contemporary 'cosmopolitans'
focus on how to avoid atrocities and alleviate the worst social inequalities.

   Wilde's understanding of solidarity is very strongly influenced by the
dichotomy between the national and the global dimension. He understands solidarity first and foremost as a protection *against* something,
namely against particularism, war, and against any kind of nationalism.
This is different from other writers working on global solidarity, such as
Andrew Mason, who sees communities as important enablers for the
obtainment of societal goods (Mason 2000). For Mason, communities
are different from 'mere associations' of people in that they comprise
'people who share a range of values, a way of life, identify with the group
and its practices and recognize each other as members of that group'
(Mason 2000: 21). Because of their shared commitment to certain values,
Mason argues, communities are necessary to advance political goals. But
he also sees a potential difficulty in the economic, social and cultural frag-
mentation in contemporary pluralistic liberal democracies. He believes
that in practice, most societies are too heterogeneous for people to identify with one another (a notion which Mason calls 'the moralized concept
of community', Mason 2000: 224). This, however, should not lead us to

throw out the ideal of political communities altogether. Mason's 'second best' ideal, and the most practicable solution, is an 'inclusive political community [. . . where] the vast majority of citizens have a sense of belonging' (Mason 2000: 225) not to each other but *to the institutions* of the community. This means that members of the community do not need to be concerned with each other, but 'they are likely to develop a sense of sharing a common fate as a result of being part of a society to which they all have a sense of belonging' (Mason 2000: 225). Such a sense of belonging can, in principle, also develop at the global level, but only if the international community gives up the principle of non-intervention in favour of 'a liberal ideal of global community' with liberal institutions (Mason 2000: 173, 179–82). An important way to reach this goal, according to Mason, is a much more extensive use of humanitarian intervention.

A key contribution to contemporary scholarship on global solidarity is Hauke Brunkhorst's book *Solidarity: From civic friendship to a global legal community* (2005). Originally published in German in 2002, this book stands out because it is one of the few works that does not take the meaning of solidarity for granted; instead, Brunkhorst attempts a (re)conceptualisation of solidarity that makes sense for contemporary global politics. For Brunkhorst, solidarity is not merely a way to organise welfare societies but it is tantamount to democracy itself. In order to make this argument, Brunkhorst detaches the meaning of solidarity from its socialist as well as its religious connotation and redefines it as a value that is political but not wedded to any ideological camps (see also, Hoelzl 2004). He argues that solidarity is, in fact, the only political value that enables legitimate forms of political rule. While this applies, in principle, to all levels of governance and government – regional, national, international and global – Brunkhorst devotes a significant section of his book to universal solidarity (he calls it 'Solidarity in the Global Legal Community'), a type of solidarity that overcomes difference and particularisation. Just like societal change in general, Brunkhorst understands globalisation primarily in terms of functional differentiation in society. An effect of expanding functional differentiation, he argues, is that nation states become less important, and also less effective in their governance. The emerging gap is filled by the de facto power of globally operating corporations and other market forces. Brunkhorst argues for the appropriation of this legitimacy gap by solidarity, enforced by a strong global civil society, which he sees as the 'putty' needed to fill the gaps that the law leaves open. Just like putty needs the bricks and stones that it holds together to rest upon them, solidarity can unfold only within the conditions of a constitutional democratic state which serve as its 'bricks'.

We will return to the theme of global solidarity in Chapter 4, in which we will include a discussion of authors such as philosophers Carol Gould (2007) and Sally Scholz (2008).

2.9   Inclusion, Exclusion and Conflict: Agonistic Solidarity

Friedrich Nietzsche and Hannah Arendt famously used the term *agōn* in reference to ancient Greek contests, which were cruel public spectacles and, at the same time, pleasurable practices of selecting the 'best', in a contest to which certain groups – including women and slaves – were not admitted. Highlighting the co-existence and mutual dependency of seemingly contradictory notions such as conflict and community, death and thriving and inclusion and exclusion in modern democracies, 'agonistic' scholarship questions the possibility and sometimes even the desirability of political communities that overcome conflict and reach eternal peace. Rather than trying to weed out conflict, they argue, political communities should aim at dealing with it constructively, abolishing its most cruel manifestations and mitigating the negative consequences of socially acceptable manifestations. Arendt (2005) saw the *agōn* as a step in the process of transforming violence into politics.

In contemporary scholarship, *agonism* subsumes a number of political and social theorists who hold that it cannot, or even should not, be the role of political systems to overcome conflict. Thus, the main question that agonists are concerned with is how difference and conflict can and should be dealt with, instead of how they could or should be overcome. The work of Chantal Mouffe and Ernesto Laclau has been particularly influential in this context (Laclau and Mouffe 2001; Mouffe 2000).

Darryl Gunson (2009: 249) provides one of the rare explicit references to agonism in the bioethical literature when he notes that solidarity, by calling for, or describing, inclusive and cohesive forces regarding a particular group, is necessarily exclusive of those outside of this group.[13] In other words, solidarity includes mechanisms that prevent it from being extended to other groups. This is the reason why some authors refuse to

---

[13] See also Heyd (2007: 11), Jaeggi (2010: 290) and Putnam (2000: 23: 'Bonding social capital, by creating strong in-group loyalty, may also create strong out-group antagonism'). The work of other authors could be seen as implicitly contributing to an (emerging) notion of agonistic solidarity: Jodi Dean (1996: 19), for example, emphasises the inherent property of solidarity to always exclude those which it does not include (see also Lenhart 1975; Rorty 1989).

treat solidarity as something a priori positive. Jeffrey Alexander, for example, in an attempt to reconceptualise the civil sphere, sees solidarity as being closely related to both inclusion and exclusion, and emancipation and repression (Alexander 2006).[14] Angelika Poferl explicitly differentiates between 'inbound' and 'outbound' solidarity: For 'inbound' solidarity in Europe, the challenge is to accommodate and meaningfully address great differences in how social inequalities are configured across Europe, and how societies differ in how they seek to address these; an argument that is vindicated by current developments in the European Union, where not only ideas about social justice but also consensus of its role in the European project seem to be farther away than ever. For inbound solidarity, according to Poferl, the great heterogeneity in how people live, suffer, and in what values they hold poses the key challenge. 'Outbound solidarity', in contrast, is largely a call for reflection on how European societies and governments should deal with the grave social inequalities, atrocities and the human cost of natural catastrophes that take place outside of Europe's borders. Poferl's vision for inbound and outbound solidarity is a 'European solidarity model' that is 'more than the sum of national practices and institutionalisation of solidarity' (Poferl 2006: 312; author's translation). It largely consists of a critical reflection of criteria for inclusion and exclusion similar to what Jodi Dean (1996) suggests.

While these nuances are very helpful, what Poferl leaves unexplored is the question of how solidarity emerges in specific groups within a population. She acknowledges the existence of 'pre-political' forms of solidarity that precede the existence of political communities enforcing solidaristic norms (Poferl 2006: 314). Her examples of such pre-political solidarity, however, are bonds between families for which the term solidarity is ill-suited (see Chapters 3 and 7). Poferl also makes reference to culture as an important source of group identities that, as she emphasises, are necessarily exclusive. In this sense, conceiving entire nations as solidaristic collectives represents an advance over more particularistic forms of solidarity. Following Wagner and Zimmermann (2003: 250), Poferl sees the nation as 'the historical answer to the problem of solidarity' (cf. Poferl 2006: 315).

---

[14] Andrew Mason, in his work on *Community, Solidarity and Belonging*, disagrees with the idea 'that a community, by its very nature, requires "outsiders", i.e. some who do not belong to it. [. . .] If this were part of the nature of community, the very idea of world community would be conceptually incoherent (. . .) [C]ommunity in the ordinary sense involves sharing values and a way of life, identifying with the group and mutual recognition, all of which are possible in principle in the absence of outsiders' (Mason 2000: 175).

At the level of the nation, access to the in-group requires two conditions, namely citizenship and participation in 'market- and welfare-regulated reproduction'. When these conditions are met, however, the access to the in-group is automatic (Poferl 2006: 315). From this perspective, national solidarity still excludes people, but it makes the criteria for inclusion and exclusion transparent.

As an explicit term, 'agonistic solidarity' has not yet been very influential in ethical, social and political theory. The question of whether solidarity should only be called such when it facilitates or supports desirable normative goals, or whether solidarity in the form of social cohesion is something intrinsically positive, is one of the under-conceptualised questions in the existing literature. This relative lack of attention has to do with the fact that the categories that are used to delineate the very groups within which solidarity takes place are typically treated as self-evident; only rarely are they unpacked. Through our own approach to solidarity, we concede that in principle, solidarity can indeed also be enacted within a group that displays hostile behaviour to those outside of the group. We will return to this difficult challenge to solidarity in the next chapter.

2.10   Conclusion

Even though this chapter cannot do justice to all scholarship relevant to solidarity, the discussion of approaches that have been particularly influential for our own thinking gives an insight into the breadth and variety of writing – explicitly or implicitly – on solidarity. The overview in this chapter includes strands of scholarship that employ a relational understanding of personhood and subjectivity, as well as approaches that treat people as autonomous individuals who deliberately choose with whom to practice solidarity. In terms of the role of groups and of communities in practicing solidarity and creating solidaristic institutions, the approaches discussed in this chapter vary considerably. They range from authors who consider difference and political opposition as constantly shifting yet inevitable facts of social and political life that solidarity has a valuable role in bridging, to those for whom the ideal state would be a society where difference does not matter. What we derive from all of these debates is an insight into the great importance of scrutinising and understanding categories and practices of group formation. Instead of taking it for granted that people within a pre-defined group consider themselves similar to each other and are willing to support each other, we need to look very closely at the circumstances in which similarities between people are recognised and give rise to action, and circumstances in which difference is more powerful. Our own understanding of solidarity thus poses a lot of emphasis on the concrete and enacted nature of solidarity. As we will lay out in the next chapter, we understand solidarity as enacted commitments to accept costs to assist others with whom a person or persons recognise similarity in a relevant respect.

3

What is Solidarity?

3.1 Introduction

The previous chapter gave an overview of several developments and themes in Western thinking that have influenced our own understanding of solidarity. This chapter presents our definition of solidarity as *enacted commitments to accept costs to assist others with whom a person or persons recognise similarity in a relevant respect.* We do this with the dual aim of providing a definition that stresses what is specific about solidarity, thus bringing more clarity to a term which has been accused of being 'vague' or 'opaque',[1] and distinguishing it from related terms such as friendship, altruism, empathy, etc. Secondly, we aim to develop a definition of solidarity that is suited for application to policy contexts in biomedicine and related areas. Our current focus is on biomedicine for pragmatic reasons; our definition of solidarity, and our suggestions regarding solidarity-based policy and governance frameworks are, however, also applicable to much wider contexts, as sketched in Chapter 8.

The introduction of our own approach starts by outlining one of its most important features – and one where we deviate from most of the existing scholarship on solidarity – namely that we understand solidarity first and foremost as something that is *enacted*, rather than as a value, feeling or obligation. A look at how practice epistemology has shaped our approach to understanding and utilising solidarity sets the stage for everything that follows later. We then highlight aspects of other scholarly traditions that we have adopted into our own understanding of solidarity, such as theoretical scholarship on the relationality of personhood. After that, we introduce our definition of solidarity in more detail, including the relationship between solidarity and reciprocity, which is a very close but not a linear one. We draw out some implications of the definition before we give an

---

[1] For a definition of vague terms, see Buyx (2008b).

43

overview of the reception that our approach has received in the literature, and how that has helped us to advance it.

3.2   Solidarity as Practice

Practice is often understood as 'skilful acting'. In this view, knowing and acting are seen as two activities or states where the first is a requirement for the second; we are assumed to apply knowledge that we have previously acquired. Practice, in other words, is seen as applied knowledge. This view includes two tacit assumptions: first, that knowing and acting are distinct, or at least separable categories and second, that knowing is typically prior to acting.

Although this view has been challenged in recent decades, it is still influential on how the relationship between knowing and acting is conceptualised in the Western world. The often-heard warning 'think before you act' is an everyday example of this. Assuming we should 'think before we act' qualifies any action that is not preceded by cognitive thought as rash, deficient and likely to cause damage. Noam Cook and Hendrik Wagenaar formulate an alternative to the dualist view, one that we espouse as part of our definition.[2] For them, practice is a purposeful engagement with the world whose meaning is derived from a given context (Cook and Wagenaar 2012: 4). They insist that

> formal knowledge emerges out of, and cannot be seen apart from, an often unacknowledged and largely tacit context of hunches, cues, bodily predispositions, expectations, appreciations, values, affects, and so on. That is, all knowledge, including formal knowledge, is embedded in ordinary experience, and, in an essential sense, gets its meaning, its life, from it.
>
> (Cook and Wagenaar 2012: 8)

Such an understanding of the relationship between knowing and acting treats practice not as the *application* of knowledge but as something that contains both knowing and acting. It is underpinned not so much by a

---

[2] Cook and Wagenaar in turn build on the work of thinkers such as Ludwig Wittgenstein, Maurice Merleau-Ponty, Hans-Georg Gadamer, Michael Polanyi, Geoffrey Vickers and Charles Taylor, as well as non-dualist traditions of Japanese philosophy. Influential in this latter respect is the twentieth-century philosopher Nishida Kataro (Nishida 1990 [1911]), who also draws attention to the importance of place as the context of practice. See Cook and Wagenaar (2012: 25), Kopf (2004) and Scott (2000). Non-dualism is, of course, one of the central features of post-modern theory as well; for a discussion of the relevance of this for the realm of biomedicine and biotechnology, see Sharon (2014; in particular, chapter 6). See also Chapter 4.

reversal of the chronological and hierarchical order of knowing and acting, but by a refusal to accept their dichotomy, and even separability (Cook and Wagenaar 2012: 9). What we know is shaped by our interactions with the world, and vice versa: we act upon what we know, and we know because we act. Knowledge is obtained from doing something – may it be learning in a classroom, or any other kind of activity that may not even feel like learning. Not only our minds, but also our bodies, our eyes and hands remember our past actions. This means that knowing always includes an element of *reenactment*; by recalling what we know, not only our minds, but also our embodied memories are called upon.[3]

Our approach to solidarity is underpinned by such an understanding of the intertwined nature of knowing and acting. We believe that a practice epistemology has several implications on understanding solidarity:

First, solidarity is most fruitfully understood as something that is enacted, and not as an abstract value, normative ideal, or inner sentiment. This means that it requires some external manifestation that is apparent to others. That is, something that expresses itself to, and engages with, the outside world, rather than being internal to a person. Just as a mere thought would not be seen as a *practice*, a sentiment, feeling, or impulse – for example, feeling loyal towards another person, or feeling empathy – does not in itself represent a solidaristic practice. An external manifestation of solidarity will typically comprise of an action by a person (or persons), but it could also take the form of a document, a policy or law, or another written or symbolic *articulation of meaning*.

We believe that the insistence that solidarity needs some form of external expression is necessary to avoid that any situation where a person relates to somebody else with sympathy or understanding could be labelled as an instance of solidarity. An example would be that we 'feel solidarity' with striking miners in a Latin American country, without basing any action upon this, however small it may be. Such inflationary use of the concept is one of the reasons why solidarity has been criticised as too vague a term (Capaldi 1999; Gunson 2009; Husted 1999; Rippe 1998). Insisting that solidarity is never merely a sentiment does not mean, however, that feelings, sentiments or thoughts are excluded from practices of solidarity. They are in fact often important elements; for example, because they play a role in motivating a solidaristic act. Inner feelings, sentiments or thoughts are, however, never *sufficient* elements of solidarity. Let us assume that a

---

[3] This paragraph draws upon personal communication with Noam Cook, London, April 2014.

person's decision to volunteer her time to raise money for a cancer charity is based on a strong sense of fellowship that she feels with breast cancer sufferers because she – or a close friend, or a family member – suffered from it as well. Merely having this feeling would not be qualified as solidarity. Through the person *acting upon* and *with* this feeling, however, it becomes part of her solidaristic practice. The *extent* or *kind* of the external manifestation of solidarity is not a decisive criterion here. A person's volunteering to donate an organ after death, following a law that mandates participation in a solidaristic healthcare system, or someone devoting a minute of her time to help somebody else – all these practices could be qualified as solidaristic practices, assuming that other criteria are met (see later).

Second, analyses of solidarity need to take into consideration concrete practices, policies and their contexts. We are conscious that solidarity has been described as a cultural or social value in the past (and has in fact often been called a specifically 'European' value, Häyry 2003, 2004, 2005; Hermerén 2008; Holm 1995; Tomasini 2010; see also Chapter 1). But it is only when this value is expressed in practice that it becomes relevant to our inquiry. A lot of recent and contemporary literature in various fields treats solidarity as a general, political ideal or a broad moral value. A reflection of the moral ideals and values that have shaped and continue to shape our societies is certainly important, and as part of such an analysis, an exploration of solidarity and its place within modern social and cultural values is worthwhile. If there is, however, no mid-level theory that connects such exploration of cultural and political values and norms with observable action of individuals and groups, then this exploration loses its power to explain individual and social practices. Similarly, if dominant values and norms in a society are analysed only on the basis of influential thinkers, works and legal documents, we cannot understand *how* they became influential. We also run the risk of conflating cause and correlation: for example, if a hypothetical country named Goodland had strong solidaristic values enshrined in its social policies, and the population of this country also donated more money to disaster relief than the population of other comparable countries, we could be tempted to explain the latter by the apparent commitment to solidarity in Goodland. This may be accurate, but it could also be that the main reason for the willingness of Goodland's citizens to donate money is a different one, such as particularly compelling charity campaigns, or the religious belief among most citizens of Goodland that those who donate will be rewarded in Heaven. Knowing whether or not the donations of Goodland's citizens are indeed instances of solidarity would require investigating *empirically* what values and norms and perceptions underpin and motivate these practices.[4] When analyses of solidarity lack attention to the manifestation of solidarity in concrete contexts and practices, they lend themselves to using solidarity as an empty label for any number of political objectives (Prainsack and Buyx 2011).

The *third* consequence of understanding solidarity as a practice follows directly from the previous point. As for any practice, *context is of crucial importance*. The difference between, for example, the movement of fingers over piano keys and playing music on the piano illustrates this.[5] Moving fingers over the keys of a piano is not practice; playing music on the piano is. The practice of playing the piano cannot be isolated from the pianist, her history, her training, etc. The practice of playing the piano is, literally, inseparable from context. We argue that the same holds for practices of solidarity. Context is vitally important in that it shapes and determines whether an action can be regarded as solidaristic. Say a neighbour, who is also a mother, picks up Irina's children from day care because Irina is stuck at work. Say she does this as an act of mother-to-mother solidarity with Irina. The same person picking up Irina's children merely because Irina pays her for her time does *not* constitute a solidaristic practice. It is only the practical situation that allows us to understand what the relevant similarity is that motivated the neighbour's enactment of solidarity with Irina.

Fourth, practice often includes values and knowledge that cannot be fully articulated nor assessed according to parameters of rationality. Saying that practice is purposeful engagement with the world is not the same as saying that practice is always deliberate and rational. What the psychologist Daniel Kahneman (2011) famously called 'system 1 thinking' – the kind of thinking that is intuitive, automatic, embodied, and that cannot be turned off – within an epistemology of practice could be seen as practice on the basis of tacit knowledge; that is, the kind of knowledge that cannot be expressed entirely in words, and that we may not be aware

---

[4] While we disagree with several aspects of her conceptual understanding of solidarity, this is exactly what sociologist Aafke Komter does in her book on social solidarity: she analyses 'giving behaviours', such as donating time or money, in the Netherlands and provides some illuminating discussion of how solidaristic behaviours vary between populations, nations and cultures (Komter 2005). For a discussion of how to explore empirically the meaning of personal and collective practice, see Wagenaar (2014).

[5] In addition to the movement of a piano player's fingers over the keys, Wagenaar writes, 'the music is an ensemble of the notes in the score, the long training of the pianist, her powers of concentration, her knowledge of other works of the composer and the interpretation history of the piece, and the thousands of ongoing and embodied judgments of interpretation that, taken together, make up her skill as a pianist' (Wagenaar 2004: 643–55).

of (Polanyi 1962).[6] This is relevant for our understanding of solidarity because solidarity often has a strong 'tacit knowledge' component. Just as we cannot exhaustively explain in words why we love some people, or why we do things for our friends, there can be something in the practice of solidarity that is embodied and cannot be explicated. In this book, we do our best to consider the reasons and motives behind practices of solidarity, and the context in which they are situated. However, we are very happy to acknowledge that more often than not, such theoretical analysis will not be able to get 'the whole picture' of why a person (or a group) does what she (or the group) does. Our inquiry thus leaves ample space for more empirical research and further theoretical analysis.

Fifth, because practice is always contextual, it draws attention to the relation between the actor and her human, natural and artefactual environments (Cook 2008). We have a strong commitment to a particular way of understanding the relationship between human actors and their environment that is compatible with, but does not flow directly from, the practice approach. Our understanding of solidarity rests upon the understanding of persons as entities that are dependent on, and whose boundaries are open to, their environments. As this is a fundamental tenet of our understanding of solidarity, we will take some time to explain the relevance and implications of this – against the thematic background we have sketched in Chapter 2. Such a relational understanding of personhood, in turn, has two main implications, namely that, first, people's interests are also typically shaped by concern for others, and that, second, we cannot distinguish neatly between self-interested and other-directed action. As we will argue later, both of these implications are essentially important for our understanding of solidarity.

3.3   Personhood as a Relational Concept

As we mentioned in Chapter 2, in Western thought, personhood, in its ideal form, is often understood to be formed by separating ourselves from others. The moment when a very young child is able to separate between herself and the outside world, and when she is able to understand herself as being *in* the world, yet as a separate, different entity, is treated as a key

---

[6] Tacit knowledge, according to Michael Polanyi (1962), is what we know but cannot say. Polanyi contrasts 'tacit knowledge' with 'explicit knowledge', namely what we know and can say. Playing a piece of music on the piano also illustrates the role of tacit knowledge: we can talk about how to play, but we cannot explain it to the extent that somebody else can do it merely on the basis of our explanation.

step of the development of her personality. Closely related to an under-standing of personhood as comprising independent individuals is the idea that the actions and decisions of human beings are typically motivated by *self-interest*. This assumption has its roots in the strong foothold that the idea of the 'rational actor' has had in the social and economic sciences in particular. Two elements of the rational choice paradigm are of crucial relevance here: first, the idea that individual action is the 'elementary unit of social life' (Elster 1989: 13),[7] and second, that the actions of people can be assumed to be motivated by the aim to increase their individual gains (in a wide sense, including financial, emotional or social status gains). A rational actor is thus one that is guided by self-interest. This under-standing of the self-interested rational actor explains why other-regarding behaviour has often been portrayed as driven by 'irrational' forces and impulses, and not by rational reflection. Historically, women's selfless care for their children, for example, has been attributed to their caring 'instincts', or their being driven by hormones. Even today, when other-regarding behaviour cannot be explained by natural impulses, it is often taken to be an exceptional phenomenon that only people of a particularly high spiritual or religious status are capable of practicing consistently. The extent to which the idea of the rational actor is inscribed in legal and ethi-cal instruments creates a range of issues for medical practice and research (Prainsack in preparation).

Although the idea of the rational actor has been very influential in scholarly work of a wide range of disciplines, philosophy has been one of the disciplines in which it has probably had the weakest foothold. As we mentioned in Chapter 1, a range of twentieth-century philosophers had alternative views of personhood, including Heidegger, Nietzsche and Gadamer. Critics of modern liberal political philosophy, such as Charles Taylor, point out that the human ability to reason is developed only in rela-tionship to others. Similar to many post-modern and feminist theorists (e.g. Strathern 1988), Taylor holds that relationality is a precondition for subjectivity, not the other way round (Taylor 1985a: chapter 7; Taylor 1989). We are who we are because we relate to others. The beginning of post-modern philosophy in the 1960s and 1970s meant an irreversible departure from the idea of the self as a fixed, coherent and bounded entity for those associated with this thinking (see Chapter 2). Since then, the influence of

---

[7] The idea that individual human action is the core unit of social life, and that societies and political institutions are reducible to the actions of individuals is known as 'methodological individualism' (see also Scott 2000).

post-modern philosophy has extended far beyond the field of philosophy, and has penetrated social theory and social sciences more generally.

A relational understanding of personhood (Mackenzie and Stoljar 2000) has profound consequences for how we conceptualise the ways people act and decide. If others play a role in shaping our identities and our interests, then very few things that we do are exclusively self-regarding or solely self-interested. Some strands of the social sciences, social theory and increasingly fields such as behavioural economics have indeed treated rational action as only one among several elements of human practice, next to other, non-rational notions such as habits, emotions and similar. The works of sociologists and social policy scholars such as Marcel Mauss (1925) and Richard Titmuss (1970) have drawn attention to the extent to which concern for others is an important element of most human practices. They also highlighted the role that other-regarding practice plays in the emergence and practice of social institutions. Especially Mauss, rather than portraying concern for others as something that is conceptually opposed to self-interest, illustrates how self-interest and orientation towards others always *overlap*. Other people are typically not physically part of us (unless we are conjoined twins), but they – in their roles as parents, friends, spouse, children – play important roles in shaping who we are, what our needs and 'interests' are and why we rejoice or suffer.[8] Although we are clearly not identical with others or with our environments, it is impossible to clearly separate ourselves from them in terms of our identity and self-understanding. It is therefore puzzling that, despite virtually everything that we do being related to others *and* to ourselves, the assumption that we can separate between the two in theory is so deeply engrained in norms and values governing our societal practices. This is also particularly evident in the practice and research of medicine.[9]

[8] Our entanglement with our non-human environments is often even closer, as it becomes part of our bodies by our food intake or the implants we carry in our bodies (e.g. Bukatman 1993; Haraway 1993).

[9] See Prainsack (2016). For an examination in the context of blood donation, see Buyx (2009). As we also expand on further down, an exception to this is public health. Due to the prominent role that binding and coercive measures play in this field, which routinely have the capacity to infringe individual autonomy for the sake of collective benefit, the tension between these two principles (or goods, depending on the definition) has received explicit attention throughout the development and from the very beginning of this field. Perhaps because of the latter, conceptualisations of personhood that accommodate non-instrumental, non-deliberate and also sometimes the unconscious nature of social relations and attachments have been more prominent in the theory of public health than in other areas of medicine (see Prainsack and Buyx 2011).

For over three decades now, and influenced by the broader debates we presented in the previous chapter, many scholars have criticised that in medicine people have been seen as separate from the relations they are embedded in. This does not mean that the importance of relationships for human flourishing was denied, but the ethical and legal instruments guiding medical practice did not accommodate or operationalise the importance of relationships in sufficient ways. For example, some mainstream understandings of patient autonomy and the related instrument of informed consent have rightly been accused of over-emphasising the independence of individuals, and of not giving sufficient attention to the important relational elements of personal autonomy (see e.g. Gilbar 2011; Koenig 2014; Maclean 2013; Manson and O'Neill 2007; Stoljar 2011; Tauber 2003). Feminist and other critical scholars have sought to address this problem at the conceptual level. Legal scholar Margaret Jane Radin (1996: 72), for example, speaks of the importance of a 'receptiveness to connectedness, to the recognition that human life is impossible without nurturing from those who care for us when we are helpless and dependent' that characterises virtually all strands of feminist thinking (see also Strathern 1988). It is this recognition of care as a central feature of human existence that also underpins Carol Gilligan's (1982) 'ethics of care', which we briefly encountered in the previous chapter. Care ethics is often seen as an alternative to the prevalent rights-based discourse. It is an alternative that foregrounds personal relationships and moral responsibilities within these relationships, and prominently recognises human vulnerability and the intrinsic human need to look out for others, and to be looked out for. Work on 'relational autonomy' in bioethics and public health ethics makes similar points (Mackenzie and Stoljar 2000; Baylis et al. 2008).[10] We need to acknowledge, Baylis and colleagues argue, that we all 'develop within historical, social, and political contexts and only become persons through engagement and interaction with other persons' (Baylis et al. 2008: 201). Not only our self-understandings, but also our decision-making and

---

[10] These authors challenge an understanding of autonomy that conceived people as 'separate from one another, each with his or her own private interests that must be respected and accommodated as far as possible [. . . I]n these circumstances, the larger social contexts that patients and research participants inhabit tend to be treated as either irrelevant or as obstacles to their autonomy' (Baylis et al. 2008: 200). Similar to what Baylis and colleagues did for the field of public health, Jennifer Nedelsky argued, as early as 1990, that legal scholarship and practice need 'a new conception of the tension between the collective and the individual, for which the boundary is not an apt metaphor' (Nedelsky 1990: 162). She argued that '[w]hat actually makes human autonomy possible is not isolation but relationship' (1990: 169).

our 'interests' are relational (see also Nedelsky 1990, 2011; Powers and Faden 2006).

Our understanding of solidarity follows some of these arguments. We do not see self-'interest' and concern for others as mutually exclusive. On the contrary, we hold that almost everything we do is self- *and* other-regarding at the same time (albeit not always to equal degrees).[11] We also subscribe to both the *causal* and the *constitutive* views of relational autonomy. This means that, in the former form, people are seen as embedded, relational beings, whose relationships to their human, natural and artefactual environments have an important impact on the development of autonomy. In the latter form, it means that people's subjectivities and interests are partly shaped by other people (Stoljar 2011, 2015). This prominent role that a person's relationships play in shaping her practice is an important aspect of our understanding of solidarity, to which we turn next.

3.4   Our Working Definition of Solidarity

Because of – and in response to – the different and often conflicting understandings of solidarity in the literature, we developed a working definition of solidarity.

> **SOLIDARITY**
>
> Solidarity is an enacted commitment to carry 'costs' (financial, social, emotional or otherwise) to assist others with whom a person or persons recognise similarity in a relevant respect.

3.4.1   Costs

Under 'costs' we subsume all types of contributions (e.g. time, effort, emotional investments or money) that people make to assist others. Small things, such as giving up our own comfort to offer somebody a seat on the bus, count as 'costs' as well as big things, such as donating an organ. It is important to note that although the acceptance of such costs for the sake of assisting others is a requirement of solidarity, it does not preclude that groups or individuals enacting solidarity also benefit from doing so. This is because although we can distinguish between purely altruistic and merely selfish motivations or acts on the abstract level, it is impossible to do so

---

[11] We return to this particularly important aspect of the simultaneity of self- and other-regarding practices in Chapter 7.

when it comes to our actual practices. As argued earlier, almost everything that we do, even the most 'selfless' things, contain self-regarding aspects: even if someone donates an organ to a total stranger, this act affirms the donor as a good person, a moral citizen, a religious person, etc. Similarly, as argued earlier, even the most 'selfish' thing is also typically other-regarding in at least some aspect. For example, even if we do something merely to improve our reputation, it could be argued that the very idea of reputation is void without other people. Because we are part of a social fabric – including our families, different communities and often also a nation – all our practices are directly or indirectly related to others. It is also important to emphasise that our personal gain from doing something for others does not detract from the value of what we are doing. It is equally important, however, to note that the expectation of a direct benefit must never be the *decisive* motivation for a solidaristic practice. To stick with our earlier example, if the neighbour picked up Irina's children from day care *merely* (i.e. for no other reason than) because she expected payment, then this would be a business transaction, and not an act of solidarity.

3.4.2   Similarity and Commonality

There is another aspect to the definition of solidarity that needs further specification. We define solidarity as practices reflecting a commitment to carry costs to assist others with whom a person or persons recognise similarity in a relevant respect. 'Similarity in a relevant respect', here, means that one has something in common with the person that *matters in a specific situation.* Here is where the understanding of solidarity as a practice unfolds its full meaning. What constitutes 'similarity in a relevant respect' depends on the specific context of the situation. If, for example, we sit on an airplane and worry about making it to a meeting on time because our flight is delayed, then our *similarity in a relevant respect* with the person next to us may merely be that all of us are going to a meeting and worrying about making it on time. The fact that the person sitting next to us may be, for example, diabetic, or vote for a political party that we detest, is immaterial for our potential solidarity with her in this situation. However, if it does turn out that we share more things in common with this person, then this could be the basis for our bond becoming stronger than merely a bond of solidarity; for instance, we could eventually become friends, which are bound together by a much denser net of connections.

The central role that similarity in a relevant respect plays in this understanding of solidarity also means that solidarity applies to practices where commonalities between people, not differences, are the decisive 'trigger' for action. If Federica recognises something that she shares in common with Jean – a shared problem, say, a shared characteristic, or a shared conviction – then this can form the basis of her solidarity with him. They may be very different in many respects, but regarding their specific soli- daristic practice, they act upon their similarities. In the case of charity, the feature that motivates somebody to support somebody else is, besides their willingness to provide support, the *difference* in the life circum- stances of the actors. David gives something to Lia because he is richer, more privileged and so forth. Here, despite things that they may share in common – e.g. that they may share the same religion – it is *what sets them apart* that underpins charitable practice. Therefore, charitable relation- ships are, almost per definition, unequal. Solidaristic practice, in contrast, rests upon commonalities *in the concrete situation or setting in which they take place.* These commonalities can become more stable if solidaristic norms govern legal arrangements, such as universal healthcare.

3.5   Three Tiers of Solidarity

In order to be able to focus our discussions on the level on which solidaristic practices take place – ranging from inter-personal to being part of the 'fabric of society' – we distinguish between three 'tiers' of solidarity (Figure 3.1).

TIER 1 INTERPERSONAL SOLIDARITY

At this level, solidarity comprises manifestations of the willingness to carry costs to assist others with whom a person recognises similarity in at least one relevant respect.

The first tier of solidarity is that which is practiced *between individual people*. If Ayse suffered from regular back pain when she was pregnant and offers her seat on a bus to Ivo who seems to have a painful back while standing up, then this represents a practice of solidarity at tier 1. Ayse rec- ognises a relevant similarity with Ivo that leads her to offer assistance. As outlined earlier, the extent of the 'costs' that a person is willing to accept for the sake of helping others does not play a decisive role.[12]

---

[12] Note that it is not implied that all practices of solidarity have the same value for personal or societal well-being; we are merely stating that there is no minimum threshold of a 'cost' that somebody accepts for her practice to be considered solidaristic.

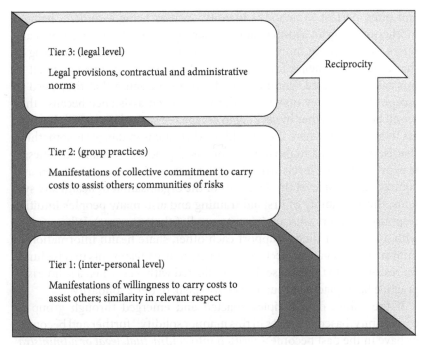

Black background: practices
Grey background: institutionalisation

Figure 3.1 Three tiers of solidarity.
Source: Adapted from Prainsack and Buyx (2014).

If practices of solidarity between people are so common in a given context or community that they are seen as 'normal', then we have an instance of tier 2 solidarity. Tier 2 solidarity applies to group-based or community-based practices.

TIER 2 GROUP SOLIDARITY

On this tier, solidarity comprises manifestations of a *shared* commitment to carry costs to assist others with whom people consider themselves bound together through at least one similarity in a relevant respect (e.g. a shared situation, characteristic, or cause).

People who are part of the same general or concrete situation typically share certain risks or positive goals that emerge out of, or define, that situation. Sharing a 'general situation' means something that is relatively stable, and often part of somebody's identity, such as being a student, being a mother or being an asthma patient. Sharing a concrete situation typically refers to something more temporary and transient, such as shopping in the same store when a fire breaks out. These shoppers form a, albeit in this case short-lived, 'community of fate' in the sense that they need to escape the fire; they may help others who need assistance because they are all bound together by seeking to escape the same danger. Helping others in a situation where their health or their life is in danger is something that is, of course, a highly institutionalised practice in many societies; it is expressed at all levels from the inter-personal, to the communal and contractual/legal level (in the forms of the organisation of healthcare systems, the availability of first aid training and also many people's intuitive response to others who are in acute need of their support). When people with a particular illness support each other, share health information to minimise the negative effects of the illness or organise events to raise funds for research into the disease they are affected with – i.e. when a solidaristic practice takes place at group level – we speak of tier 2 solidarity.

If the values or principles enacted and emerged through group or community-based practices in this manner solidify[13] further and become – or have in the past become – written into *contractual, legal or administrative norms*, then we have instances of tier 3 solidarity.

> **TIER 3 CONTRACTUAL, LEGAL OR ADMINISTRATIVE NORMS**
>
> At this level, solidarity is institutionalised in the form of contractual, legal or administrative norms.

Tier 3 represents the highest level of institutionalisation of solidarity, typically in the form of legally enforceable norms. Examples include welfare state and welfare society arrangements, progressive taxation or legal and administrative arrangements underpinning publicly funded healthcare systems such as the British National Health Service (NHS) or German Statutory Health Insurance. Other examples are contracts between different private actors and international declarations or treaties, such as virus sharing agreements in the context of pandemics. Such legal, contractual and administrative arrangements can be described as institutionally 'solidified' enactments of people's willingness to accept costs to assist others with whom similarities in a relevant respect are recognised – either by

---

[13] This notion of 'solidification' was coined by Rahel Jaeggi (2010).

them directly, or, in the case of tier 3 solidarity, by state actors and institutions that act on their behalf.

The three tiers of solidarity as described in the definition stand in a particular relationship with each other. While the 'lower' tiers of solidarity often exist without the 'higher' levels, these higher levels have typically – but not always – been preceded by lower levels. In other words, solidaristic norms and provisions at tier 3 have often emerged out of initially more informal practices of solidarity at the inter-personal (tier 1) or communal or group level (tier 2). But of course, not all inter-personal practices at tier 1 actually solidify into practices and norms at tiers 2 and 3.

3.6 Distinctions and Clarifications

In Chapters 5–7, we apply our understanding of solidarity to a number of cases and contexts, putting practical 'flesh' on the bones of this concept and showing how it can be put to work. Before we do that, some further clarifications of important aspects of this definition of solidarity are necessary. These discussions also prepare the ground for the final section of this chapter, where we respond to our critics.

3.6.1 Solidarity and Autonomy

In line with the relational understanding of the person, we also subscribe to a relational account of autonomy. As outlined earlier, we subscribe to a relational understanding of autonomy in both of the senses described by American philosopher Natalie Stoljar (2015):

> If relationships of care and interdependence are valuable and morally significant, then any theory of autonomy must be 'relational' in the sense that it must acknowledge that autonomy is compatible with the agent standing in and valuing significant family and other social relationships. 'Relational' may also deny the metaphysical notion of atomistic personhood, emphasizing instead the idea that agents are socially and historically embedded, not metaphysically isolated, and are, moreover, shaped by factors such as race and class.

It is sometimes assumed that there is opposition between solidarity and autonomy, and that those arguing for solidarity inevitably aim to 'override' personal autonomy. This view is mistaken. It would only be the case if autonomy were to be understood in a very narrow sense as the right to self-determination of atomistic, self-interested individuals. Such a notion of autonomy would indeed be in a tension with many accounts of solidarity, and also certainly ours. But if we understand autonomy as the right of persons to shape, through their decision-making, their own fate in collaboration with and with concern for others, then personal autonomy is a characteristic of solidaristic practice. To qualify as a solidaristic practice, following the recognition of similarity, there must be *choosing* and *deciding* to assume costs to assist others.[14] Although we do not assume that this act of decision-making is always a rational act in the sense that it seeks to enhance individual gain, it includes at the very least some kind of intentionality. Usually, when a person decides to engage in solidaristic practice, this decision is an expression of her plans, motives, values or relational circumstances. As such, solidaristic practice is most meaningful when a person has decided to engage in it free from pressures and desperate needs. Solidarity thus flourishes most where the social, economic, political and environmental conditions for life are such that they enable and encourage meaningful practice, instead of narrowing down options and limiting decision-making capacities.

3.6.2   Conditions of Possibility for Solidarity

In societies where discursive, political and economic structures are in place that emphasise and foster concern for others and where the well-being of individual people is seen as closely connected to the well-being of others, these structures provide a 'glue' between the three tiers. They provide the background conditions for solidarity to grow and proliferate. If such structures are not in place, then solidaristic practices at each of the tiers can emerge, but they would hang 'in thin air'. In such a situation, solidaristic practices are unlikely to proliferate, flourish and solidify.

Emphasising what connects people over what sets them apart is one of the most important features of solidarity. However, such a focus on what binds people together also bears the risk of concealing inequalities and power asymmetries. When we analyse specific instances of solidarity, it is thus important that we do not look merely at the specific interaction between people (tiers 1 and 2), or only at the specific law or rule that prescribes a solidaristic practice (tier 3). Instead, we should also consider the political, economical and cultural context of that practice. Although instances of solidarity among people or groups can take place even in a society with the worst possible circumstances for solidarity to flourish,

[14] On the contractual and legal level 3, there is no literal choice involved, of course, but, as we stress in several places in this book, individual practices from lower levels which entail choice are a vital precondition for solidaristic laws and regulations.

for solidarity to become institutionalised and to become part of the 'social fabric' of a society, it requires certain conditions of possibility. These conditions include a predominant discourse that promotes concern for others, consideration for weaker people and the willingness to share, over values such as competitiveness and economic success. They also include trustworthy institutions and a certain level of economic and political stability. In other words, the more people can trust societal institutions, the more they can trust each other, and the less people need to be afraid, the more likely it is people and groups will practice solidarity, and institutions will be designed according to solidaristic principles. What may sound like a circular argument describes in fact a basic socio-psychological dynamic: confidence begets confidence, trust begets trust, solidarity begets solidarity. Solidarity alleviates vulnerability by decreasing the distance between the most and the least vulnerable in a society, and it does so by foregrounding similarities that then give rise to action.

3.6.3 Vulnerability

Many authors see solidarity as something that is directed mostly towards vulnerable people (Habermas 1994, NCoB 2009). The role vulnerability plays in our framework lies in the notion of similarity. We have emphasised that one of the core features of solidarity is that it foregrounds similarities between people, and that these similarities are determined by the specifics of a concrete practice or setting. As argued earlier, while two people, or members of different groups, may be very different in many respects, one single similarity, if it *matters enough* in a concrete situation, could give rise to solidarity. If we have, for example, experienced a serious illness earlier in our lives, we may donate money and provide other means of support to others who suffer from the same disease, even if we have never met them in person and they live at the other side of the world. The shared experience of this illness becomes a defining moment in our practice of solidarity – although there may be nothing else that we see ourselves having in common with the people whom we are helping.[15]

---

[15] We thus disagree with David Heyd (2015: 58) when he says that '[w]e feel solidarity, rather than sympathy, with fellow academics; but we feel sympathy, rather than solidarity, with the victims of an earthquake in a faraway country'. It could be the other way round; with whom we enact solidarity and with whom we feel sympathy depends on what characteristic, common goal or shared experience matters in a specific situation. If we are afraid of a tornado hitting our home it may matter less that our colleague Anil is a fellow academic, than the fact that Anil lost his house in a storm some years ago.

The shared experience is what 'makes us' do something to assist these people. This 'doing something', in turn, is typically something that affirms, helps or supports others, and not something that harms them. It is in this sense that vulnerability matters: despite the fact that what motivates our action is a commonality that we share with others, in the concrete situation in which solidarity is enacted, it is them, and not us, who are in need of support. That they are vulnerable and in need of support, however, only determines the direction of the support in the concrete instance of solidarity. It does not change that the commonality between us, and not our differences, gave rise to our action. In that latter sense, despite only one of us being in need in this particular moment, we act within a situation of fellowship.

3.6.4   Solidarity vs. Friendship and Love

We have so far used examples for solidaristic practices that mostly played out between strangers; indeed, one of the implications of our definition is that in solidaristic practices, the recognition of similarity can occur despite people not knowing each other at all. For a solidaristic practice to occur, people need know only about the relevant similarity they share; and this holds at all three tiers of solidarity. But of course solidarity does not need people to be strangers; people practicing solidarity may know each other as neighbours, colleagues, acquaintances, etc. The better people know each other, however, the more likely they are to be bound together by stronger bonds than solidarity. While there can be solidarity of the kind we have described between neighbours and colleagues, the stronger the emotional bonds and the closer the relationship, the more solidarity becomes redundant. The main difference between solidarity, on the one hand, and friendship and love, on the other, is that friendship and love bind people together through so many and such deep bonds that their willingness to help each other does not require the recognition of similarity in (only) one relevant respect. Friends, families and lovers are usually bound together by emotions, and by a multitude of shared values, habits, practices, experiences and plans so that they are a community of fate in a much 'thicker' and deeper sense than is typically the case for solidarity. Solidarity is subsidiary to these thicker bonds (see also Heyd 2015; Chapter 7). Solidarity thus is, in other words, particularly pertinent to situations where no other ties exist to bind people together.[16]

---

[16] We readily acknowledge that within relationships such as acquaintances or colleagues it can sometimes be difficult to clearly distinguish whether a practice is a solidaristic practice

3.6.5   Solidarity and Reciprocity[17]

Many authors see reciprocity as closely related to, or even synonymous with, solidarity.[18] Indeed, the relationship between these concepts is such that for solidarity to spread and institutionalise, a certain level of reciprocity is needed. But how exactly does reciprocity support the practice and institutionalisation of solidarity? As a first step, we need to differentiate between direct (or immediate) and indirect (or mediated) reciprocity.[19] Direct reciprocity applies to situations where a person receives something 'in return' for something else in one discrete transaction. Exchanges of goods, services or favours are directly reciprocal if they take place between the same group of actors, and without a significant time lap. Peter giving Tanya money in return for Tanya handing over her car, Lou cooking dinner next Wednesday because Ali cooked dinner for her last Wednesday and next week will be Lou's turn are instances of direct reciprocity. Indirect reciprocity, in contrast, applies to situations where somebody does or gives something without expecting to receive the same thing from the same person in the same transaction. Keith giving blood hoping that someone else will do this so that he will get blood if and when he needs it – without knowing whether or when he will need it and who would help him – would be an instance of indirect reciprocity.

As mentioned earlier, if reciprocity is the decisive or even the only motivation for a practice, then that practice cannot be called solidaristic. If Peter's interaction with Tanya is motivated only by Peter's desire to own her car, then handing over money is not a solidaristic practice. If Tanya recently lost her job, however, and Peter recognises 'similarity in a relevant respect' with Tanya because he (or somebody close to him) has experienced unemployment as well, and this is the main reason for buying a car from her instead of from somebody else, then the interaction could be solidaristic. Similarly, if Keith gave blood for the *decisive* reason that he hopes

---

based on the recognition of similarity in a relevant respect, or already a practice based on affection, closer to friendship. This is not troublesome – in most cases, after some analysis it will be possible to make a distinction, and those cases where the relationship and the motives at play cannot be distinguished in practice do not detract from the value of keeping these concepts apart analytically.

[17] The following paragraphs owe a lot to Albert Weale's insightful comments on solidarity (personal communication with authors, see also Weale 2001).

[18] In fact, in an earlier article, one of us (mistakenly) identified reciprocity as the central, defining element of solidarity (Buyx 2008a).

[19] For a detailed discussion of direct vs. indirect reciprocity (including its sub-types) and their relationship to solidarity, see Molm et al. (2007). See also Lévi-Strauss (1969) and Takahashi (2000).

somebody else will do so when he needs it, then his giving blood would not be an act of solidarity. This does not mean that Keith would not be helping others, or that his help would therefore be less valuable; it just means that it would be an expression of something else than solidarity. If receiving something in return is the decisive motivation for a practice, then this practice cannot be seen as solidaristic. But particularly at higher levels of institutionalisation, indirect reciprocity can play an important role of stabilising solidaristic arrangements, and overall attitudes of reciprocity will help maintain and enliven solidaristic policies and laws. We will return to the relationship between solidarity and reciprocity in Chapter 7.

3.7 Responses to Our Definition and Critique of Our Approach

Since the publication of our first works on solidarity in 2011, our approach has been reviewed and criticised in several places. We are grateful for this engagement with our work. We would like to respond to some of this criticism in order to pre-empt misunderstandings and also to highlight how these critiques have informed and further focused our thinking on solidarity.

In their essay 'Solidarity: A Moral Concept in need of Clarification', Angus Dawson and Marcel Verweij (2012) criticise our description of how solidarity is expressed between individual people (i.e. at the inter-personal level, tier 1 solidarity).[20] They hold that situating solidarity at the inter-personal level is a misnomer, because they believe that what we describe actually takes place at the group level. They argue that latter is the case because

> [. . .] the basic definition of Prainsack and Buyx already involves a joint or collective commitment to bear costs of helping or protecting others – which goes further than the one-person-to-one-other relationships that the authors envision at the first level. This suggests that on their own account of solidarity some idea of a *group* in which people *share* commitments to others in that group is necessary, even at the first level.
>
> (Dawson and Verweij 2012: 3, original emphases)

We fully agree with Dawson and Verweij that solidarity is most powerful, and perhaps most important, when it is practiced within a group, and potentially across an entire society, supported by norms and stable practices. We have also emphasised that conditions that emphasise mutuality, shared experiences or common goals that bind people together in a

---

[20] An initial response to Dawson and Verweij (2012) was published in the same journal in the same year: see Prainsack and Buyx (2012b).

society are conducive to solidarity. At the same time we disagree with the authors that even when solidarity is practised between two people, this requires a group identity to come into play. As we have explained earlier, for a solidaristic practice to emerge between two people, the person enacting solidarity needs to perceive that she and the other person are similar in a relevant respect. This similarity – that in turn gives rise to the solidaristic action – could consist of something that many people share in common, such as being female, or it could be something more transient that connects only the two people in question, e.g. that they are surprised by a storm during a hiking trip. If this shared experience of weathering a scary storm is the bond that makes Laura do something for Mie that she would otherwise not do, then it is unclear why 'some idea of a group' (Dawson and Verweij 2012: 2) is required for this solidaristic practice to emerge. A practice that takes place in a dyadic relationship between two people can, of course, extend into more widely shared practices within larger groups, but solidarity certainly does not require 'pre-existing groupings'.

Dawson and Verweij then add another point, namely that it is unclear whether we treat solidarity as a moral or a normative concept, and whether we 'contribute to active debates about how solidarity might help us understand what is right and wrong in public health and health care practices' (Dawson and Verweij 2012: 3). Our overriding aim in our earlier work has been to obtain a better understanding of what the analytical and political value of solidarity is and can be. To clarify the analytical value of solidarity, it was necessary to define its core elements and to see what sets solidarity apart from related concepts. To understand the political value of solidarity, we need to explore in what ways solidarity-based frameworks and arrangements differ from those that are not, and what the societal surplus value of solidarity-based approaches is. Much of this book is devoted to the latter.

We will delve into the normativity of our account in much detail in Chapter 4, so here is a short answer: while largely descriptive, our understanding of solidarity has important normative and political dimensions. These normative implications pertain to our very understanding of personhood in the first instance, and to how we envisage flourishing societies in the second. Our approach is informed by relational positions that understand people's identities and preferences as influenced by their human, natural and artefactual environments. Based on such a relational understanding of personhood, we argue that policies reflecting people's willingness to accept costs to help others are preferable to policies that do not accommodate or consider solidarity. As pointed out earlier, we also consider political, economic and discursive circumstances that prioritise values such as concern for others over values such as competitiveness as desirable. These are normative positions that are underpinned by our conviction that solidaristic practices and policies regularly lead to happier people and more flourishing communities. They are not, however, sweeping endorsements of a *particular* normative version of solidarity of the kind Dawson and Verweij seem to expect – and present themselves, with considerable difficulties (see Chapter 4, where we discuss their work in more detail).

In another article, Angus Dawson and Bruce Jennings (2012) explore why explicit references and discussions of solidarity have been so rare in public health ethics to date. They object to some elements of our framework, mostly around the three tiers of solidarity (Dawson and Jennings 2012: 72–3).[21] Dawson and Jennings call our tier 2 – the group-based practice of solidarity – 'the real heart of solidarity' and argue that it is unclear why inter-personal and contractual/legal manifestations of solidarity should be called solidarity at all. While, again, we agree that group-based solidaristic practice is a powerful form of solidarity, we maintain that it is indeed analytically fruitful to distinguish between charity, love, contractual obligations and solidarity also at the inter-personal and contractual/legal levels. Dawson and Jennings then present their own understanding of solidarity as 'a value that supports and structures the way we in fact do and ought to see other kinds of moral considerations' (Dawson and Jennings 2012: 73). They describe three key forms of solidarity: 'standing up beside', 'standing up for' and 'standing up with' somebody, which all signify related but different relations between the person(s) enacting solidarity and those to whom solidarity is directed (see also similarly Jennings 2015; Jennings and Dawson 2015). The authors also contend that unlike us, they do not consider 'costs' to be a requirement for solidarity. While the emphasis on solidarity being something relational unites us with Dawson and Jennings's work, we believe that a key weakness of their approach is that it does not allow to differentiate between solidarity and other forms of providing support and assistance: people could be standing up with, for and beside others out of love, pity or even for merely strategic reasons. We thus maintain that for an understanding of solidarity to be useful, it requires other criteria in addition to the provision of support. Lack

---

[21] Like Dawson and Verweij (2012), Dawson and Jennings (2012) criticise that our understanding misses the 'heart' of solidarity, namely a primary or exclusive (this remains unclear) focus on the 'constituting' group level of solidarity. We will respond to this reading of our account, and the weaknesses of theirs, in Chapter 4.

of differentiation between related but distinct concepts only muddies the waters. It also contributes to the idea that solidarity is a vague and thus practically and politically useless concept.

A very helpful critique of our limitation of solidarity to humans comes from Melanie Rock and Chris Degeling. Inspired by anthropologist Tim Ingold's notion of 'being alive' that integrates human beings ontologically with the rest of the natural world (Ingold 2011, 2012; Ingold and Palsson 2013), and by Annemarie Mol's and John Law's work on embodiment and enactment in non-human animals (Law and Mol 2008, 2011; Mol 2002), these authors argue that there is no apparent reason why our understanding of solidarity should not apply to non-human animals. They contend that our own work on solidarity has 'emphasise[d] human life to the point of virtually excluding consideration of non-human life as an ethical matter' and thus label our approach as 'humanist solidarity' (Rock and Degeling 2015: 62). They argue for what they call 'more-than-human solidarity', which acknowledges

> ... people's embodied effort to be of assistance to non-human animals and places, which arise from the materiality of enmeshments between human bodies, non-human bodies, and places (following Ingold 2011). [. . . W]e highlight that 'others' with whom people recognise sameness and shared circumstances can – and do – include non-human animals or plants.

> (Rock and Degeling 2015: 3)

In contrast to Dawson and Verweij, and Dawson and Jennings, respectively, Rock and Degeling endorse the core elements of our definition, as well as our three-tier conception of solidarity. They suggest to amend, however, our definition to apply also to 'non-human animals and places'. Rock and Degeling's critique is spot-on in the sense that (a) we should indeed have made it explicit that we limit the range of actors that we discuss as practising solidarity to humans, and on the basis of what rationale and (b) this limitation of the range of actors to humans does not follow from the other elements of our definition. In other words, it would be possible to replace 'people' in our approach with a wider group of entities, without the need to adjust any other part of the definition. In principle, all entities with whom or which we can recognise fellowship in the sense of 'similarity in a relevant respect' could be on the receiving end of our solidaristic practice, irrespective of whether they are human or not. For example, if we accept a risk to our health as a 'cost' of comforting a horse suffering from an infectious disease, this can be an instance of practising solidarity if we do this because we recognise our own vulnerability in the suffering of the horse ('similarity in a relevant respect').[22] Although we agree with Rock and Degeling that humans can enact solidarity with non-human entities, we will retain the anthropocentric focus in our own work: given the focus of this book in the biomedical domain, we limit our argument to the domain of human practice.[23]

Another critique of our work which has helped us to draw out more explicitly some implicit elements of our approach comes from political philosopher Meena Krishnamurty. In her article on political solidarity, Krishnamurty (2013) states that

> Their [Prainsack and Buyx's] view fails to give an account of how those individual citizens, who are characterized by political solidarity, ought to interact with one another outside of acting in ways that express a willingness to take costs on to help one another. If one citizen acts so as to take on the costs of helping another, but does so while demeaning or insulting her/him, say, by berating her/him for needing help in the first place, then this would not count as a genuine instance of political solidarity [i.e. Krishnamurty's version of solidarity]. This suggests that how individual citizens interact with and treat one another are important to the phenomenon of political solidarity.

(Krishnamurty 2013: 130)

Whether or not our approach is vulnerable to this criticism depends on how one understands the meaning of the term 'assistance' in our definition. Krishnamurty is right insofar as we did not make it explicit whether 'assisting' someone could include harming or demeaning them at the same time in a significant way, and we gladly take the opportunity to do so now: we take assisting to be an overall – that is, in sum – positive, capabilities-increasing act. In our definition, people's willingness to assist others is based on the recognition of similarity – of something relevant that is mutually shared between them. It is this similarity that leads to a relationship between the person(s) who assist(s) and the one(s) who receive(s) assistance. This relationship also regularly requires an emotional engagement with the other person, as Krishnamurty herself acknowledges. Theoretically, it is possible that a solidaristic practice harms the recipient(s); what is intended as supporting somebody else is

---

[22] This could, in principle, be extended to plants as well, and to drive the argument even further: in cultures and situations where objects are seen as animated, it would be conceivable that humans engage in solidaristic practices because they recognise similarity in a relevant respect with them.

[23] We acknowledge but cannot enter here into the debates about the kinds of actions and behaviours usually ascribed to humans that animals might also exhibit.

not always perceived as such on the receiving end. An example for the latter would lie in the argument that welfare payments could harm those who receive them as they enable actions that are detrimental to the person's happiness. Similarly, the food that we cooked for our ill neighbour could be contaminated and make her even sicker, or the crutches that we send to a country where people suffer injuries from landmines could be seen as a deprecating gesture by them. In all three cases, however, harmful effects would never be the *intention or goal* of solidaristic practices or arrangements, but instead unfortunate results of our practices or policies, which should lead to their reconsideration and improvement. This point also underscores the importance not only of critically reflecting on our criteria of including and excluding people from certain groups, but also of giving careful consideration to how the particular form and substance of our support is likely to affect the recipient(s). In cases where harming the recipients is knowingly accepted and merely disguised by a solidaristic rhetoric, the practice or policy in question does not meet our requirement of solidaristic action. We readily agree that we do not have an account for all behaviours 'outside' of solidaristic practices – but there is the law, there are accounts of justice, and many principles that govern our conduct we would point to (see, e.g. Wilkinson and Pickett 2011). Solidarity does not have to do all the work alone.

It is possible that Krishnamurty conflates solidarity with charity when she voices her concern about the harmful effects on its recipients. Charity is indeed typically characterised by a top-down and asymmetric interaction or relationship; in fact this is one of the key differences between charity and solidarity, as explained earlier. In some situations, charity can be accused of robbing those on the receiving end of their dignity, demeaning them by forcing them to lay open their needs and vulnerabilities, and 'grovel' for help.[24] This can be the case particularly in contexts where a subjective and legally enforceable right to assistance – as in welfare society arrangements – is replaced by making those in need dependent on charity. This kind of potentially patronising or demeaning asymmetry, however, is not part of solidaristic practice as we understand it. On the contrary, such asymmetry does not meet the criteria of our definition. A person who acts to carry costs, but berates or demeans the person aided while doing so is not acting out of solidarity as we understand it. She does not recognise similarity with her beneficiary while she demeans them for wanting aid.

---

[24] Elisabeth Anderson (2000) makes a structurally similar argument against the asymmetries in luck egalitarianism and the resulting potential losses to dignity in her seminal article.

In fact, she expresses the opposite of similarity, namely that the recipient is lesser than herself.[25] The same holds if we replace 'person' with 'institution' and move to solidarity on higher levels of institutionalisation. What Krishnamurty talks about in her critique is no instance of solidarity – not by her account, but certainly also not by ours.

A weakness of our approach is that according to our definition, solidarity could be enacted in support of aims and causes that we reject, such as torture or terrorism. The difference to the scenario discussed earlier – that solidarity could harm its recipients rather than benefit them – is thus that here we are concerned with the effects of solidarity on those *outside* of the relationship or group, not within. An example for this would be a situation in which members of a terrorist group, whose aim is to kill everybody who does not subscribe to their own beliefs, practice solidarity *within* the group. Their mutual solidarity would make the group stronger and more effective in killing people outside. This example illustrates two important things: first, that solidarity in itself is not always positive, and second, that in order to assess whether a concrete instance of solidarity is desirable, we need to take a look at the context of the practice (see also Scholz 2015).[26]

The first point explains that except for the inter-personal level, solidarity usually involves – explicitly or implicitly – the drawing of a boundary between an in-group and an out-group. A group of farmers who cover for each other in times of illness might exclude farmers who do not live in the same village. Solidarity among workers of all countries excludes capitalists. Most national systems of 'universal' healthcare exclude non-residents. As Jodi Dean (1996) argued, to soften this exclusionary element of solidarity as far as possible, our solidarity should be 'reflective' in the sense that we scrutinise the boundaries we draw against the groups that we belong to. Our own definition of solidarity entails the same argument: by emphasising that solidaristic practices are always underpinned by the recognition of similarity in a relevant respect between people or groups, it highlights the social process of 'making' similarity, and enjoins us to focus on what connects us to others over what sets us apart. Seeing some people as similar to ourselves (and thereby others as different) is indeed a social practice and not a disinterested recognition of objective facts. When somebody argues that smokers and overeaters should be excluded from receiving

[25] We thank Pete West-Oram for this latter observation.
[26] This is one of the aspects in which we take a different view on solidarity from, e.g. ter Meulen who states that 'solidarity can also be regarded as an *intrinsic* value, meaning the unselfish dedication to a fellow human being who is in need' (ter Meulen 2015: 4). Here, ter Meulen seems to mistake solidarity for an unspecific kind of altruism.

certain healthcare services, then this person makes in fact two arguments, one explicitly and one tacitly: the explicit one is that smokers and alleged overeaters are less deserving of support than non-smoking people with healthy eating habits. The tacit argument is that smoking and eating too much are behaviours that are so morally significant that they delineate two groups, namely those who care about their health and those who are careless (see also Buyx and Prainsack 2012).

While every practice of solidarity includes processes of 'othering' to some extent – group solidarity most significantly – whether or not this is problematic depends on the context. That universal healthcare excludes non-residents is a problem, because many immigrants living in precarious circumstances have nowhere else to turn. That solidarity among workers excludes CEOs, or that the solidarity between village farmers excludes those in the adjacent village, in contrast, is less likely to be a problem, because CEOs typically have sufficient resources to advance their own causes (or because their causes do not deserve our support), and farmers in the adjacent village are likely to have a similar system of solidaristic support. Thus, solidarity cannot be seen in separation from the role that we want a particular solidaristic practice to play in society. Solidarity manifests itself at different levels, from the inter-personal level to the 'fabric of (modern) society' (Houtepen and ter Meulen 2000b: 374; our tier 3 solidarity). At the same time, solidarity is only one practice among many others, and plays out in societies that are at the same time governed by other, sometimes normatively much stronger (deontic) principles, including justice principles, the rule of law, etc. (see more on this in the following chapter). Overall, for any well-ordered, flourishing society that espouses such norms, it would hardly be desirable, say, for the values of a violent organisation – one that bases their mutual solidaristic practice on prioritising a common ethnically or religiously defined characteristic – to solidify into more widely shared or even legally prescribed norms. Indeed, in pluralistic liberal democracies this is factually impossible, because sectarian communities would not gain the majority support that would be needed for their value system to be more widely adopted or even institutionalised. In undemocratic theocracies or racist regimes, however, this danger exists, and even in liberal democracies it is possible that solidaristic practices at inter-personal and communal levels effectively exclude minority groups. Both would be highly undesirable.

We are not suggesting that inter-personal (tier 1) and group-based (tier 2) practices of solidarity that emerge on the basis of particular specific traits should be forbidden or even discouraged beyond what is already prohibited by existing civil and criminal norms that prevent racism or other forms of undue discrimination. Instead we suggest that solidaristic practices that are capable of increasing tolerance, mutual support and well-being across society should be actively promoted. This distinction, of course, presupposes an understanding of what a decent and flourishing society needs (Margalit 2009; Ould 2014; Wilkinson and Pickett 2011). Politics, policy, civil society work and even commercial activity can help make more visible what unites people than what sets them apart from each other. While such solidarity cannot be enforced against people's will, it can be facilitated.

3.8   Some Political Implications of Our Understanding of Solidarity

Rock and Degeling's (2015) examples about humans practising solidarity with animals shed light on another important aspect of solidaristic practice: it also often expresses a refusal to put a price on things. Rock and Degeling's aforementioned example of comforting a dying horse illustrates this perhaps most compellingly: there is no expectation of reciprocity – a dying horse will not be able to give anything back in any direct way, nor will it be able to spread the word about the good deed of the person. Neither is there any other expectation of direct personal gain that could justify such a practice in terms of any form of economic cost–benefit balance (unless we regard the satisfaction that comes out of doing something good to others as a 'direct personal gain', which would then lead to the abolition of the concept of self-interestedness altogether). This non-calculating (Häyry 2005: 204) and non-calculable characteristic of the enactor and enactment of solidarity is expressed in a very strong form in the case of assisting a dying animal, but it is also present in many other practices of solidarity between humans. Again, while a practice embedded in a context of reciprocity does not preclude that the practice can be solidaristic, if the expectation of getting something back is the *decisive* motivation for a practice, then the practice cannot be considered solidaristic. This means that the self-interested calculation of personal benefits is incompatible with the practice of solidarity.

Solidaristic practice is thus imbued with meaning as well as personal and social value, but not with price and market value. The consequences of this are profound in the sense that our version of solidarity can be seen to imply a rejection of some subject positions geared at reasoned behaviour and effective self-governance. It replaces this subject position with one that includes a more holistic sense of well-being, where the well-being of the actor is inseparably connected to the well-being of those around her (such as those articulated also in visions of the 'solidarity economy'; for an overview, see Ould Ahmed 2014). We argue that this subject position is not only in line with recent developments in the theoretical debates around the concept of the person as relationally embedded (see earlier and Chapter 2), but also much more suited to the context of biomedicine and healthcare policy making, where narrow conceptions of well-being are increasingly criticised (Venkatapuram and Bunn 2012).

3.9 Conclusion

This chapter has introduced our understanding of solidarity, and explained its key components. We discussed our three-tiered system of solidarity, describing solidarity at the inter-personal (tier 1), communal (tier 2) and at the level of contractual, legal and administrative norms levels (tier 3). We discussed the relationship between these three tiers and introduced some further clarifications of our definition. Subsequently, we outlined some of the key points of criticism of our concept of solidarity to date and took this criticism as an opportunity to explain some aspects of our work in greater detail, and to expand on other aspects that had been insufficiently developed or misunderstood in our earlier work.

We then clarified that although our understanding of solidarity has normative implications, it does not ascribe normative value to the concept of solidarity itself. Because solidarity almost always excludes some people from its benefits, we need to look at the societal and political structures that the practice is embedded in, and what values those who practise solidarity are committed to serving, to assess the value of solidarity in a specific instance. An understanding of solidarity as practice brings with it that context is always part of the practical situation. It is one of the sources of meaning of a practice. It does not, however, determine people's action in a linear way: while the similarities and differences to other people that we see are shaped to a large extent by the concrete situation and by the discursive, political and economic landscapes that we are part of, whether or not we act upon is a matter of choice and commitment.

We explained that this is where our account takes a normative form. One simple yet important political normative argument in line with our understanding of solidarity is that solidaristic practices that are likely to increase the well-being of all members of society are worthy of support. We also take it for granted that this overall goal is worthy for any society.

In many contexts, this will mean that solidarity practised on the basis of common traits shared by wide groups of people, or even all people, is preferable over solidaristic practice based on more specific – and thus more exclusive – characteristics. Especially where fundamental interests of humans are at stake, such as in healthcare, the aim should be not to exclude anybody a priori from a solidaristic practice. When less fundamental interests are concerned, solidarity based on the recognition of specific characteristics – such as admiration for the same film maker as the basis of helping somebody out by paying for her movie ticket – seems comparably unproblematic. Again, the main focus on exclusion precludes a practice to count as solidaristic in our understanding in the first place.

The next chapter is devoted to the normative content and use of solidarity. We will give an overview of what we consider the three main strands of normative scholarship on solidarity – group solidarity, political solidarity and universal solidarity – and then situate our own approach in relationship to these traditions.

4

Solidarity: Normative Approaches

4.1 Introduction

In previous chapters, we sketched some of the lines of thought that have influenced our own understanding of solidarity (Chapters 1 and 2). We then presented our definition of solidarity as enacted commitments to accept costs to assist others with whom a person or persons recognise similarity in a relevant respect (Chapter 3). We explained the elements of our definition, relating them back to the bigger debates sketched in previous chapters. We also engaged with some of our critics in the process. In this final chapter of the theoretical part of this book, we will situate our understanding of solidarity in the debate around the concept's normative content, aiming to contribute to the critical discussion of the role solidarity can play as a normative principle.[1] In other words, we will draw out what normative conclusions can be drawn from our understanding of solidarity regarding the conduct of people and the organisation of society. Before we do so, we will briefly comment on a phenomenon that seems to be more common in connection with solidarity than with other terms, namely the crypto-normative usage of the term.

4.2 Solidarity: Descriptive and Crypto-Normative Usage

4.2.1 Descriptive Solidarity

As discussed in Chapter 1, solidarity is often used as a descriptive term to capture various 'bonds that bind people together' (Arts and Verburg 2001). It is taken to denote different types of mutual attachments within social groups, or, more generally, reasons for social cohesion, and for 'the relevant sense of belonging together in a society' (Houtepen and ter Meulen 2000b). Kurt Bayertz sees as an important function of solidarity

---

[1] By this we mean that we will examine accounts of solidarity that are normative in that they say what solidarity should be about, and that argue that solidarity is (always) a good thing.

that it serves as an 'inner glue' (*inneres Bindemittel*) of societies (Bayertz 1998: 23).[2] Depending on the type of society in question, this 'glue' can consist of civic friendship (harking back to Aristotle's concept of *philia*, applied widely to individuals, families, tribes, states, etc.),[3] or capture less intimate and personal forms of interconnectedness in bigger, modern societies and nation states (Bayertz 1998).

Descriptive uses of solidarity – where solidarity is used to describe certain social bonds or relationships – are mostly found within the social science literature. Outside of the social sciences, descriptive uses are relatively rare; more often, the descriptive side is taken to be one important element of a fuller understanding of solidarity whose most important element is its normative meaning. In many writings about the modern welfare state, discussions start out with solidarity being used descriptively to capture some essential features of the state in question, such as particular forms and institutions of mutual support in a society. Ruud ter Meulen and Rob Houtepen, writing about the Netherlands, see solidarity as a requirement 'to keep the fabric of modern societies intact' (Houtepen and ter Meulen 2000a). This social fabric has recently been perceived to be under threat, starting with the retreat of welfare states in continental Europe at the end of the twentieth century, and being fuelled again by economic and political crises, such as the financial crisis of 2008 and following years. More and more people, it is argued, seem to oppose transfer payments and other social services to those with lower social economic status.[4]

4.2.2   Crypto-Normative Usage of Solidarity

Particularly when it is used to justify specific policies, solidarity is often referred to but not unpacked. It is mentioned in passing, or it is introduced

---

[2] Bayertz distinguishes four types of solidarity: besides the aforementioned type of solidarity as 'inner glue' of societies, he speaks of solidarity as brotherhood, of welfare state solidarity and of solidarity as a strongly normative group label. Bayertz does not subscribe to or give priority to any of these understandings.

[3] 'Wanting for someone what one thinks good, for his sake and not for one's own, and being inclined, so far as one can, to do such things for him' (Aristotle Rhetoric 1380b36–1381a2).

[4] See Bertelsmann-Stiftung (2012); Poferl (2006); see also Houtepen and ter Meulen's (2000a, b) writings on the European welfare state, ter Meulen et al. (2010) and Komter's (2005) empirical studies on solidarity in the Netherlands. Ter Meulen, in a recent article, describes a 'narrowing of solidarity' towards what he calls 'interest' solidarity. According to him, people are less willing to engage in pro-social behaviours and support others. Instead, they have a reciprocal expectation of having their interests met through solidary systems, e.g. public healthcare systems (see ter Meulen 2015: 5). A practice where the decisive motivation rested on reciprocity would not meet our criteria of solidarity (see Chapter 3).

as a descriptive concept and then normative statements are derived from it, as if a mere reference to solidarity could justify that normative claim. Frequently, the description of solidarity as a descriptive statement about modern welfare state arrangements thus crosses over into a normative appellation. Solidarity in such cases is applied with dual connotations; first as a description of a particular state of affairs, such as social cohesion, group empathy or communal engagement, which is also, secondly, taken to be positive and desirable. This, in turn, leads to appellative or prescriptive statements. Solidarity is often described as being under threat and taken to be in need of protection or support – without any argument provided to justify such claims. Such crypto-normative usage of the concepts has undoubtedly contributed to the understanding that solidarity is a 'vague', empty label (e.g. Capaldi 1999), that authors writing about it are prone to committing naturalistic fallacies, or that they only 'tap into the associated feelings' without providing reasoned argument and explanation (a phenomenon that Sally Scholz aptly calls 'parasitical' solidarity, Scholz 2008: 12). It has therefore been our explicit goal throughout our work on solidarity to highlight the potential of the term to be misused as a stand-in for reasoned argument and debate in a number of fields (see Prainsack and Buyx 2011).

4.3   Solidarity and Normativity

It is relatively straightforward to define terms such as substantive human rights, or justice, as normative concepts, namely concepts that capture claims about how things should be and how we ought to act. From the early beginning of classical philosophical thought, such as Plato's discussions of various definitions of justice in his *Politeia*, justice has been described, defined and used as a normative concept. Human rights were explicitly developed as the prescriptive instruments of implementing a normative understanding of rights that everybody is entitled to, by virtue of being human. Debates rage on in political philosophy, political theory and related fields about what the right conception or theory of justice is, and what the moral status and scope of human rights can be.[5] As such, we might disagree about a concept's scope, structure and content; for example, we might subscribe to a deontological theory of justice, or to a

---

[5] We referenced a number of important works on the right definition of justice in Chapter 2. For debates on human rights, see e.g. Nickel (2014) who provides a substantive bibliography.

consequentialist one. However, we would not deny that any such conception or theory provides us with norms about how to order our world and what to do, telling us our moral obligations and duties, and giving us guidance on how to develop policy and practice.

Cast in explicitly philosophical language, the definition and debate of concepts such as justice fall into the realm of deontic normativity (see e.g. Heyd 2012). The normative character of judgements in this category relates to 'what ought to be done, to duties and obligations, to justice and rights' (Heyd 2012). Moral requirements of this kind are usually abstract, but accompanied with specific criteria of how to fulfil them, and with established sanctions when they are violated. As philosopher David Heyd puts it, the deontic sphere of morality 'is often taken as describing the minimal conditions of morality, the basic requirements of social morality that secure a just society' (Heyd 2012). As such, they are fixed, abstract and often claim universal validity.[6] This is the sphere of theories of justice, and of any rights- or claim-based theory. Heyd contrasts this with the axiological sphere of normativity that is concerned with the nature, types and criteria of values, value judgements, as well as with character, goals and ideals of human agents.[7]

There is often an implicit expectation that the deontic kind is the main – or even only – kind of normativity relevant to ethical discourse and policy making, and that normative theories that do not offer abstract, fixed or universal principles or criteria of 'what ought to be done' are therefore failing to provide any clear guidance of how to act, and what policies to develop and choose. We believe that this assumption is mistaken and that there is substantive normative and policy guidance that can be derived from concepts that do not fall into the realm of deontic normativity, and that, in addition, are not exclusively normative, but have an important empirical and descriptive dimension – as is the case with solidarity. We will focus on this in the later parts of this chapter.

---

[6] Universality is not a necessary requirement; there are accounts that define and argue for deontic duties and principles within e.g., a particular nation state, or a particular community (see later in this chapter).

[7] In his recent article, Ruud ter Meulen employs a similar distinction along the lines of the classic philosophical dichotomy between two concepts that both are subsumed under 'morality' in the English language: Kant's morality *Moralität*, namely abstract rights and duties, with 'justice interpreted as a matter of universal duties between individuals, which can be justified on the basis of rational deliberations' (ter Meulen 2015: 10) and Hegel's work around *Sittlichkeit* (the ethical life) comprised of particularistic 'conditions in which the individual first and foremost finds his own self' (ibid).

4.4   From Axiological to Deontic: The Normativity of Our Understanding of Solidarity

As stated in Chapter 3, one of the aims of our approach is to improve the analytical value of the concept of solidarity. We also presented ours as a first and foremost a descriptive approach, enabling us to distinguish solidarity from related concepts and proposing a number of defining elements that help to determine whether specific practices or institutions are solidaristic or not. We posited that solidarity, in its most bare bones form, comprises enacted commitments to carry costs – in the widest sense of the word – to assist others with whom a person or persons recognise similarity in a relevant respect. This understanding of solidarity has normative dimensions, but these normative dimensions are primarily not of a deontic, but instead of an axiological kind. They are concerned with states of affairs and human agents, goodness and ideals and 'unlike its deontic counterpart, [these are] open-ended. Virtuous character traits, ethical ideals, or the goal of promoting human happiness have no fixed measure and can in principle be always improved and further perfected or realized' (Heyd 2012).

We would argue that particularly at the inter-personal level of solidarity, where individuals interact directly with each other, solidaristic practices fall mainly into the axiological domain. That is, these practices are enactments and expressions of who a person is, and wants to be. The recognition of similarity in a relevant respect, and the subsequent helping of someone based on that recognition, is not underpinned by some universal principle. Nor is it the application of an abstract and general, fixed understanding of, e.g. the human condition. Instead, such practice is transient, particularistic, context-dependent and shaped by the experiences, values, psychological states and the human, natural and artefactual environments of the person(s) engaging in the practice (see also Haidt 2001). At the inter-personal level, we thus take it, solidaristic practices are almost exclusively axiological.

Many solidaristic practices could, in addition, be classed as supererogatory; that is, in Urmson's classic description, praiseworthy though non-obligatory acts (Urmson 1958). Duties and claims based on rights are usually understood as obligatory; certainly, following them is not supererogatory. If a person helps someone with a heart attack because she is a consulting physician in an emergency room, then doing so is this person's professional duty and not normally a supererogatory, especially praiseworthy act. The same holds for all legal or moral duties that come with obligations we ascribe to people and institutions. In contrast, and to

reduce a complex debate[8] to what is pertinent for our discussion of solidarity, supererogatory acts and behaviours cannot be mandated. They are
voluntary and optional (sometimes, depending on the risks involved, they
can be classified as 'heroic'). In our understanding and, importantly, at the
inter-personal level of solidaristic practice, they arise out of the recognition of similarity in a relevant respect. This could invoke some criticism
by those who would take solidarity as a normative concept of the deontic
kind only, with clear duties of solidarity, and the opportunity to mandate
solidaristic behaviour (see 'our critics' in Chapter 3).

What are the implications of these distinctions for our understanding of
solidarity? Particularly at the inter-personal level, most solidaristic practices will be of the axiomatic, supererogatory kind. There is wide consensus that the axiomatic realm is, on the whole, subsidiary to the deontic
realm – at least on the level of practical policy, and the norms societies
govern themselves with. In other words, to achieve a decent society, first
we need to establish minimum conditions of justice and the related institutions necessary to implement and enforce these conditions, before we can
focus on fostering solidaristic practice. This means that when we ask which
concepts should have the strongest normative power within our societies,
solidarity cannot, and should not, replace justice; instead, the normative
values of the two concepts complement each other as they inform overlapping yet different kinds of practices. Most importantly, while justice is typically thought and acted into being in a top-down manner, solidarity often
emerges bottom-up.[9] Justice is destined to guide the creation of mechanisms for the allocation of resources in the widest sense of the word,
ranging from the distribution of tax burdens to healthcare to the right
to vote, often enforced by state or regional forms of power. Solidarity, in
contrast, requires that people *actually* recognise similarities with others
(at least at the inter-personal and communal levels, i.e. the first and second
tiers of our three-tier system). At least at the inter-personal level (tier 1),
solidarity can therefore be understood as a prerequisite of justice (Gould
2010), but it cannot be mandated and sanctioned in the way duties of justice can. Even at the level of contractual and legal solidarity (tier 3), where
solidaristic arrangements can be enforced by law, the stability of these

[8] There is an interesting debate about the exact definition and nature of supererogation
that we bracket here (but see e.g. Gamlund 2010; Heyd 1982; Kamm 1985; Mellema 1991;
Portmore 2003; Raz 1975; Vessel 2010).
[9] This is so for most mainstream understandings of distributive justice (Lamont and Favor
2014), and many global justice accounts (Brock 2015); an exception is e.g. justice as virtue
(see Slote 2014).

contractual and legal arrangements over time depends on whether they correspond with actual practices 'on the ground'. Here, at the level of contractual and legal obligations, solidarity does in fact directly overlap with justice. In sum, however, while justice is a thoroughly deontic – and more so, a universal – principle, solidarity is the 'putty' that fills some of the gaps that justice leaves open, for inter-individual, prosocial and supererogatory behaviour.[10]

Solidarity is thus a concept that helps us to make explicit when and how axiomatic practices cross over or change into deontic practices (which are codified as rules, duties and even laws). When solidarity practised between people changes into practices that are shared more widely in groups, and even more so when these practices become normative and start to shape contracts, laws and administrative norms (tier 3), they take on an increasingly deontic form.[11] For example, a patient with a chronic condition helping another patient with the same or a similar condition – out of a recognition of similarity in a relevant respect – to make changes to her house in order to get around more easily has no duty nor obligation of solidarity to do so. If she accepts costs that are beyond minimal, she performs a supererogatory, solidaristic act.[12] If both these patients become members of a patient support group, which has formed on the basis of a shared situation and

---

[10] Supererogation and altruism are, of course, not synonymous. Supererogation is an attribute or quality of several classes of practices. The fact that both altruism, for those who use this term, and solidarity are supererogatory does not have any bearing on our overall rejection of altruism as a term that implies a false dichotomy (namely the dichotomy between self- and other-regarding action; see Chapter 3).

[11] Ashley Taylor introduces the interesting distinction between 'expressive solidarity' (solidarity *with*) and 'robust' solidarity (*within* a group). The latter is based on bi- or multi-directional, sanctionable reciprocity and as such would fall into the deontic category. The former is concerned more with motivational factors and is taken to be uni-directional. While this distinction does not neatly map onto our practice-based understanding, it is useful to highlight that our account would be mostly 'expressive' on the inter-individual level 1, and evolve towards more robust solidarity, with accompanying growing expectations and implementations of reciprocity, on the higher levels. See Taylor (2015) and Chapter 3.

[12] It is also interesting to note that on this inter-personal level, there does not have to be any expectation of reciprocity; solidarity could manifest itself as an ad hoc, one-off act of help (see discussion on reciprocity in Chapters 3 and 7). Even if there is an unspoken or unconscious expectation of reciprocity in an indirect sense, this is not a precondition for solidarity at this level. For solidarity to effectively solidify further into higher levels of institutionalisation, however, either as a group-based practice or in legal, contractual or administrative provisions and norms, there will need to be a general sense of reciprocity in society. An expectation that those who contribute to solidaristic arrangements and practices will not be left alone if they ever need assistance is thus an important 'background condition' for solidarity to grow and stabilise.

shared experiences with a disease, the willingness to accept costs to help others within the group is a constitutive element for the group. Through this process of institutionalisation, and by virtue of their becoming fellow members of the support group, people's mutual help would cease to be supererogatory and cross over into a practice more akin to an obligation or duty (depending on the group's policies, forms of sanction, etc.). And where solidaristic practices have been institutionalised as national laws, such as the obligation of citizens to contribute to a solidarity-based health-care system, supererogation is no longer a condition for the practice to emerge, as it can be enforced by law. On these higher levels of institutionali-sation, solidaristic practices between people or groups as well as solidaristic norms – for example, laws that institutionalise mandatory contributions to a public healthcare system – could be described as practices where deontic instruments serve the enactment of axiological goals and ideals, and where axiological ideals and behaviours have been transferred into the deontic sphere. We can capture the aforementioned problem that in democratic societies, solidaristic laws and regulations, in order to become durable, need to be based on actual practices that people engage in voluntarily and not merely to avoid social or legal repercussions. When there are no actual axiological practices to support these norms, such laws and regulations would amount to little more than 'deontic shells'.

We will focus on the implications of grounding solidarity in the axi-ological sphere later. Before we do this, we discuss some of the explicitly normative approaches to solidarity that have recently gained prominence in philosophy and neighbouring disciplines, and contrast them with our approach.

4.5   Normative Solidarity: Three Approaches

Despite the relatively peripheral role that the concept of solidarity has played in modern moral philosophy and social theory, a number of nor-mative accounts of solidarity are currently being developed. This literature is growing and as such, any typology we develop here can only be prelimi-nary. Moreover, these approaches differ in many details, and imposing a classification on them runs the well-known risks of levelling nuances on the one hand, and disregarding overlap on the other. Nonetheless, it is pos-sible to make out three main strands within this scholarship that diverge with respect to the source and the scope of normative solidarity. They can be subsumed under the rough headings of deontic group solidarity, politi-cal solidarity and universal solidarity.

4.5.1 Deontic Group Solidarity

Among contemporary normative approaches to solidarity, a discussion of deontic group solidarity is the most common type. Rooted in narrative and communitarian philosophical accounts sketched in Chapter 2, this strand of philosophical thought focuses on the importance of particular moral notions that emerge and are supported within particular groups and communities. Scholars sometimes posit themselves in opposition to 'mainstream' universalist (deontic) approaches that revolve around concepts such as justice, freedom, individual rights and liberties, etc., emphasising the importance of the particularistic normativity of particular communities and groups (see our discussion of communitarianism vs. liberalism in Chapter 2).

In accounts of solidarity that stand, broadly speaking, in this tradition, solidarity is the source of privileges, entitlements, duties and obligations that all members of a particular group share or recognise and enact towards each other. These accounts strive for the explication and justification of norms of the deontic kind, with duties and obligations to all group members. Philosopher Simon Derpmann, in one of the few recent monographs on solidarity as an explicitly normative concept, provides a succinct definition of this kind of solidarity: 'solidarity is understood as *a moral relation* between persons belonging to *a particular group*' (Derpmann 2013: 12, original emphasis, our translation). The joint commitment to shared values justifies the duties and obligations of solidarity within the group. Having and accepting such obligations, in turn, is taken by Derpmann to reinforce the group's cohesion and thus its intra-group solidarity: 'Solidarity must be based on the motivating conception that agents have an obligation towards other agents' (Derpmann 2009: 305). Derpmann emphasises the necessity to refute a 'neutral' moral standpoint, a central feature of influential liberal and egalitarian theories, in favour of particular, community-derived reasons for moral claims, duties and obligations that flow from a particular shared worldview, particular shared values or a particular shared situation or context (Derpmann 2013: chapters 6 and 7).[13] Translated into the language of political philosophy,

---

[13] Group solidarity is typically seen as a result of shared values and a shared commitment to a common good, which are enacted as long-term, constant arrangements of solidarity (see the following examples of communitarian group solidarity). However, as Klaus-Peter Rippe (1998) points out, a variation of this kind of normative group solidarity could be more transient, originating in shared situations or circumstances that result in short-term group commitments. Speaking in the language of our own definition of solidarity (Chapter 3), such 'project-related' group solidarity is taken to play out on lower levels of

solidarity of this type is seen to stem from a shared 'thick' understanding of the good life and the common good among groups of people. Such a thick understanding of the common good also includes an understanding that risks or challenging and threatening circumstances that the group finds in itself are shared as well. The latter is also an important element in Angus Dawson and Marcel Verweij's understanding of solidarity: 'A core idea of solidarity is that the group as a whole shares the risks, burdens or possible threats' (Dawson and Verweij 2012: 1).

Prominent examples of this kind of group solidarity have also been developed by Alfred Tauber and Daniel Callahan (Callahan 1998, 2003; Tauber 2002). As discussed in Chapter 2, both are eloquent critics of what they perceive as the precedence given to an individualistic perspective where moral and practical policy decisions are concerned. They diagnose and criticise an overemphasis on the rights, interests and preferences of the individual to the detriment of common and public values, goods and resources. Callahan, for example, has long argued that the focus on individual autonomy is one of the root causes for the bad situation of the US healthcare system (Callahan 1998). Resources in the healthcare system, Callahan criticises, are predominantly devoted to improving the situation of individuals through (often high-tech) medical intervention and care; as a result, preventive and other, often structural measures[14] to improve the health of the population are left underfunded (Callahan 1998).

Group solidarity is seen as one of the social values that could balance out such overemphasis on the preferences of individuals and help give more weight to the shared common good of a community (Tauber 2002). In the context of healthcare, Callahan specifies the common good as the collective provision of a decent – not perfect – level of care for every member of the group suffering from pain or illness. Solidarity in this context means that in order to provide this level of healthcare, a degree of self-sacrifice by each member of the group (who, individually, would most likely prefer 'perfect' instead of just 'decent' care) is required (Callahan 1998: 171–2).

Solidarity, here, is tied to the membership of a specific group that shares particular values, convictions or situations – if only to be a member of the same nation, religion or gender. Since only members of the same group have duties of solidarity towards each other, Derpmann argues, solidarity

---

institutionalisation. It is more common, however, for authors who write about different kinds of normative group solidarity to envisage more stable structures of solidarity-based commitments and duties.

[14] These structural measures range from education to addressing the social determinants of health.

cannot extend beyond the group. Both group membership and the commitment to group values thus precede any actual practice of solidarity, and the practice itself, expressed in duties, obligations and respective entitlements, is restricted to the group. In other words, the entitlements of this kind of group solidarity – e.g. duties of assistance and support by and to other group members – have to be gained by entry into the group (citizenship within nation states, or by becoming a group member; see also Poferl 2006) and by commitment to the group's joint values and goals. Non-members of the group are therefore excluded from solidaristic practices. Thus, accounts of group solidarity have a strong focus on inclusion and exclusion – whether this is made explicit or not.

Little attention, however, is paid to the process of 'grouping', that is, how groups come into existence and according to what criteria distinctions between groups are drawn both by their members and by those outside the group. This is surprising, given the importance of groups in these accounts. It also leads directly to the most obvious strand of criticism, which runs along the lines of well-rehearsed arguments against non-universal moral theories, including communitarianism.[15] This criticism relates to the claim that the source of any moral claims and any duties of solidarity in theories of group solidarity is a joint understanding of the common good, a shared worldview or a collective commitment to particular views and values. However, as has been pointed out by many authors in the debates between liberal and communitarian political philosophical theories, it is problematic to simply *presuppose* or *assume* such shared understandings, particularly, where big entities such as entire nations and the norms that govern them are concerned. Pluralistic societies are characterised by the acceptance of a broad variety of values. Defining a particular common good, from which moral obligations flow, runs the risk of unduly disregarding or even silencing views that are not in accord with this presupposed common good.[16] It has been pointed out that at best, particularistic moral theories have a tendency to assume the status quo as morally binding, and at worst can become conventionalist or even autocratic, because the process of 'grouping' – who is part of the group, and why – is not considered

---

[15] We summarise these long-standing and complex debates here extremely briefly; see Chapter 2 for an overview of the arguments around non-universalist theories, communitarianism, etc. (see also Bell 2013, Dancy 2013; Gaus et al. 2015, all of which also provide extensive references).

[16] This is particularly relevant for those who would assume nation states to have defined common goods, because citizenship is usually something a person is born into, and not something she chose deliberately.

and therefore also cannot be criticised (Bell 2013). Liberal thinkers, as
e.g. Stout (1988) summarises, sometimes criticise communitarian visions
not because they see liberal visions of societies as fairer or more just, but
because the communitarian alternative, to them, bears even greater dan-
gers: 'Communitarians are to be distrusted because they call us into a kind
of solidarity with others in public life that would be disastrously totalitarian, threatening our private bonds and spiritual freedom' (Stout 1988: 233;
see also Bell 2013; Dworkin 1989; Frazer and Lacey 1993; Kymlicka 1989).
But criticism of communitarianism does not come from liberal thought
alone: Loewy and Loewy (2007: 262), for example, call 'parochial communitarianism' the way in which '[s]ome religions may include only their
own members and some secular groups of persons may limit such obligations to other members of their own race or community'.

The above arguments against the role of communities and groups
within communitarian thought have purchase in the case of solidarity as
well. In a group whose members are seen to owe each other solidaristic
support, it is unclear who is entitled to define what this support should
consist of, and on what basis. Callahan's quasi-anthropological sugges-
tion that it is the quest to reduce human suffering and vulnerability that
forms (part of the) common good, and that this shared quest thus gives
rise to solidarity, might have some plausibility. However, in order to
explain and justify inclusion and exclusion within groups whose members are solidaristic with each other, and in particular, in order to justify
policy decisions based on this kind of solidarity, such assumptions are
insufficient. Human vulnerability and suffering are universal (as others
who use them within their global solidarity arguments have pointed out
in great detail, see later), and in order to claim them as the basis of a common good that is, at the same time, *limited to* members of a particular
group or nation, it would need to be shown empirically that these very
generic similarities are indeed recognised by the members of the group
as similarities in a relevant respect – but are not, at the same time, recognised with anyone else.

Other supporters of group solidarity, like Derpmann, or Dawson and
Verweij, insist that a specific idea of the common good within a group is
a precondition for solidarity. They do not elaborate on the way in which
this common good should be chosen or defined, however, or by whom.[17]

---

[17] In the final chapter of his rich philosophical examination of solidarity, Derpmann (2013:
chapter 7) offers some general criteria for how 'reasons of solidarity' (*Gründe der Solidarität*,
our translation) could be evaluated, and what types of group solidarities should not be

It remains unclear why a particular common good – say, using public money to pay for more high-tech healthcare services – and not another – say, using these resources for levelling the socio-economic gradient[18] – underlies, or should underlie, the constitution of a group. Moreover, these authors remain silent on how any common good gives rise to solidaristic duties and entitlements. One could think a group's common good rested on evidence that members supported a particular common good, but authors such as Dawson and Verweij explicitly reject consent, choice and 'signing up' as playing any part in group solidarity (which they call 'constitutive solidarity').[19] It is thus unclear where the commitment to a particular common good – say, prioritising the reduction of socio-economic inequality over paying for more high-tech healthcare services – would, and indeed, should, come from. However, if such a common good is taken to give rise to solidarity, as group solidarity theorists assume, then its emergence and affirmation require argument, or evidence of actual practice by people. In the absence of either, it is unclear how and why the groups that are the very foundation of this kind of solidarity come into existence in the first place. To quote Dawson and Verweij: constitutive solidarity 'is emergent from who we are as members of that group. (. . .) Arguably, it only makes sense to talk of solidarity if there are in fact sufficiently strong bonds within a group already' (Dawson and Verweij 2012: 2). Presupposing existing groups in this way, with 'already strong bonds' in place, could reconfirm a reactionary status quo.

The most likely explanation for why authors such as Dawson and Verweij pay so little attention to the processes and criteria of group formation is that they take groups as a given, as something that is already there. Such an understanding disregards entirely the fact that groups can be formed *because of* practices of solidarity. There is no reason to assume that groups always, and certainly not necessarily, precede solidaristic practice. When after a natural disaster, for example, people donate money to

---

acceptable, but he does not offer any specific guidance as to how such criteria should be applied, and by whom, and what the resulting common goods could look like.

[18] These examples are a deliberate allusion to long-standing discussions about whether it is the extent of state-of-the-art healthcare, or addressing the social determinants of health (income inequalities, relative deprivation, etc.) that have the biggest impact on public health. Valid arguments have been made for both, with the overall evidence pointing towards the latter approach (Daniels 2008; Marmot et al. 2010; Sigerist 1943; Venkatapuram 2011).

[19] 'Its' [constitutive solidarity's] existence is not dependent on consent, on "signing up", on any quasi-contracts or sense of reciprocal or mutual benefit. It pre-exists individuals and endures after them' (Dawson and Verweij 2012: 2).

provide disaster relief, provide spontaneous shelter for those affected or log on to social media to help locate missing persons in their area, new groups are in the making (Anderson 1991). In such cases, solidarity is indeed constitutive of a collective identity which may become more stable and fixed but which may also disperse and reconfigure differently in a different context. If, as Dawson and Verweij suggest, 'constitutive solidarity' is understood as 'emergent from who we are as members of that group', then this misses the point that people enacting solidarity with others may not be members of the same pre-existing group at all; instead, they see similarity between themselves and an emerging group of others with whom they are building relations *in the enactment* of solidarity.[20] Group solidarity accounts that do not reflect upon the status, emergence and delineation of the groups that they rely upon can thus run the danger of reconfirming static, conventionalist understandings of who is – and indeed, should be – practicing solidarity with whom. At worst, they could condone sexist, nationalistic and racist rationales that have given rise to collective identities in our societies.

4.5.2   Political Solidarity

Related to group solidarity are different understandings of 'political solidarity' that have been explored in political theory. These authors reflect more explicitly – and often critically – on processes and criteria of inclusion and exclusion. Hence, the relational and group-specific elements of solidarity, and more specifically, the moral relation between members of a particular community, are emphasised in these approaches as well. In one of the best-known and most influential articulations developed by philosopher Sally Scholz, political solidarity is understood as 'a relation that forms *a unity of individuals* each responding to a particular situation of injustice, oppression, or social vulnerabilities' (Scholz 2008: 12–13, our emphasis). Political solidarity here is exemplified in the form of political action that stems from relational bonds between people who 'unite around some mutually recognized political need or goal in order to bring about social change' (Scholz 2009: 208) – with corresponding accountability and duties of solidarity of cooperation, social criticism and activism (ibid: 210).

The understanding of the term 'political' in 'political solidarity' usually denotes the active responding to situations that are considered socially

---

[20] This paragraph relies on the argument we make in more detail in our response to Dawson and Verweij in Prainsack and Buyx (2012b).

unacceptable, irrespective of geographical boundaries between people. Because of this emphasis, and in contrast to scholarship focusing on group solidarity as discussed earlier, the political solidarity approach critically reflects the criteria and processes of inclusion and exclusion. The groups and communities within which solidarity is or should be practiced are neither treated as static nor (regionally) presupposed, e.g. based on state borders or citizenship; instead, they are fluid and changeable and can 'emerge' around common causes (Scholz 2008: chapter 4). Shared understandings of e.g. situations of oppression and shared goals to alleviate these are often seen as the moral causes underpinning concrete expressions of solidarity. The focus on concrete and often goal-oriented ('project-related', Rippe 1998) shared understandings in the political solidarity strand thus differs from more generic notions of the good life that group solidarity presupposes.

While such accounts of political solidarity better reflect the heterogeneous nature of modern societies, they can also, like group solidarity, run into difficulties when they are probed to account for why and how such shared understandings come into existence. They equally struggle to explain on what grounds membership and inclusion in the political solidarity group would or should be determined, particularly in view of corresponding duties and entitlements. One way to provide such an explanation would be by referring to the analysis of existing empirical data on emerging phenomena of mutual help and common causes – that is, recognising the importance of the contextual analysis necessary to understand when, how and why similarities have been or are being recognised between people and groups.

In the absence of recognising the importance of such contextual analysis, the selection of what kinds of common causes underlie an account of political solidarity requires some argument; it also influences what the particular account can offer in terms of relevance for the analysis of actual phenomena. For example, because of its explicit foundation in cases of injustice or oppression, Scholz's strong normative account is applicable to a surprisingly narrow set of situations – it does not allow for a conception of solidarity outside of perceived social inequities and vulnerabilities.[21]

---

[21] This would mean, in effect, that several of the topics commonly associated with solidarity in the biomedical sphere, including our case studies in this book – organ donation, databanks and personalised medicine – would only come under the remit of Scholz's political solidarity if there were cases of social vulnerabilities, oppression, etc. This might indeed often be the case, but certainly not in all cases where we might think that a solidarity perspective could be fruitful.

While we greatly sympathise with an approach that focuses on solidarity where it is assumed to do the most good, we believe that the restriction to injustices and oppression is not necessary and indeed limits an otherwise rich and inspiring theory.

Other accounts of political solidarity see as the key 'unit' for solidaristic action not an otherwise undefined group that is bound together by a common cause or a shared notion of the common good, but the (nation) state. An example for the latter is the work of the political philosopher Meena Krishnamurty, who argues that '[t]o the extent that we are concerned with political solidarity, it is a relation that takes place between *those within a shared state*, that is, *among fellow citizens*' (Krishnamurty 2013: 129, our emphasis).[22] Citizens are taken to share affective bonds, be it because they share common points of reference from a shared history, as advanced by political scientist David Kahane (1999), or 'attitudes of collective identification, mutual respect, mutual trust, and mutual support and loyalty toward one another' (Krishnamurty 2013: 129).

Accounts that develop political solidarity with specific reference to nation states and modern democracies, such as the ones by Krishnamurty and Kahane, suffer from one of the issues discussed earlier with regard to group solidarity: to a significant degree, nation states are historical artefacts. In times of increasing globalisation, pluralism and multiculturalism, it is difficult to see why fellow citizens share mutual respect, support and trust that give rise to solidarity simply by virtue of being citizens of a nation state. Empirical evidence to this effect would be needed for this position to be compelling; the mere assumption that citizens of a given state entity are more likely to provide solidaristic support to other citizens than with other people – such as their relatives on the other side of the world, or their fellow Muslims, Jews, Buddhists, Christians, etc. in another country – is unconvincing. This unexamined assumption also puts such conceptions of political solidarity in danger of remaining merely programmatic (see also the discussion of global solidarity in Chapter 2).

---

[22] Interestingly and in contrast, Scholz calls this kind of solidarity 'civic solidarity' (Scholz 2008: chapter 1). According to her, solidarity that refers to the relationship between citizens within a political state is distinct from (her kind of) political solidarity, which emerges through cohesion between people united by a common political commitment and conviction, regardless of their 'categorical identity' (Calhoun 2002) pertaining to nation or territory. As mentioned, there is some overlap between the three clusters of accounts we describe here; it would be possible to class Krishnamurty's account as belonging into the group solidarity cluster; however, we follow her own description of her account as 'political solidarity'.

We should note here that Krishnamurty tries to avoid this issue by not deriving specific duties or obligations of solidarity and instead restricts the normative function of her political philosophy to a 'developmental' and 'motivational contribution' with regards to justice: 'relations of political solidarity play an integral role in engendering a firm commitment to justice, in the developmental and motivational senses, among citizens' (Krishnamurty 2013: 134). This comes close to what we have described earlier as a recognition that solidarity is mainly axiological, and is also an element common to the third type of normative solidarity, universal or global solidarity, which we discuss next, and which transcends group categories altogether. However, this motivational element is not easily compatible with the actual borders of most nation states: there is no reason why the developmental and motivational contribution that relations of solidarity, according to Krishnamurty, give rise to, would be restricted only to citizens – unless it was the fact of citizenship *itself* which gave rise to these, and that in turn would be in need of a specific argument and justification. Thus, despite providing some interesting analyses of the role state institutions can play in fostering the social bases of political solidarity, Krishnamurty's understanding of political solidarity remains an ideal to aspire to; the true normative power in her account stems from a classical deontic, broadly Rawlsian conception of justice.

4.5.3   Universal/Global Solidarity

A number of authors have recently developed accounts of universal (or, with regards to corresponding political dimensions, global) solidarity. All of these accounts move away from a focus on specific groups or national communities and instead try to develop an understanding of solidarity that includes all humans (or even animals, see Rock and Degeling 2015). This strand of scholarship tends to draw strongly on Jürgen Habermas (1984; 1986; see also Chapter 2).[23]

Some of the literature that tries to argue for solidarity entailing all human beings takes what Krishnamurty calls 'the developmental or motivational' route. Scholars assume that solidarity can aid the implementation or the

---

[23] Here we focus on the newer accounts of universal and global justice that also take into account the policy contexts in which we are specifically interested in for this book (e.g. medicine, public and global health, etc.). This is the reason why we do not devote much space to Habermas's particular account of solidarity, which forms part of his discourse ethics, and where universal solidarity is tied to discourse and interaction (see Habermas 1984, 1986, and discussions of his work on solidarity, e.g. by Sterno 2009).

validity of other universal and explicitly deontic concepts. Political philosopher Carol Gould (2004, 2007, 2014), for example, uses the term 'network solidarity' to refer to solidarity across borders. Gould understands
solidarity as one of the 'fundamentally social bases of the norms of global
justice' (Gould 2014: 7). According to her, such solidarity is distinctly different from historical instances of group solidarity in that it denotes a 'conception more suitable to the new forms of transnational interrelationships
that are being established' (ibid: 99). Referring to Rorty's work, and against
a background understanding of general human solidarity,[24] the more specific notion of solidarity she develops is based on 'fellow feeling'. It derives
from identification with – often remote – others and leads to shared commitments to establish justice to aid them: 'The shared values that charac-
terize these solidarity relationships consist, then, in a shared commitment
to justice, or perhaps also, in more consequentialist terms, to the elimina-
tion of suffering' (ibid: 110). Further, solidarity presupposes empathy, 'yet
moves beyond this to a readiness to take action in support of others', focus-
sing on aid that is most beneficial to them (ibid: 111).

Gould's network solidarity comes close to Scholz's understanding of
political solidarity we described earlier,[25] which applies to people joining their fate with respect to shared goals and commitments irrespective of national borders. Where Gould's network solidarity differs from
Scholz's political solidarity is that Gould, in contrast to Scholz, understands global solidarity as entailing an explicit emphasis on human rights
and global justice: solidarity, Gould argues, can raise awareness of the fact
that there are shared needs for notions of global justice. She also argues that
because solidarity brings the interconnectedness of people to the fore, it can
help to justify a reconsideration of how resources in transnational contexts
are distributed so that they increase global justice. Solidarity further desig-
nates, for Gould, 'a willingness to acknowledge need in everyone else and
to act in general ways to support their human rights, especially by working toward the construction of transnational institutions that can allow for

[24] Gould describes general human solidarity as 'a limit notion, or what might be called a
horizon of possibility, where it refers to a disposition that each can have to act in solidarity
with some others' (Gould 2014: 109).

[25] Again, we underline that the distinction in the three strands of scholarship is to some
degree arbitrary, as they overlap. However, because accounts in each of the three strands
share central features that mark out important differences, we believe it is justified to group
them in the way we have done; on a pragmatic level, it aids a summary presentation of
contemporary normative accounts of solidarity overall.

their fulfilment worldwide, or by participating in social movements that take such egalitarian rights fulfilment as a goal' (Gould 2007: 155).

With the idea of overlapping network solidarity/solidarities, Gould strives to avoid the formulation of a purely abstract concept of human solidarity that was famously criticised by Richard Rorty. Rorty argued that the universal, collective 'we' that such a concept of solidarity presupposes is too abstract and too big to make any sense philosophically (Rorty 1989: esp. 190 ff.). Gould retains some idea of a general human solidarity, but her central interest lies in smaller, overlapping solidarity networks that are more specific than just a disposition towards mutual aid. One of the main characteristics of such solidarity networks is that they can cross borders and 'apply to relations to others at a distance. This move will only be possible, however, if we take solidarity to denote a relationship to individuals or groups smaller than the universe of human beings generally' (Gould 2007: 149). The solidarity networks she envisages as underlying a number of transnational and global actions and political initiatives are related to specific goals and practices; they 'work to construct forms of global justice on the ground'.

Gould's framing of network solidarities as a means to motivate a more effective implementation of justice and human rights provides another interesting example of the bridging function of solidarity between the axiomatic and the deontic. Solidarity, for Gould, is the human disposition that enables both the feasibility as well as the actual emergence of the norms, laws and sanctions that are grounded in justice and human rights (Gould 2007: 162). Such an anthropological understanding is in line with empirical findings on the general relational nature of human existence (helpful overviews and many references in: Bierhoff and Küpper 1997; Mackenzie and Stoljar 2000; Taylor 1985c; Voland 1997; see also Chapter 2).

Lisa Eckenwiler, Christine Straehle and Ryoa Chung, in their recent work on health inequalities and health worker migration, strive to extend the 'affective affinity' they see as the basis of Gould's conception of solidarity by including relational and structural aspects and a focus on the commonality of shared problems (this comes close to our notion of recognition of similarity in a relevant respect). Their understanding builds on Iris Marion Young's work, for whom people 'dwell together' in complex relations of structural interdependence that might transcend national borders and that emerge around and might contribute to injustices (Young 1990). According to Young, because of structural injustices, we are motivated to acts of solidarity that may have global reach. This, again, is echoed in Gould's dispositional motivation that solidarity provides for

constructing and implementing universal concepts such as global justice
and human rights. Eckenwiler and colleagues extend this and argue that
to explain the motivation for action that solidarity provides, a relational
understanding of personhood is required: 'If we conceive of individuals
as ecological subjects who are intersubjectively defined, and thus interde-
pendent, we can motivate solidarity beyond affective ties' (Eckenwiler et al.
2012: 383). Eckenwiler and colleagues fall short, however, of explaining
how the deontic elements of their solidarity-based 'obligations of mutual
cooperation, and collective responsibility for global public health' (ibid:
388) come into existence. Nevertheless, their contribution adds the vital
dimension of a concept of a person, both as an explanatory category (what
are the subjects that act in solidaristic ways like), as well as a source of
normativity for solidarity. The concept of personhood plays a central role
in the normative dimension of our understanding of solidarity as well (see
previous chapters).

Another strand of normative work on solidarity that does not fall neatly
in one of the three categories we have developed here is the work of political
theorist Jodi Dean (1996). In her notion of reflective solidarity[26] she aims
to combine solidarity with a positive approach to differences, thus putting
the spotlight on the aforementioned issue of inclusion and exclusion that
remains unexplored in some accounts of group solidarity. Seeing differences between ourselves and others, for Dean, is inevitable; however, we
should be conscious and critically reflective of how and why we separate others from ourselves. Dean's notion of reflective solidarity 'refers to *a mutual
expectation of a responsible orientation to relationship*' (Dean 1996: 29,
original emphasis). Responsibility, here, means that we are accountable for
excluding others, and 'orientation to relationship recognizes that we can
acknowledge our mutual expectations without hypostatizing them into a
restrictive set of norms'. Dean's main normative argument is thus a proce-
dural one: reflective solidarity should 'require us to rethink the boundaries
of community, the demarcation between "us" and "them". [. . . It] conceives
the ties connecting us as communicative and open. This openness creates
a space for accountability, enabling us to grasp the ways this notion of solidarity no longer blocks us from difference, but instead provides a bridge
between identity and universality' (Dean 1996: 30). According to Dean,

---

[26] A similar term – 'reflexive solidarity' – is used by Houtepen and ter Meulen (2000b: 367)
when they suggest that linking the work of political theorist Herman van Gunsteren (1998)
with Anthony Giddens's (1994) work 'offers important clues to develop a joint approach to
democratic citizenship and reflexive solidarity' (see also Beck et al. 1993).

then, our main ethical duty with respect to solidarity is that we reflect on practices and institutions of exclusion regarding both their criteria and their scope, and the underlying substantive values and norms. Dean's mobilisation of solidarity amounts to a call for tolerance, communication and inclusion. While she does not explicitly work towards a universal or global understanding of solidarity, her approach is applicable across borders and would indeed enjoin us to reflect upon the differences with whom we do not share location, country, ethnicity, etc.

4.6 Conclusions

We have argued that solidarity, in our understanding, is a descriptive–normative concept grounded in the axiological sphere. Depending on the level of institutionalisation, some enactments move towards the deontic. This entails that solidarity is suited neither to be framed nor applied in the way clearly deontic concepts such as human rights, or justice, can be. That is, solidarity cannot be framed as ideal theory, without regard of actual practical conditions and empirical evidence for practices and behaviours. Nor can it be applied as a normative ideal; that is, a theoretical ideal of how people should act, without regard of how, and why, they actually *do* act. Some of the normative approaches to solidarity we have discussed try to develop such conceptions, with various degrees of attention to actual empirical evidence and data, and run into several problems we have sketched in this chapter. Again, the importance of contextual analysis must be stressed. It should also be noted that not conceptualising solidarity as a normative ideal entails an acceptance that there will be some solidaristic practices that can be considered problematic – for other ethical, or even legal reasons – and that this cannot be done away with in our account (see our remarks on this in Chapter 3).

Our own approach differs from accounts of group-based and political solidarity insofar as these presuppose the existence of certain groups (families, neighbourhoods, nations) as quasi-natural reference communities within which solidarity is, or should be, practised. We stress the importance of paying close attention to the processes of how groups emerge; that is, to 'grouping'. Our approach shares several features with the third strand of the literature that we discussed, namely global or universal understandings of solidarity. First, again, we deem solidarity to be largely axiological. While the authors mentioned do not use this terminology, both Gould's and Scholz's 'motivational' roles that solidarity plays towards constructing and establishing justice and human rights seem to be underpinned by an axiomatic understanding of solidarity, with the latter helping to implement and secure deontic principles. Secondly, a central element of our definition of solidarity – similarity in a relevant respect – is inspired by Dean's work. Importantly, this mandates a focus on what connects us, instead of what sets us apart. We believe that this goes some way to uncover problematic practices that could appear to be solidaristic (e.g. in, say, racist communities) as not solidaristic: any practice that has a central, decisive focus on exclusion cannot be solidaristic by our definition (see also Chapter 3).

Thirdly and importantly, like Eckenwiler and colleagues, our understanding of solidarity rests on a relational notion of personhood that sees people's identities, interests and actions as shaped also by their relations to their human, natural and artefactual environments (see in detail Chapter 3). Such a 'thick' understanding of personhood is vital for a fruitful understanding and employment of solidarity. Particularly at the interpersonal level, solidaristic practices are also expressions of who one is as a person. Even more importantly, enacting solidarity also entails intentional action. The enactment is intentional and thus, an act of personal autonomy (which we understand as relational autonomy, see Chapter 3). For people to flourish, we need societies that allow for relational practices to be supported and flourish – which in turn includes fostering solidaristic practices within society overall.[27] And in order that solidarity grows, we need to order our societies so that solidarity practices and policies are preferred and supported.[28] As we will see in more detail in the second, applied part of our book, this line of argument is where the political and policy guidance part of our solidarity understanding comes from. In fact, it develops considerable normative as well as transformative force when applied to governance and policy making: there are surprisingly few policies that explicitly recognise, embody or foster solidarity as we understand it, or at least allow for the practice to thrive. Suggesting that policies that recognise or are compatible with solidarity are to be preferred over those that, say, focus primarily on the protection of individual rights results in recommendations for changes to governance that can be quite controversial, as we will show in the second part of this book.

---

[27] For the important exceptions to this – namely, problematic solidaristic practices – see the previous chapter.

[28] While we acknowledge that our understanding of solidarity therefore chimes best with a democratic, pluralistic setting where there is a wide variety of opportunities and choices, we believe that it is also possible to have recognition in a relevant respect in severely autonomy-restricted settings. In these latter settings, solidarity is less likely to grow and institutionalise.

PART II

Solidarity in Practice

Solidarity in Practice I: Governing Health Databases

5.1 Introduction

New opportunities and technologies for large-scale data linkage and datamining have rendered databases one of the key resources for many areas of public life. In fields as varied as medical research, marketing and government, databases have become indispensible resources for generating knowledge and innovation. They are sources of great social benefit, and also of concern. Ethical and regulatory challenges arise from the virtual ubiquity of databases and the increasing digitalisation of datasets, and also from increasing possibilities to link and search digital datasets (e.g. Mittelstadt and Floridi 2015; NCoB 2015; Pasquale 2015; Prainsack 2015a). Moreover, many of the datasets established and used today lend themselves to both aggregation and 'drilling down', namely the automated searching for information throughout different hierarchies of records or files. This means that it has become much easier to go back and forth between the individual and aggregate level. As sociologist Lawrence Busch (2014) points out,

> In times past, the few [large-scale datasets] that existed were such that users were either forced to work with aggregates (e.g., census data), or they consisted of massive tomes (e.g., telephone directories) or huge files (e.g., real property or medical case records) from which individual records could be retrieved. However, with few exceptions, those [datasets] designed for aggregate analysis were such that *drilling down* was impossible, while those designed for drilling down were such that *aggregation* was all but impossible. All were both expensive and time consuming to collect, and even more expensive to analyze (our emphasis).

Because different datasets can be linked together much more easily, it is becoming increasingly common for insights obtained at the aggregate level to be used to make probabilistic 'predictions' about individuals. An example for this is the practice of consumer scoring (Dixon and Gellman 2014). Here, perfectly innocuous looking pieces of information about a person – such as the frequency of her grocery purchases, for example, the length of time she has been with her current employer or the type of car she drives – are used to assign a score to a person based on the statistical correlation of these pieces of information with relevant behaviours or characteristics, such as defaulting on a mortgage, suffering from a chronic illness or causing a car accident.[1]

The types of information that are used for such predictive analytics schemes are those that were found to correlate with a certain relevant characteristic at the aggregate level, while the causal relation between the two may be entirely unclear.[2] That predictive analytics yields a certain proportion of false positives and false negatives is seen as inevitable, as in any case of actuarial reasoning. For banks that are interested in people's health risk score when they assess mortgage applications, for example, it does not really matter if the scoring mechanism errs in the assessment of Susan Khan, if the prediction is accurate for 49 other people out of 50. The bank knows that their model will include a few false positives as well as false negatives, and it plans accordingly – it spreads its risk. To a specific person, however, a false assessment matters a lot; her mortgage application may be declined without her being aware of the reason, and there is no way to seek redress or even to correct the incorrect information. As Dixon and Gellman (2014) point out, in their chilling report on consumer scoring in the United States, as of yet there is no legal right for individuals to see their scores, or to know what types of information goes into the scoring algorithm. If scores are based on wrong information, then it is usually impossible for the affected person to rectify the mistake. The penalties for erroneous information are typically so low that scoring companies and credit bureaus do not pay much attention (Pasquale 2015: 191). This situation is troubling as it introduces a new decision-maker into our lives that is not transparent to the public and not accountable to anybody (see also Rieder 2005).

Against this backdrop it is apparent that not only data collection as such, especially linkage and datamining practices, but also questions revolving around access to data and information pose a range of ethical, regulatory

---

[1] For a recent example of the latter, see Hickey (2015). See also Prainsack (2015a).

[2] For example, a company specialising on health risk scoring may have found that out of all people in a large aggregate dataset, those who displayed a combination of seemingly random behaviours – such as buying vitamin supplements online, and purchasing fewer than five offline purchases with their credit cards per month – have a significantly increased risk to suffer a life-threatening illness in the following 12 months. Although it is unlikely that there is any direct causal connection between these criteria and the illness, the company will nevertheless use them to score individual people because the system is sufficiently reliable at the aggregate level.

and social challenges. This is particularly so in the domains of medicine and healthcare. In these areas, data are often sensitive to start with, even before linkage and mining occurs. At the same time, the pressure to 'share' data – with other researchers, public and private enterprises or the public as a whole – is bigger than ever. Some of that pressure comes from the pervasiveness of the idea of big data itself, as we discuss in the next section: because large datasets are available, so the argument goes, we need to utilise this resource and not let it go to waste. We are thus in need of new approaches to the governance of databases that strike a proper balance between the value of creating public benefit and the protection of personal goods, while at the same time counteracting the profound power asymmetries underlying much of the collection and use of personal data in our societies.

We believe that solidarity is a concept that can help us strike this balance. As described in detail in the previous chapters, we understand solidarity as enacted commitments to accept costs to assist others with whom a person or persons recognise similarity in a relevant respect. Using a solidarity-based perspective, we argue that a solution for governing health databases entails the overcoming of the dichotomy between personal and common benefit. We argue further that giving up this dichotomy moves different concerns to the foreground: instead of a focus on technical aspects such as informed consent or a conceptual focus on individual autonomy, a solidarity-based approach shifts our attention to shared societal benefit and shared societal responsibilities. It treats data sharing, information privacy and data protection as both collective and personal goods.

5.2   Power of Big Data

The notion of 'big data' is probably one of the most pervasive buzzwords in both scientific and public discourse at the moment. Yet it lacks a clear definition; it is used to describe both a paradigm and an approach for making probabilistic predictions about people and things on the basis of large datasets. Some authors argue that only the entirety of data representing a phenomenon – $N =$ all – deserves to be called big data (Harford 2014). Many understand it as both a cluster of technologies and processes to organise and search data with the help of analytical software in order to identify patterns and correlations (see also Cohen 2012). Because of this focus on correlation, Viktor Mayer-Schönberger and Kenneth Cukier describe the key tenet of the big data paradigm as a shift away from the 'age-old search for causality'. Instead of starting with the exploration of causes, these authors argue, 'big data' allow us to discover patterns and correlations that can lead to 'novel and invaluable insights [. . .] If millions of electronic medical records reveal that cancer sufferers who take a certain combination of aspirin and orange juice see their disease go into remission, then the exact cause for the improvement in health may be less important than the fact that they lived' (Mayer-Schönberger and Cukier 2013: 14). This is exactly the rationale that underpins the kind of consumer scoring that we described earlier.

A second characteristic of big data, besides the 'abolition' of causality, is a changing attitude towards the accuracy of individual measurements. In the context of 'small data', according to Mayer-Schönberger and Cukier, it is important for every single data point to be correct. In the context of big data, in contrast, the larger scale makes up for the inaccuracies in single data points such that the signal can still be located in the noise. If, for example, a person measured her temperature once a day, it would be important for each measurement to be accurate if she wanted to obtain a reliable fever curve over the course of the week. If she measured her temperature every 3 s, then it would be practically irrelevant if a few of these measurements were incorrect.

Scholars have called for a critical examination of the assumptions that the notion of big data brings to the table (Davies et al. 2012). One of the issues, as pointed out at the beginning of this chapter, is the notorious problem of conflating correlation and causation; to stick with the example of aspirin and orange juice, knowing that 80 per cent of the cancer patients in this study benefitted from this measure would not enable us to predict whether or not a particular patient will benefit from it. When the causes for a particular effect are not known, the utility of the information for individual patients is limited, regardless of the size of the dataset – because even if something has an effect on most people, it does not mean that it will have the same effect on us. Neither is it true that a larger scale of data can always compensate for inaccuracies at the level of individual data entries. If there is a problem with the recording of the data, then a larger scale of data will also scale up the inaccuracies (Spiegelhalter 2013).

There is also a shift towards linking datasets and using predictive analytics in and across more and more domains of life. The result of this is that any piece of data stemming from somebody is personal: it is personal in the sense that it can lead to the person's identification, or it can disclose something about her when linked with other data or information. The question is thus not how 'personal' the data are that are collected or stored by or about a person, but instead how *intimate* the information is that can be inferred. If somebody used the comments on a new research study that Lucas posted on *Facebook* or *Twitter* for a research project, for example, then these data allow less intimate inferences about our friend Lucas than if he shared his personal diaries or his genetic carrier status online. But given the possibility for data integration and data linkage, any data point, as innocent and trivial as it may look, could lead to probabilistic assumptions being made about a person that could be of an intimate nature, as in our examples about the likelihood of future hospitalisation or the prevalence of a chronic illness earlier. Assumptions regarding our lives and our health can be made even on the basis of the topics we write or tweet about, on the basis of the pictures we 'like' or share online or on the basis of the purchases we make with credit or company loyalty cards. Lucas's comments on a particular research study on a social media platform would disclose, at the very minimum, that Lucas reads scientific literature. The more easily datasets can be linked, the more tempting it becomes for companies and organisations to use data from and about people to make probabilistic 'predictions' about them, their future and also possibly their families and 'friends' on social media. It has been suggested that healthcare providers use this kind of data mining to identify 'risky' (read: costly) patients and offer different treatment to them than to low-risk patients (Eagle and Greene 2014). Patients who 'overuse' emergency rooms, for example, can be identified with the help of predictive analytics and pre-emptively targeted with advice to avoid that they end up using the ER (Society of Actuaries 2014). The flip side of such special treatment for high-risk patients could be a worsening of care, or, in a worst-case scenario, the loss of insurance cover altogether in countries that do not provide health insurance for all – which is one of the reasons that public healthcare is such a fundamentally important concern in today's societies (we will discuss this in detail in the next chapter).

While actuarial reasoning and risk stratification are widely used practices within private insurance, we are concerned about the adoption of predictive analytics in ever wider areas of healthcare. The stratification of people according to their actual or potential 'cost' to the system is diametrically opposed to the spirit of solidarity. Solidarity, as we lay out in Chapter 3, is reflected in people's commitments to accept 'costs' to support others with whom they recognise similarity in a relevant respect. When it comes to health, we all share in common that we are vulnerable to disease, and that we will need healthcare at some point in our lives. Although our specific health risks may be different, we share in common that we all face risks. Singling out people to whom we attribute particular risks, whether they are due to alleged moral failings – such as smoking (Buyx and Prainsack 2012) – or characteristics that we cannot be held accountable for – such as an inherited risk for a particular cancer – runs against the solidaristic principle that mandates that we act upon what connects us to others and not on what sets us apart. Health risk scoring, as mentioned earlier, would use both types of information to aid decisions that are likely to have tangible or even serious consequences for the people about whom they are made.

In sum, contemporary health databases do not represent merely a scaled up version of databases before the era of digitalisation and big data approaches. Databases today comprise the creation, collection and use of more types of data in the personal, clinical and public domain, and at much higher volume. These new challenges mean that we cannot simply scale up existing ethical and regulatory frameworks. As we argue in the next section, a solidarity-based approach not only suggests new practical solutions, but also moves different issues to the fore.

5.3   What Databases are Suitable for Solidarity-Based Governance?

Before we go into the meat of our solidarity-based approach to database governance, a few qualifiers of the types of databases and settings for which such solidarity-based governance would be suitable in general are in place. There are many different ways to classify databases, without there being a universal typology. Databases can be distinguished according to what types of data they hold, who owns or uses the data or for what purposes data are used, to name only a few important parameters. Of particular relevance for us here is whether or not data are digital and computable. If data are digital and computable, this greatly increases the potential for mining and analysis. We will introduce three additional criteria that are important for a discussion of database governance and solidarity (see also Prainsack in preparation).

5.3.1   *Do People Know that They are Contributing Data for Health-Related Research?*

The first aspect concerns the extent to which people are aware, or even actively involved, in the provision (i.e. creation, collection or recording) of data. The answer to this is not always straightforward. A person who is told about her positive HIV status may not participate actively in the recording of this information with health authorities, although she may have read a leaflet or been told by a healthcare worker about this and thus is aware that this information will be registered. A person whose smartphone geolocation data are 'donated' by her mobile phone provider to researchers studying the movement of people in urban metropolitan areas may be aware that her phone data are used by the company for billing purposes, marketing and similar purposes, but she may not know that they are used for research. Similarly, while people who use a mood diary to keep track of changes in their psychological and emotional well-being, and even those who use *Facebook* accounts, are actively involved in the creation or collection of health data, nevertheless they might not be aware that these data are used for research (a situation which, in the case of Facebook carrying out studies on their users without their explicit consent, recently led to significant controversy; see Meyer and Chabris 2015). Finally, most people who look up symptoms online are contributing data for marketing purposes, because websites often pass on data to *Google Analytics* or other services. Unless the user read the entire terms of service, she may not be aware of this (Libert 2014; Merchant 2015).

What is important in this respect for our model of solidarity-based database governance is that data collection that people have not agreed to, or are not even aware of, cannot be seen as part of a solidaristic practice. This is because solidaristic practice always includes intentionality and decision-making (see Chapters 3 and 4). Even institutionalised practices of solidarity, such as welfare society arrangements, entail that people are aware of what they contribute. They may not always have a say about what they contribute – such as in the case of tax payments, on the highest levels of institutionalised solidarity – but there needs to be a minimum level of transparency about what the costs are of the arrangement. Lack of knowledge of having 'donated' data precludes such a practice to qualify as a solidaristic practice; on the contrary, it raises the suspicion of exploitation.

5.3.2 *Do the Databases Serve Public or For-Profit Interests Primarily? Does the Database Aim at Creating Social Value?*

It is often impossible to establish exactly whether a particular database serves for-profit or public interests. The source of funding is not a reliable criterion: besides many databases receiving funding from both public and private sources, some publicly funded databases also allow data to be used for commercial purposes, and vice versa. An example of this would be data from personal health records held in public clinics also being used by pharmaceutical companies, as envisaged by the English care.data initiative: announced early in 2014, the initiative claimed to enable the 'sharing' of patient data held by the English National Health Service with researchers and corporate actors in the United Kingdom and abroad. The initiative encountered strong public opposition, because of how difficult it was for patients to opt out; its implementation was postponed until a yet undetermined date in the future (see e.g. Sterckx et al. 2015; Weaver 2014). Another example for the marriage of for-profit with non-profit motivations from the reverse direction of a commercial company seeking to increase public benefit would be data philanthropy (see Prainsack in preparation). For-profit companies or organisations that routinely collect large amounts of data as part of their core business 'donate' these data, with personal identifiers removed, to researchers who use them for public benefit.[3] Other formats of linking for-profit and non-profit activities are much older, such as corporate social responsibility programmes that companies have run for decades. Similarly, researchers at universities with links to industry are the rule rather than an exception in some disciplines. The point that we want to make here is that it can be very difficult, if not impossible, to determine the 'social value' of an organisation's activities just by looking at whether it is a commercial enterprise or a public initiative. This means that the distinction between the for-profit and non-profit nature of an institution hosting or running a database is not a suitable criterion for us to decide what governance form would be appropriate for database governance and whether it could be considered as a solidarity-based endeavour. Whether it can be considered suitable for solidarity-based governance depends upon the database serving an objective that those contributing to it endorse as a common goal, and on financial incentives not being the sole or decisive motivation for participation. Instead, the key motivation to contribute should be the willingness of people to support others, reach a common goal or create some other kind of social value – understood in the broadest sense of the word as something that improves the life of most citizens (by improving healthcare, social care,

---

[3] Geolocation data and call logs held by telephone companies, for example, can be mined in order to learn about likely disease outbreaks, based on the idea that disease outbreaks correlate with changes in patterns of movement of people in a particular area (see also Wesolowski et al. 2012). Geolocation data from mobile phone companies can also be used to monitor the movement of people after a natural disaster in order to aid the distribution of emergency relief (Bengtsson et al. 2011), or to improve the understanding of the spatial distribution of diseases (e.g. Stresman et al. 2014).

by making life more affordable, etc.).[4] In the context of biomedicine and healthcare, to which we restrict our focus in this chapter, it is relatively easy to find examples of creating social value through a database endeavour; wherever the goal is health- or treatment-related research, such as in research biobanks, social value is one of the results of the activities. However, it could still be possible that other structural features of a database preclude it from being regarded as solidarity-based, despite being situated in the health context. This would be the case for databases that collect health data from individuals and that could be utilised to generate socially valuable information and results, but where the primary goal is to link this to, say, participants' purchasing behaviour, and any useful analysis or aggregation of data with a view to improving individual or population health was not performed. This is why the other two criteria are equally important, and whether they apply will have to be decided by looking at each particular case.

5.3.3   Are Participants Compensated or Paid for Participating?

It is possible that people contribute to a database, even one that is set up with the sole aim to create social value, *merely* because they expect a personal benefit, such as a payment or direct reward. If such a direct personal benefit is the sole reason for a person to contribute data, this precludes their contribution from being classified as solidaristic. We hypothesise, however, that most people – although they may *also* expect a personal benefit – do not contribute *merely* out of self-interested motivations. Existing empirical research into why people contribute to biobanks strongly supports this hypothesis (Critchley et al. 2012; Hobbs et al. 2012). Moreover, the important thing for us here is that the contributions of *most* people to a database can be seen as a solidaristic practice for it to qualify as a solidarity-based database, not whether it is the case in every individual instance (Table 5.1).

When all three requirements are fulfilled, we can assume that people deciding to contribute to such databases do this to support others with whom they recognise similarity in a relevant respect (in the case of databases, this 'similarity' may be limited to a common human vulnerability).

---

[4] By using such a broad definition, we bracket an ongoing and interesting discussion about what social value is (see Rid and Shah's forthcoming special issue of *Bioethics* on the term and its definition in the context of medical research).

Table 5.1 *Requirements, types and examples of databases that are suitable for solidarity-based governance. Examples were deliberately limited to the health domain*

Criteria	Examples for Databases that *Do Not* Meet this Criterion	Examples for Databases that *Do* Meet this Criterion
Requirement 1 Knowledge: people knowingly contribute to the database	Self-diagnosis websites that track people covertly; credit bureaus or other companies that associate 'scores' to people according to specific criteria without informing people	Biobanks where people are required to give consent; health data repositories and commercial DNA testing websites with clear policies on consent
Requirement 2 Social value: database does not serve primarily commercial interests and seeks to create social value	Databases for marketing and other commercial purposes	Databases in academic research institutions, charities, etc.
Requirement 3 Appropriate incentives: database does not provide significant incentives for participation	Prize draws; databases paying their participants considerable sums of money (i.e. enough to influence their decision-making); databases that are primarily providing diagnostic services	Databases that do not pay participants and do not provide personalised results, or those that do give individualised results but this is regularly not the only reason for participation (e.g. UK Biobank)
Conclusion	Database *not* suitable for solidarity-based governance	Database suitable for solidarity-based governance

5.4   Our Approach: Solidarity-Based Databank Governance

As argued earlier, we assume that most people who knowingly (requirement 1) contribute to a database that aims to create social value (requirement 2) are also willing to accept certain 'costs' when they decide to participate – unless the expectation of a direct personal benefit is the only reason for participation (requirement 3). These 'costs' are the risks involved in the participation. Risks will always include that of unauthorised re-identification; perhaps ironically, organisations that seek to maximise social value by making data openly available to the public – such as the Personal Genome Project – typically expose participants to the highest risk of re-identification. Institutions running the database (the 'data controller')[5] need to do what they can to keep the risk of re-identification to a minimum. This can be done, for example, by institutions hosting data for health research asking all collaborators or secondary data users to state explicitly that they will refrain from attempting re-identification (NCoB 2015: Recommendation 12; see also Widdows 2013).

5.4.1 What 'Costs' of Participating in Databases are Acceptable?

As argued earlier, we assume that those who knowingly contribute data to a database that seeks to create social value without offering undue incentives can be assumed to do this within a solidaristic framework. This, in turn, means that they accept the risks inherent in participation. These risks are the 'costs' each participant assumes to assist others when signing up or donating to a database. This assumption can only be upheld, however, if these risks are within the range of what a reasonable person would normally expect, due to the nature of the database, or if they have been made aware of particular other risks. For example, unless people are told otherwise, they will assume that databases will run data analyses with personal identifiers removed, unless there is a need to do otherwise that has explicitly been stated. An example for the latter are the Personal Genome Projects that were initiated in the United States and now have sister projects in other countries including the United Kingdom.[6] Personal Genome Projects are proactive in informing potential participants of the fact that confidentiality and privacy cannot be guaranteed, and are, in fact, very unlikely to be upheld.[7] The stance that re-identification can never be

---

[5] In the context of the new General Data Protection Regulation of the EU, a data controller is 'the institution or body that determines the purpose and means of the processing of personal data'.

[6] The Personal Genome Projects comprise scientific research studies as much as societal ones: their mission is to make genomic and other health-related information publicly available. Participants to the Personal Genome Projects have undergone rigorous vetting processes ensuring that they are aware of the risk of their health-related information being made available online in an identifiable manner.

[7] For the sake of full disclosure: Barbara Prainsack is a member of the Advisory Board of the Austrian Personal Genome Project, and she has collaborated with several members

excluded entirely has now become widely accepted across projects working with patient data (see also Gymrek et al. 2013).

5.4.2   Practical Tools for Solidarity-based Governance

The task of making potential data contributors aware of *atypical* risks
is the responsibility of the organisation or person collecting the data.
Furthermore, because it is impossible to foresee all future data uses, and
to predict all possible risks (see also Widdows 2013), the best way for
database-hosting institutions to disclose their commitments to prospective participants is in the form of a 'mission statement'. We envisage such a
mission statement to provide insights into the 'value system' of a database,
including where the funding comes from, how it is governed and what it
hopes to achieve (Prainsack and Buyx 2013). Mission statements will need
to be updated regularly in light of changes to the governance, research
goals or intellectual property strategy of the database or organisation running it. If an independent governance body finds that the changes are so
fundamental that they constitute a change to the overall value system and
mission of the database, then participants will need to be notified and re-
consented and receive the option to opt out of further research.

Sean Cordell makes a similar argument when he argues, for the case
of biomedical databases in particular, that '[m]ore helpful in determining
what this *kind* of large scale biobanks should be doing [. . .] would be a
specific understanding of the particular and characteristic *way* in which it
serves the good of the public health, and the public interest' (Cordell 2011:
288; original emphasis). Such a mission statement could consist of a paper
document, an online tutorial, a video introduction and/or an online application that should also contain up-to-date information about ongoing
research projects and other relevant aspects. It would not be the only, but
an integral element of the 'participation agreement', which in turn serves
as a shorthand for the cluster of practices and documents that take place
at the moment of a new data donor or participant signing up. Besides the
mission statement, the participation agreement could also contain 'traditional' consent forms, which, however, would be expected to be shorter
and more concise and understandable; boilerplate language required by
law or ethics committees can be separately attached in another document
and available for viewing any time. An ideal participation agreement
would entail the following elements:

---

and participants of the US Personal Genome Project. Alena Buyx is Advisor to the German
Reference Genome.

1. the mission statement, detailing the 'value system' and overarching goals of the database, including information on commercial interests;
2. information about the *types of* research questions and projects that the database supports at the time of recruitment, with an explicit acknowledgement that these might change in the future without participants being contacted (although descriptions of current research projects should be available on the database's or institution's website);
3. statement of future use: the participation agreement should include a statement that the database – and thus the data of the participant – may be used for research that cannot yet be envisaged (subject to research ethics approval wherever laws and regulations require this);
4. re-contacting and feedback: potential participants should be informed of what kind of data and information (including incidental findings) they will have access to, and how. For example, will they have access to their raw data? Will they learn about the main findings of the study? Will they need to obtain this information proactively, e.g. by logging into a secure website, or getting only aggregate data on a publicly available website? Or will no data and information be available to them? The latter scenario, albeit not desirable, is not in principle incompatible with our approach, as long as participants are told that they will not have access to this information;
5. potential participants should be given an indicative list of risks and benefits associated with the participation as they can currently be foreseen, with an explicit note that this list may be incomplete.

Many of the elements of the participation agreement that we propose are not new; for example, UK Biobank already includes a kind of 'mission statement' in the materials handed to potential participants (e.g. Widdows 2013). Moreover, many of the governance changes we suggest resonate well with ongoing initiatives in, e.g. 'reflexive' or 'proportionate' governance (Laurie 2011; see also Academy of Medical Sciences 2011).

5.5 Distinguishing Features of a Solidarity-Based Database Model

5.5.1 Voluntariness and Consent to being Governed

In our previous work on this topic, we argued that our solidarity-based framework is unlikely to be suitable for a database for which profit-making is its main or overarching objective (Prainsack and Buyx 2013).[8]

---

[8] We formulated our previous argument in relation to biobanks – that is, repositories storing materials derived from, or pertaining to, biological materials. However, there was nothing in our framework that prevents us from expanding it more broadly to databases.

We still uphold this assessment overall, but our argument is now more nuanced: as laid out earlier, any database that seeks to create social value and does not serve exclusively for-profit goals, and to which people knowingly contribute data, and that does not provide incentives for participants is suitable for solidarity-based governance.

Two more important features of our solidarity-based model need highlighting: first, the explicit acknowledgement that people who knowingly and voluntarily contribute data and other goods to a database are willing to accept some 'costs'. That many people are willing to do this does not mean, however, that everybody should be expected, or socially pressured, to do it. It is important within our framework that people can decide as freely as possible whether they want to contribute data. At the inter-personal level, solidarity is typically not something that can be demanded; only at higher levels of institutionalisation, social, contractual administrative or legal provisions and norms can solidaristic practice be made mandatory. For health databases in particular, considering mandatory participation would be justified only when there is an urgent public need, which will not normally be the case. Thus, at the point of their data being entered in the system, people need to be able to decide whether or not they want to sign up to the 'deal' they are offered in the mission statement. It is perfectly compatible with a solidarity-based framework if such a deal entails that people give an initial 'consent to a governance scheme' (Koenig 2014: 34) and agree for other people – typically independent governance boards – to make decisions on the further use of their data on their behalf. This applies as long as these further uses remain within the remit of the initial mission that they consented to. This also means that people who are not capable of giving consent (children, people who are unconscious, etc.) cannot sign up to a database employing a solidarity-based governance framework.

5.5.2   *Partnership, Veracity and Transparency in a Solidarity-based Approach to Database Governance*

We also emphasise that people's willingness to accept 'costs' must not lead to the conclusion that they are less deserving of safeguards if they were not happy to participate. In contrast, people's willingness to accept costs to help others mandates that they will be treated *as partners* in the endeavours that the database serves. This means, in turn – and this is the second distinguishing feature of our approach – that certain requirements of veracity and transparency apply to how the database is governed. Participation agreements that give a wider flavour of the nature and mission of the database that people are contributing to, instead of revolving around risk management, are one manifestation of this.

The value of *veracity*, as promoted by Jeantine Lunshof and colleagues (Lunshof et al. 2008; see also later), plays an important role in guiding our model for the governance of databases. Veracity in the practice of running a database does *not* mean that everything that the institution running the database knows about the research project or the governance structure needs to be told to participants at the time of signing up. Such an approach would do nothing but impose unmanageable amounts of information on participants, rather than support a good understanding of the core commitments and stakes of the database. What the value of veracity does mandate, however, is that information on aspects that – as empirical research has shown (e.g. Haddow et al. 2007) – people care about, such as the aim of the research, who will benefit and commercial and conflicts of interests, should be conveyed to potential participants upfront. Another aspect that should be conveyed is according to what principles or criteria the institution intends to decide what research to take on, and with whom to share data.

Veracity is best understood as a disposition to treat data donors and research participants in a particular way, namely as what we call 'information equals'. Research institutions and data contributors are not, of course, equal in every respect, especially not in terms of the resources available to them. At present, however, there is a gross asymmetry between the two parties in what they are expected to hand over: while data contributors are typically expected to share different types of information (e.g. clinical and familial data) with the database, most databases do not give contributors access to anything. Such asymmetry would be justified if it was necessary to protect social or personal goods, but at present it mostly serves intellectual property protection interests of institutions. Taking data contributors seriously as 'information equals' does not mean that both sides need to have access to the exact same amount or type of information, which would pervert the very idea of a database and raise serious issues about the confidentiality of data from other donors. It means that organisations collecting and using data choose carefully what type of data they collect or ask for instead of using anything they can get their hands on (see Prainsack 2015a), and that they support participants in making meaningful decisions throughout the duration of the relationship with the database. The institutions hosting or running the database should make up-to-date information about their mission, projects and commercial interests available on their website; in other words, the information that is given to prospective participants in the context of a participation agreement should also remain available for existing participants. This information could be available in a password-protected 'members' section on the institution's website, or in a publicly accessible place, depending on the type of database. Veracity also means that databases should, wherever meaningfully and reasonably possible, give data donors or participants access to the raw data held about them (Angrist 2015; Lunshof et al. 2014). By 'raw' data we mean the data that are entered into a repository (see also Gitelman 2013; Leonelli 2014). Whether the repository operates within a research or treatment context is irrelevant here.

Giving data donors and participants access to such raw data, if they so desire, is an important matter of principle: if participants and data donors are taken seriously as true partners in the endeavours that the databases serve, then they need to be able to access whatever data about them are held in systems. While it is true that such raw data could include mistakes or inaccuracies (Janssens and Cecile 2014), if participants are aware of this possibility, there is no reason to assume that raw data are more dangerous to them than they would be for research. Being able to access their raw data would enable people to submit these data to secondary analysis, to store it for future reference or even to donate it to (other) research projects if they so wish.[9]

Importantly, the relationship between *veracity*, understood as an attitude of respect towards data donors as equal partners of those running and hosting databases, and *transparency* is not linear: more transparency does not automatically enhance veracity, and veracity does not require all kinds of transparency in all situations. As Koops (2013: 201) notes, in the most general sense, transparency in the context of databases can be defined in terms of openness to public scrutiny. Because something can only be open to public scrutiny if it is accessible and comprehensible, transparency includes these requirements as well. In this regard, transparency is different from openness. For example, data from an experiment in a physics lab can be 'open' in the sense that it is publicly accessible; the lab experiment however is not transparent if it cannot be understood by members of the public. The lab data would thus require explanation and annotation

---

[9] The argument that people should have access to the raw data that databases hold and process about them does not, however, mean that people should be actively encouraged to download their raw data (Lunshof et al. 2014). The important point is that people should have the option of accessing their raw data if they desire to do so. For those who do, the engagement with the data – even if only in the form of thinking about what to do with them – will help to increase data literacy, and, most importantly, it will enable them to have an overview of what data about them are processed in various kinds of databases. As mentioned earlier, people could also donate these data to other research projects, or they could deposit them into data commons, e.g. openSNP.org; openhumans.org, etc.

to meet the requirement of public scrutiny.[10] While it is not possible to determine in advance which kinds of transparency best serve the principle of veracity in the context of specific database governance cases, they should be carefully considered when thinking about veracity towards data donors and participants.

It will not always be easy for institutions hosting databases to be transparent to data donors and participants. Transparency frequently requires time, money or other resources. Making raw data available to data donors could also incur costs for the database; besides the costs for the necessary infrastructures, it also means that databases would lose exclusive access to the raw data. In a solidaristic framework, however, it should be expected that both sides – institutions and data donors – are willing to accept some costs to support others. If the costs of providing access to their own raw data to data donors, for example, are too high in the context of a particular biobank, that is, if it required excessive resources which would thus be channelled away from research-related activities for public benefit, then a solidaristic framework would mandate that participants refrain from expecting access to their raw data. If, however, raw data access – and other measures to increase transparency – require only moderate effort and marginal resources from a biobank, then a solidaristic framework requires that these measures will be undertaken.

5.6   Implications of a Solidarity-Based Approach for Consent and Returning Findings

In the previous sections we have laid out what types of databases are suitable for a solidarity-based approach, outlined the approach itself and introduced veracity and transparency as important principles that need to underpin database governance. In the following section we will discuss how a solidarity-based approach would look like in practice, specifically regarding two 'hot issues' in healthcare database governance, namely consent and the return of findings.

---

[10] Furthermore, Heald (2006: 29–35) distinguishes between process and event transparency, and between retrospective and real-time transparency. Heald also distinguishes between 'nominal' and 'effective' transparency according to whether something merely 'looks' transparent, or whether it is indeed accessible and comprehensible for members of the public. This distinction is not relevant for our discussion, as we would assume that transparency is always effective; otherwise, we would not call it transparency but tokenistic openness. Other distinctions that Heald makes – e.g. between vertical and horizontal, and between upward and downward transparency – are not discussed here.

5.6.1   What Type of Consent Fits
Solidarity-Based Database Governance?

What kind of model of consent is appropriate for solidarity-based databases? The principle of informed consent was introduced in medical ethics after the Second World War in order to protect individuals against possible harm, such as unwanted treatment or other intrusions into one's bodily integrity (Sutrop 2011: 376, see also Harmon 2009; Mason and Laurie 2011: chapter 4; Sommerville et al. 2012; Widdows 2013). While the principle has been supremely important in changing medical care and research from largely paternalistic practices to practices where patient-participants decide what will be done to them, there have been worries that this notion has become overshadowed by narrow interpretations of individual autonomy. These interpretations, critics argue, run the risk of understanding consent not only as one of the manifestations of autonomy, but also as a quasi-synonym for autonomy itself (McGuire and Beskow 2010; critically: O'Neill 2003; Wilson 2007; see also Chapters 2 and 3). Particularly in modern litigious cultures, informed consent could be seen as having assumed the role of a 'stamp of approval' for medical practice (see also Stark 2012 for an exploration of the beginning of this history in the United States in the 1950s). This also applies to research where participants state that they have understood the risks involved in their participation and have willingly agreed to accept them, and consequently cannot hold a research institution, or a databank, responsible for any harm resulting from activities that were carried out as described. Consent, thus, has become a tool to manage risks, and is often used with a view to 'taming' the uncertain and unknowable into actionable and contained tasks and objectives. As a result of legislation and regulation requiring ever stricter informed consent from research participants, significant resources are channelled into developing and implementing policies and protocols to document that participants have been informed about, and agreed to, what will be done with their samples and data. This is clearly mandated in scenarios where the risks for research participants are considerable (e.g. health risks).

In connection with health-related biobank-based research, however, to cite a common situation in the biomedical domain, current risks for participants are regularly very small, both in terms of the nature and the degree of risk.[11] In many instances of such biobank-based research, the

---

[11] The infringement of data protection standards and physical harm would be examples for a particular nature of risk. In the context of biobank-based research, the degree of the former is medium to low, depending on the concrete context; the risk for the latter is extremely

most significant risks for individuals are the possibility of involuntary and/or unauthorised identification, and possible scenarios of discrimination that may emerge from it. To the best of our knowledge, instances of actual discrimination based on a participant's involvement in a biobank (including large genetic research studies or cohorts) are extremely rare.[12] Moreover, in the case of virtually all research biobanks, it is impossible to predict all the ways in which data and samples will be used in the future. Informed consent models trying to achieve full risk reduction and disclosure at the moment of joining are doomed; they are not in line with the speed of change in modern research, and, moreover, impose great burdens on researchers and ultimately mislead participants, thus jeopardising medical and research endeavours. We return to this point later.

With this in mind, and considering that participants of solidarity-based databases would be expected to accept some costs – which could consist of e.g. residual risks of re-identification – broad consent models are most suitable for solidarity-based biobank governance.[13] Broad consent means that participants agree to a wider range of possible uses of their data, instead of specific uses (Hoffmann 2009). This also implies, following standard understandings of broad consent, that data donors do not need to be re-consented when their data are used for further research projects, as long as the new research does not contradict the mission of the database that participants signed up for. In cases where the new research does conflict with the initial mission, participants need to be re-contacted. In cases when it is unclear whether or not there is a conflict, we argue that an independent governance board will be best placed to decide this. Depending on the size, scope and nature of the database, such an independent governance board could be a permanent body with specific tasks around the governance of the database, or an ad-hoc group of experts with relevant expertise, including patients, to avoid adding an undue bureaucratic burden. The important thing is that members of the governance board do not have any conflicts of interest and are independent in their decision-making, and that they cannot be relieved of their duties if they make decisions that are unpleasant for the owners or shareholders of the database.

---

low to absent (physical harm is not a direct result of somebody's participation in a research biobank).

[12] Note, however, the conflict between the Havasupai Indians and Arizona State University (see Harmon 2010).

[13] UK Biobank, for example, decided to use a broad consent framework, complemented by additional ethics and governance mechanisms (Widdows 2013: 74).

5.6.2   Access to Data and Returning of Findings

What does this mean for the obligations of databases to return findings to participants? We have argued that, within solidarity-based databases, participants should be able to access and download their own raw data (understood as the data that the database holds about them). Such access to raw data – for people who want to have it in the first place – would help people to make meaningful decisions about who should be able to hold and use data from and about them, and to what purpose. But what about the other end of the pipeline, namely information that was obtained from an aggregate dataset, or information pertaining to individuals after it was analysed or interpreted – in other words, what about all the findings that can be generated from the data people contribute? In the case of genomics, for example (Table 5.2), interpreted information includes risk calculations or personal predispositions pertaining to individuals. (These could be either probabilistic inferences from population-level data, or they could be so-called 'incidental findings' – a clear misnomer in this context – from individual-level data or a combination of both.)

We argue that any database that operates under the solidarity regime should strive to make research findings at both personal and aggregate[14] levels available with as few barriers as possible, weighing interests of data protection of people against other personal and collective benefits. With regard to findings that pertain to specific people, including the so-called 'incidental findings' in the context of medical research – that is, findings that emerged as a 'by-product' of investigating something else – we support the 'U.S. Presidential Commission for the Study of Bioethical Issues' (2013) recommendation that medical research institutions should devise policies that suit the specific situation of their database. For findings that can have a significant impact on health, however, we strongly recommend that databases encourage participants to obtain this information (the initial contact could be made electronically, and the findings themselves would be conveyed by a medical specialist or a genetic counsellor). Where incidental findings are clinically actionable, the database should have a system in place to enable participants to access this information.[15]

---

[14] For a discussion of returning aggregate findings from genomic studies to participants, see Kerasidou (2014).

[15] For details of what such a system could look, see Green et al. (2013), Jarvik et al. (2014) and Wolf et al. (2012).

Table 5.2 *Dissemination, feedback and re-consent in solidarity-based databases*

Type of Data/ Information	Example	Solidarity-based Governance Suggests:	How Should Data/ Information be Made Available?
'Raw' data stemming from specific people	DNA data: read-out from the sequencing machine. Blood test data: uninterpreted lab results	Participants should have access if providing access does not divert significant resources from core research activities for public benefit. More resources should be made available when data are clinically actionable	Online platform allowing people to download their own raw data (if initiated by individual participant)
Interpreted information pertaining to specific people	DNA data: the type of information that genetic counsellors would give to patients. E.g. carrier status, personalised risk information. Blood test data: Interpretation of normal vs. pathological ranges, health implications, etc.	Participants should have access if providing access does not divert significant resources from core research activities for public benefit. More resources should be made available when data are clinically actionable	Either web-based or face-to-face disclosure of information, depending on type of information. Also who the initiating party is depends on type of database and information
Aggregate datasets	De-identified results from blood tests of all people in a database	Participants should have access only if there is no undue risk for re-identifying particular individuals	Online platform allowing people to download aggregate data; request downloader to upload videotaped commitment to refrain from re-identification

5.6.3   *Further Practical Implications*

Rather than prescribing particular policies, a solidarity-based approach obliges those operating databases to communicate to potential participants openly whether and why results will be fed back, and what harm may result from either having or not having results fed back to them. This means that the policy of not feeding back even clinically relevant, actionable findings to individual participants would *in principle* be compatible with our approach as long as (a) the consequences of the finding for the health of the person are not significant and (b) the possible consequences of this mechanism are communicated to potential participants at the time of signing the agreement. Such policies could provide significant disincentives to research participation unless a compelling reason and rationale for this approach is provided by the database. One possible rationale for this kind of policy could be that – as it is the case with UK Biobank, for example – a project is supported by public funding and feeding back findings to individual participants would come at the cost of research that could reap tangible benefits for more people.

To honour the principle of veracity, solidarity-based governance requires that databases make general information on ongoing research existing to participants and the public wherever reasonably possible (in light of available resources and data security concerns). This information will normally be accessible online. Finally, we argue that aggregate datasets should be accessible to participants only if the possibility that individuals can be re-identified is very low (which will regularly *not* be the case).

In sum, arrangements of participants' access to data and findings in a database, in our model, will be made with a view to the best way to spend resources to increase public benefit, not *primarily* to foster individual benefit. For publicly funded databases with notoriously limited resources in particular, it would be acceptable that participants who are interested in seeing data and information generated by the database (beyond those that we would recommend to be fed back in any case) need to take the initiative of accessing the data via online platforms or other repositories, without this service being provided to them proactively and individually by the organisation hosting the database (see Table 5.2).

5.7   Solidarity and Autonomy as Guiding Principles in Health Database Governance

In our model, the autonomy of the person from whom the data in the database come remains an important guiding principle, particularly at the stage of providing people with meaningful information on what a particular database is about. Rather than being confronted with technical language detailing protocols and risks, potential participants should, to paraphrase Sean Cordell's words, understand the characteristic way in which a database operates, and for what goals. Autonomy thus expresses itself in such a way that it is possible for a person in her capacity as an autonomous person to choose to accept a certain level of risk and uncertainty (as we do in almost all realms of life; see our discussion of autonomy and solidarity in Chapters 3) and consent to be governed instead of expecting to be asked to consent to every specific use of their data further down the line. As noted earlier, in our model, participants would not need to be given the choice to opt out of new research projects as long as the goals of the new project are consistent with the stated goals of the database at the time when participants signed up. It will need to be determined on a case-by-case basis at what point the initial values and goals of a database have changed sufficiently to require re-consenting.

Databases such as research biobanks that have trusted intermediary or custodian arrangements in place can include these to make this decision. Some or even most of the databases might fall under the remit of research ethics committees or review boards. However, we explicitly do not recommend that ethics committees be entrusted with this task. This is the case not only because of the additional workload, but also because they may not be familiar enough with the database and the specific kind of research to accurately assess the extent to which a commitment to a particular value has changed in practice. Instead, governance boards, trustee boards or oversight committees with, in turn, light-touch external oversight structures should be given this task as appropriate.

In sum, the relationship between participant and database in a solidarity-based model is understood to be a reflection of the fact that the participant is willing to accept some costs to help others, and in turn trusts the database to hold up its end of the bargain. This interpretation of the relationship between the participant and the database entails a shift: from a dominant or exclusive focus on individual autonomy (and the related efforts to respect and protect it through governance) towards including a recognition that the participation of many participants, most often in research-oriented databases, can be understood as a solidaristic practice. For example, participants would accept costs by ceding some of the benefits they may have in an exclusively autonomy-based approach, such as more control over the future use of the data, or being informed individually about incidental findings that may be relevant but not clinically action-able. In a solidarity-based model, while it would be desirable for partici-pants to have all these opportunities, it would be acceptable in principle to ask them to consent to not having them. In sum, a solidarity-based model implies that ensuring individual control over data at every step of the way is not the main nor ultimate goal, although, as we argued, the idea of infor-mation equality implies that participants should have access to informa-tion wherever reasonably possible.[16]

5.8   Harm Mitigation and a Focus on 'Fixing the System'

As mentioned earlier, informed consent procedures are effectively aimed at preventing and minimising risk. That is, despite the refinement that database procedures have undergone in recent years, most instruments are still designed to inform participants about the risks inherent in par-ticipating in order to protect their autonomous informed consent, and to protect the database. This could perpetuate the implicit expectation that once participants are duly informed of as many risks as possible and of all efforts in place to prevent these risks from materialising, they will be 'safe' – which they never are. An exclusive focus on risk prevention can, at its best, reduce risks and make participants feel secure. At its worst, it can foster a mistaken expectation of participation being completely risk-free.

As explained earlier, our solidarity-based framework allows for an open acknowledgement that there will always be risks. It explicitly includes the option for participants to accept these as the costs of helping others. In cases where a participant's consent is a requirement for a database to include their information – which is often the case in medical research contexts – we have argued that broad consent is thus acceptable. In all cases, in order to reflect such willingness of participants to accept costs when engaging with databases, we suggest curtailing the current strong emphasis on risk prevention. Instead, a shift should occur towards more emphasis on devis-ing strategies for harm mitigation in cases where actual harm occurs. (By 'actual harm' we mean instances of, for example, discrimination against a person whose data and samples are stored in a database by an insurer or employer.) The difference between risk and harm here is that a risk, on the one hand, is something that has not yet materialised, i.e. it is something

---

[16] There are already successful databases where the relationship between participant and biobanks resonates with our approach, such as UK Biobank – without, however, explicitly mobilising the concept of solidarity (see e.g. Laurie 2011).

that is considered prospectively. Harm, on the other hand, is something that has already materialised and is thus considered retrospectively. Stronger emphasis on the latter would mean that we increase the scope for action *after* an undesirable event has taken place (e.g. by making available funds to compensate affected individuals for the harm that they suffered), instead of focusing all our resources on preventing the happening of the undesirable event before it has taken place.

We thus suggest that the owner or funder of a database governed according to the solidarity model sets aside a particular sum each year, or a particular proportion of the total funding, to pay into a 'harm mitigation fund'. The same governance boards or trustee boards that make decisions on re-consenting (or informing, depending on the type of database) should decide on applications from people to receive pay-outs from the harm mitigation fund. The explicit function of the harm mitigation is to provide financial support in situations when there is no legal right to compensation (or when the compensation obtained through legal means is not considered sufficient). Who exactly makes decisions on pay-outs, and according to what principles, will depend on the particular organisation running the database. In any event, the decision on the use of the money in harm mitigation funds will need to be made by people who have no financial or other conflicting interests in the database, and these bodies should include representatives of data donors. The institution of the harm mitigation fund thus embodies the conviction that merely obeying the law does not always render a particular practice ethical (Prainsack and Buyx 2011).

The implementation of harm mitigation funds does not, however, imply that compensation is the only way in which the occurrence of harm to a contributor or participant in a database should be addressed. The spirit of solidarity mandates that the problem is addressed not only at the level of individual redress but also at the systemic level.[17] Anecdotal evidence suggests that many people who became victims of privacy breaches do not only want redress, but typically also want the system to be fixed (personal communication with authors). Databases should thus devise a way in which lessons from perceived or actual harm brought to the attention of the oversight bodies could be fed back into the design of procedures and practices of the database.

In the biomedical realm in particular, the creation of harm mitigation funds could also help to justify the diversion of resources away from admin-intense consent procedures (e.g. by having shorter consent and

---

[17] We are grateful to Angeliki Kerasidou for helpful discussions on that point.

information documents and/or using online portals, by not needing to re-contact participants if their donations will be used for novel research, by easing the requirements for research ethics approval, etc.). Resources saved this way should go towards substantive research activities, public engagement initiatives or similar health- and health literacy-related activities. The slightly larger probability that participants will face negative consequences resulting from their participation is a cost that those signing up would declare to be willing to carry. And those who would actually be affected by harm would be compensated by newly created mechanisms.

5.9   Conclusion

Based on our understanding of solidarity as enacted commitments to accept costs to assist others with whom a person or persons recognise similarity in a relevant respect, we propose an approach to database governance that builds upon people's willingness to contribute data to databases that are used for public benefits. Instead of the predominant focus on risk management, we suggest posing stronger emphasis on harm mitigation. At the same time, a solidarity-informed approach acknowledges a right of access to data and information also for the originators of the data, if the idea of a research partnership is to be taken seriously (see Lunshof et al. 2014).

We argue that our model avoids some of the pitfalls of previous approaches, as it allows moving beyond overly restrictive and burdensome, exclusively autonomy-based database governance models, without running the risk of becoming a tokenistic exercise that exists primarily to grant legitimacy to the exploitation of people's data for commercial purposes. Our approach gives rise to an understanding of benefit that is both personal and societal (see also NCoB 2015: 3.29), and that needs to be balanced against understandings of risks and harms that are equally both personal and societal: if somebody accepts the 'costs' of contributing their data to a database to help create public benefit, then this person must not be left alone when she suffers harm as a result. Solidarity, we argue, enables us to find solutions that accommodate the ways in which the personal and the societal levels are intertwined, without sacrificing oneself entirely for the sake of the other.

6

Solidarity in Practice II: Personalised Medicine and Healthcare

6.1   Introduction

There has been much excitement, and much concern, around the idea of tailoring healthcare delivery more closely to individual characteristics of patients. Different terms have been used to capture this idea. In the United Kingdom, the term 'stratified medicine' refers to the clustering together of patients according to specific characteristics that determine preventive or treatment trajectories. These characteristics can be very broad, such as gender, or very specific, such as the sharing of a genetic marker that influences drug response (MRC 2015). Policy-makers and scholars in the United States often use the term 'precision medicine' to refer to the stratification of patients according to more and more specific criteria into ever more fine-grained groups (NAS 2011). Pan-European initiatives such as the European Science Foundation's 'Forward Look on Personalised Medicine for the European Citizen' (ESF 2013) have, despite the problematic connotations of this term, continued to use the term 'personalised medicine' because of the higher level of recognition it has had, compared to other terms that were more common in specific regions or nations within Europe (such as 'individualised medicine' in Germany; see Grabe et al. 2014).[1]

In the remainder of this chapter, we will use the term personalisation to refer to this overall idea (and under 'personalised medicine' we will also subsume personalised healthcare). But regardless of the specific terms used, all these labels refer to the idea that the 'one size fits all' mode in prevention, diagnosis and treatment should be replaced by a more tailored approach. An important enabler for the rising popularity of the notion of personalised medicine had been the Human Genome Project. Throughout the 1990s, the Human Genome Project had been accompanied by hopes that the ability to read the human genetic 'code' – at the time frequently

[1] One of us (Prainsack) was involved in the ESF Forward Look as one of its chairs.

referred to as 'The Book of Life' – would enable us to understand and eventually cure a wide range of diseases (Holdrege and Wirz 2001; Kay 2000). As is well known, the Human Genome Project has not delivered on this particular promise. It has, however, generated important insights into DNA-based human variation. After the official end of the Human Genome Project in the early 2000s, there was a growing sense of urgency for this knowledge – which had been obtained with the help of considerable public and private funds – to deliver clinical benefits. Utilising knowledge about how genetic variants influence drug metabolism was seen as one of the lower-hanging fruits; so much so that during the first years after the Human Genome Project, the notion of personalised medicine was largely synonymous with the matching of treatments to particular molecular (typically genetic) markers that patients carried.

Such an understanding of personalised medicine that is limited largely to differences between groups of people sharing specific genetic markers has encountered considerable resistance. Besides the critique that personalised medicine, understood in such a way, tailors treatments to groups and not to individual patients, and that the name personalised medicine was thus a misnomer, commentators have also disliked the focus on high-tech approaches. They have also argued that most of the solutions that personalised medicine proposes are out of reach for most of the world's population, and that they come at the cost of the personal touch in medicine (e.g. Bayer and Galea 2015; Doz et al. 2013). Some authors believe that personalised medicine will give rise to a radically individualised medicine and to people who care solely about their own needs, instead of considering collective health-related needs and interests (Dickenson 2013; see also Shapiro 2012).

It is primarily the latter claim, namely that personalised medicine inevitably fosters a kind of healthcare where people fend for themselves and care solely about their own interests that we seek to scrutinise – and counter – here. We argue that personalisation in medicine and healthcare can have the opposite effect: it can bridge the gap between the needs and interests of individual patients on the one hand and collective needs and interests on the other. This potential of personalised medicine to bridge the levels of the personal and the collective, however, will not unfold on its own. It needs to be actively harnessed. This is where solidarity comes in. The notion of solidarity, understood as people's willingness to accept costs to support others with whom they recognise relevant similarities, can help us to maximise the positive potential of personalised medicine. This is the case for two main reasons: first, because of its inherent imperative to base practice and policy on what people share in common and not on what sets them apart, solidarity makes us favour inclusion over exclusion in cases where it is not clear whether exclusion may have negative impacts for the excluded. This helps to avoid the scenario that personalised medicine will be used as an 'excuse' to exclude people from services or treatments that are too expensive. Second, solidaristic practice and policy allows to make active use of the fact that many people are willing to support others with whom they recognise similarities in a relevant respect, which has tangible implications at all levels of healthcare. Taking solidarity seriously often means that our systems and protocols should encourage actions that help others, even if there is a – typically moderate[2] – cost for participants in the system. Costs may occur in the form of financial contributions to a public healthcare system, in the form of participating in disease research or in the form of foregoing an intervention that we are entitled to but that is not very useful or meaningful to us. At the same time, society has the collective obligation to support people who are willing to accept costs for the sake of helping others when something goes wrong. In the previous chapter, we proposed the introduction of harm mitigation mechanisms that health databases and, in principle, any other type of database should set up to help those who are negatively affected as a result of their participation. At the level of society more generally, the most important harm mitigation mechanism is publicly funded healthcare.

Our argument in the remainder of this chapter will proceed as follows. The first point will be to show *how* the notion of personalisation in medicine and healthcare can, in principle, bring the personal and the collective levels closer together.[3] We show how current visions of personalised medicine, as they are expressed in some prominent policy reports, position papers

---

[2] In Chapter 3, we specified that most of the time, the costs (financial and other kinds) people assume within solidaristic practices will be small. For people to accept bigger costs, the bonds that they feel connect them to others (i.e. their recognition of similarity in a relevant respect) will regularly need to be very strong. We return to this point in Chapter 8.

[3] We do not mean to claim that the personal and the collective levels were ever fully separated in medicine. The objective of laboratory medicine, for example, was to carry out experiments that would then inform the treatment of individual patients. The difference to contemporary personalised medicine, however, was that laboratory medicine took an idealised version of a 'standard patient' as its reference point (see Foucault 1973; Tutton 2012, 2014), whereas personalised medicine is increasingly doing away with the idea of a uniform standard (see also Prainsack, in preparation). At the same time, this oscillation between the population and the individual level is one of the bottlenecks in personalised medicine. Patterns observed in aggregate data are often mere correlations between, for example, behaviour X and characteristic Y, with no indication as to what the underlying dynamics and causalities are (Mayer-Schönberger and Cukier 2013). It is thus very difficult to know what can be inferred from them for specific individuals.

and articles in recent years, operate with a notion of 'radical' difference, where every person represents a unique case of physiology or pathology at every stage of her life course (see also Prainsack 2015b). We argue that despite this radical approach to difference, health information at the level of individual people remains meaningless without reference to a larger group. Besides the fact that routine clinical care continues to operate with population averages as comparators for individual health data, or standardised recommendations for large groups (e.g. dosage recommendations for children), the oscillation between the individual and the population level is, in fact, also a feature of the 'big data' approaches that personalised medicine is embedded in. Such approaches look at patterns that are observed in aggregate, i.e. population level datasets to see what they mean for individuals (see Chapter 5). Data from individual patients are used to create the algorithms for such analyses, and to detect new patterns. Using this observation of an iterative interaction between the personal and the collective level within personalised medicine as a starting point, we then discuss four concrete ways, based on solidarity, in which the positive potential of personalised medicine can be enhanced.

6.2   The Changing Meaning of Difference in Medicine

We already noted that in the last decade, the meaning of personalised medicine has started to widen beyond genetics and genomics. Although some authors still refer to the use of genomic biomarkers when they talk about personalisation (Hamburg and Collins 2010; Hogarth et al. 2012), others – including reports and policy papers by organisations such as the US National Academy of Sciences (NAS 2011) and the European Science Foundation (ESF 2013) – regard personalisation, also referred to as precision medicine, more broadly as the consideration of both molecular and non-molecular differences between people (see also Desmond-Hellmann 2012; Özdemir et al. 2013; Topol 2012). Research into how genes are expressed and regulated, how external stimuli are involved in these processes and also the wider availability of computational tools to integrate different types of health information have facilitated this shift.

This shift represents not only a move away from an almost exclusive focus on molecular information to the inclusion of wider ranges of data for the goal of 'personalising' medicine, but also a change in the meaning of difference. The notion of difference within more recent understandings of personalised medicine assumes that individual patients are different on so many levels that they cannot legitimately be lumped together in groups

(Prainsack 2015b). The aforementioned Report on precision medicine by the US National Academies of Science, for example, called for the replacement of inevitably coarse and inaccurate symptom-based disease taxonomies with data-rich characterisations of individuals at various stages of health and disease. Its authors envisage a kind of 'Google Map' of health data at the level of individuals, comprising static (e.g. genome sequence) and dynamic data (changeable characteristics such as gene expression, lifestyle or postcode; see also Topol 2015). They argue that such a new taxonomy would serve both clinical and research needs much better than the taxonomies in use today (NAS 2011). Because every patient is different, as this new vision of personalised medicine assumes, their health and their diseases are different as well: individual differences in our genetic makeup, in our gene expression, in the microorganisms inhabiting our guts and bodies, in our lifestyles, diets and so forth render each of us, as well as our physiologies and pathologies, a unique expression of a particular state of health and disease in any given moment in time.[4]

6.2.1   From the Representation of Groups to Radical Difference?

At the end of the 2000s, Science and Technology Scholar Steven Epstein addressed the notion of difference in his book *Inclusion: The Politics of Difference in Medical Research*. Epstein carefully traced the emergence of the 'inclusion-and-difference paradigm' in US medical research (Epstein 2007). In Epstein's book, difference features primarily in the context of *representation*: the turn to difference in US medical research stemmed from the idea that different groups in society needed to be represented as adequately as possible. The groups that were seen to be in need of representation were defined mainly on the basis of classifications that society already operated with, such as age, gender and race. These mostly demographic categories typically referred to characteristics that were not easily malleable: 'race', gender and social status are relatively stable, and age is not something that people can change themselves. The disease

---

[4] An implication of this view is that one of the gold standards for medical research, the randomised controlled trial, has come under attack: some argue because every person is different we should move to alternative methods of studying difference instead, such as in silico modelling or in-depth studies of individual patients (N=1 studies; see ESF 2013; Schork 2015). Science writer Carina Dennis referred to the idea that individuals render themselves available for detailed in-depth study as 'the rise of the narciss-ome' (Dennis 2012) – thus echoing earlier worries by writers who have been criticising the emphasis on the individual in medical practice and biomedical ethics for a long time (see the discussions of works of e.g. Onora O'Neill, Daniel Callahan and others in Chapters 2–4).

labels that epidemiology operated with were also relatively broad-brush diagnostic labels, lumping together people with countless different trajectories, comorbidities and often widely differing symptoms. Visions of personalised medicine today continue to operate with many of the 'old' demographic, clinical and epidemiological labels, but they include more and more categories that are dynamic and malleable. For example, instead of treating all people with an Autism Spectrum Diagnosis as a homogeneous group, brain imaging enables the stratification of patients into much more fine-grained subtypes (e.g. Di Martino et al. 2014). In contrast to the processes that Epstein described in his book, within current visions of personalised medicine, difference is no longer oriented towards the representation of *groups* that are defined according to stable labels, but towards the representation of *individual patients* in as many datasets as possible (Ausiello and Shaw 2014). Here, again, difference seems to have become radical: it is not oriented towards any population average but takes the individual patient as its point of reference. If groups become so small that they end up including only one person, they are no longer a group; difference, then, becomes the property of individual people.

6.2.2   Bringing (New) Groups Back in

But this is not the whole story. We still need to draw connections to others to know what our own data mean. Clinicians still operate with population averages to determine whether our blood pressure or our lab results are within the range of the 'normal'. In addition, data-driven medicine gives rise to new, often very short-lived and ad hoc groups when comparing our data to others (Prainsack 2015b). A person who uses online symptom checkers such as *Curetogether* (curetogether.com), for example, is algorithmically matched with other users who have similar combinations of symptoms of similar severity. She can then see what remedies have worked for patients who are similar to her, thus putting her into a different group that will change as soon as new users have entered their own data into the system. Even in the face of calls for $N = 1$ studies and the creation of digital data doubles of individual patients to personalise healthcare, groups have not disappeared from medicine. If anything, they have become more fluid.

Another way in which personalised healthcare can bring the level of individuals and collectives closer together is, perhaps curiously, connected with the increasing use of digital data and algorithm-based decision-making. As mentioned earlier, 'big data' approaches in medicine are based on a continuous dialogue between the individual and the population level, where patterns observed at the population level are examined for possible inferences for individual cases (depending on the individual characteristics of specific patients), and data from individual patients are used to create the algorithms in the first place. Thus, there is a continuous feedback loop between the personal and the population levels.

At least conceptually, then, personal and collective dimensions are deeply intertwined within personalised medicine. Does this mean that we can lean back and let algorithms take care of things? Clearly not. The continuous loop of feedback between the individual and the population level can only consider information that is part of the system in the first place, and that is available in digital and computable formats. If personalisation in medicine and healthcare was realised with naïve trust in the power of such information, and the idea that collecting more and more data about individual patients will 'cure' us, to paraphrase a term by Gina Neff (2013), then we would indeed run the risk of exacerbating existing inequalities (Pasquale 2015; Prainsack 2015a). If, however, we understand personalisation as pertaining to wider characteristics than merely molecular or digital information, if we create ways for aspects that are meaningful to specific patients to gain more importance in medical decision-making (Gawanda 2014) and if we create or maintain healthcare systems that provide safety nets for people who fall ill, then we will not need to choose between what philosopher Donna Dickenson calls 'Me Medicine' and 'We Medicine' (Dickenson 2013).

The next section will discuss four specific implications of a solidaristic perspective on personalised medicine. As our examples show, employing a solidaristic perspective does not amount only to specific technical configurations of diagnostic or therapeutic practices, or the healthcare system as a whole. It rather implies a particular approach towards organising 'personalised' healthcare in such a way that it supports people to lead meaningful lives of which their human and other environments are always a vital part.

6.3 Personalised Solidaristic Medicine and Healthcare: Four Examples

6.3.1 Social Biomarkers: Personal Meaning Instead of Algorithmic Prediction

There are a lot of unresolved problems around what the quality of clinical and other data used to aid clinical decision-making can be. The question remains open whether it is prudent to act upon patterns and correlations that we merely observe without understanding the underlying dynamics (Flam 2015). Notwithstanding, algorithmic prediction is seen by some proponents of personalised medicine as the future of medicine. IBM's 'Watson' software, which is currently available in *beta* (trial) mode, is an example of this. Watson promises to support the decision-making of medical professionals by mining published literature, health records and other patient-specific information in 'real time'; and to suggest potential diagnoses and suggestions for treatments (IBM 2014).

Resorting to ever-improving algorithmic regulation poses significant problems, however: not only because it pushes the 'human touch' element out of medicine but also because it raises thorny issues around the possibility of technological errors. Decision support systems based on predictive analytics also give greater power to commercial providers who make it practically impossible for medical professionals or patients to open up and 'tinker' with their model. In the past, US case law has used human interference with computer decision software 'as a reason to shield the software vendor from liability' (Cohen et al. 2014: 1144). This could be a deterrent for doctors, patients or hospitals to modify or even ignore decision-making algorithms to better suit their own needs or follow their clinical instincts.[5] An alternative approach to algorithmic regulation would be to personalise medicine and healthcare by giving more room to information that is meaningful to people, namely information that has the capacity to make a positive and important difference in people's lives. Such meaning would be both personal and subjective. Enabling personal meaning to assume a more prominent role in medical decision-making would amount to a shift away from an understanding of personalisation narrowly focusing on genetic and other molecular biomarkers. It would mean including 'data' that represent things and aspects that are meaningful to patients, such as their experiences, living circumstances or preferences.[6]

---

[5] Although IBM, in their marketing information on Watson, are careful to avoid the impression that they are building a computer designed to replace human brains, the question of what happens when a human doctor ignores the probabilistic 'advice' of Watson still remains open. Will doctors who overrule the recommendations of their digital 'peer' be blamed if things go wrong? Will they be audited for the proportion of cases in which they deviate from Watson's judgement? These are thorny questions that will have to be solved in a principled way.

[6] A note of caution is merited here: not everything that carries the label 'patient-centric' is meaningful to patients. Some types of information that have 'patient' in the title are not actually collected by patients, or patients have not been involved in deciding that and how they will be collected, or both. Examples are the so-called patient-reported outcomes (PRO), which were introduced by the healthcare service providers and oversight authorities

How can we include information on things that matter to patients? One of the authors has proposed the inclusion of 'social biomarkers' into the kinds of evidence that we use in personalised medicine (Prainsack 2014b). Social biomarkers consist of contextualised, meaning-full information reflecting people's life circumstances, value systems and preferences. They include different kinds of data characterising a person's physiology and pathologies, such as cancer markers, cholesterol values, etc. They also indicate a person's most important social bonds, her preferences and – if the person wants to include these – also her spiritual and religious commitments. Social biomarkers thus include information not only on decisions that a person has taken with regard to situations where she would be unable to give consent (e.g. emergency treatments, resuscitations, etc.), but also regarding who the people closest to her are, what religious representatives, if any, should be consulted, etc. These data would not need to be set in stone; like other health-related data that change over time – such as gene expression, blood pressure or weight – they could be modified over time to adjust to changes in the patient's circumstances or preferences.

Approaches subsumed under the label of 'systems medicine' move in the right direction but they do not go far enough in allowing patients and their carers and families to shape what information is used and how it is included into decision-making. Many of the previous calls for more attention to be paid to information beyond the patient's body, including lifestyle, socio-economic factors or toxin exposure, treat these factors as parameters to improve clinical outcomes, and not the well-being of the patient in a wider sense (e.g. Cesuroglu et al. 2012; see also Ausiello and Straw 2014 who focus on 'passive data capture' via wearable sensors and mobile phones). The main aim of including social biomarkers in clinical decision-making would be, however, to put emphasis on the broader goals of healthcare beyond the traditional triad of prevention, treatment and cure. In line with the ethical debates around the proper goals of medicine (Anderson 2007; Cassel 1982; Hanson and Callahan 1999), good healthcare not only seeks to prevent, treat and cure diseases, but also ensures that people can live

---

including the US Food and Drug Administration (FDA) to obtain *information collected by patients*. Historically, PRO have 'focused on tightly controlled, structured data elements intended to meet the expectations of a specific audience (such as the FDA)' (Howie et al. 2014: 1222–3). They can range from very specific questions asking patients to quantify their responses (e.g. pain scores) to answers to open questions. This means that not all data generated or collected by patients can be considered as PRO, and not all PRO are patient-centric in the sense that they provide information that the patient considers meaningful for herself.

and die in a way that is dignified and meaningful to them.[7] This would be the core of genuinely personalised healthcare; and including social biomarkers would be one step towards it. But it is admittedly difficult to achieve: there can be considerable tensions between the goal of supporting shared decisions that are meaningful to patients on the one hand, and the goal of cost-containment on the other, if the solution that corresponds best with a patient's value happens to be the most expensive one (Stark and Fins 2013). Moreover, we have yet to work out how healthcare providers should be paid for the provision of services that can take a lot of time and may not result in an intervention that is reimbursable (see also Shapiro 2012).

Creating room for people to bring to the table information and data that are meaningful to them for the purpose of personalising their healthcare could, upon first sight, look like blowing into the horn of 'Me medicine' that Donna Dickenson warns of (Dickenson 2013). But we expect that creating more room for personal meaning in medicine will actually do the opposite: if we hold that people are intrinsically connected to each other, and that only few of our actions are purely self-interested, then it is farfetched to assume that the collection, sharing, discussion and use of personal health information would regularly be a solipsistic and self-centred activity. Genetic data always relate to others, not only because they can disclose information about biological relatives of the person who they came from, but also because people often want to know their 'genetic risk' out of concern for others: because they are convinced that having this information will help them with their reproductive decision-making, or because they want to share this information with their friends or families (Taylor 2012; Turrini and Prainsack 2015; Widdows 2013).

That personal data are not personal to only one individual also applies to non-molecular data and information. Because families share parts of their biology, and often large parts of their social lives with each other, any information pertaining to biological and social characteristics of family members may be relevant for others as well. Moreover, it is well known that people share clinical health information in other social networks, beyond the family, for many reasons – coping with a diagnosis, sharing experiences, worries, advice, etc. (Naslund et al. 2014; NCoB 2010). For these reasons, all health data – not only genetic information – are social in at least two ways:

---

[7] See textbooks of medical ethics, including Beauchamp and Childress (2012) and British Medical Association (2012).

because they pertain to more than one person, and because people make sense of them in connection and in collaboration with others. Because health information is not merely 'data doubles' (Haggerty and Ericson 2000) of our physiologies and pathologies in a technical sense, and because it also reflects our personhood in a much more holistic way – namely by including parts of our meaningful relations to others – people need to have a say in what information about them is used and how. Such a closer and stronger relationship between people and their health information – both information that is collected in the clinic and information that they bring forward from their personal and social domains – can not only facilitate better shared decision-making in the clinic, but also support new solidaristic practices. By having better insight in the factors that are considered in decision-making about their own healthcare, we expect that many people will decide to forego interventions that are not meaningful to them, contributing to the avoidance of waste (Malhotra et al. 2015). Many will do so merely because they have a better understanding of what is helpful to them, but at least some will do so also out of consideration for others. To be clear, we do not promote a scenario where people are pressured into sacrificing themselves for others. Instead, we seek to make better use of opportunities to avoid waste where this is a decision by, and partly to the benefit of, the person who foregoes an intervention. In addition, we expect that people's greater agency in deciding how information on their own health and lives will be used will make many people want to make this information available for research benefitting others. The latter point is the focus of our next example of how new policies can foster solidaristic practice in the realm of personalised medicine and healthcare.

6.3.2   A Step to Meaningful Data Sharing: Patient and Participant Access to Raw Data

In Chapter 5, we discussed how a solidarity-based framework affects the relationship between those from and about whom personal data are collected and those who are using the data. We argued that if data donors are taken seriously as 'information equals' by the institutions and organisations that are using their data, then there needs to be greater symmetry in what both parties have the permission and opportunity to do. We suggested that one way to achieve such greater symmetry, based on veracity and transparency, and emerging out of a solidarity-based perspective, is the call to grant patients and participants access to their own 'raw data' held in databases (Angrist 2015; Lunshof et al. 2014). We noted that the specific details of a solidarity-based database governance model could look as if it supported the agenda of increasing individual control and choice. We countered this claim by saying this would only be true if we assumed that accessing and using individual-level raw data would normally be a solipsistic, individual-centred activity. We also held that with all the evidence that we have about people using their own health data so far, this is a relatively unlikely scenario (see Harris et al. 2014; see also Turrini and Prainsack 2015). We argued that people's personal information – be it financial, health-related or otherwise – normally relates to themselves and to others at the same time. It is plausible to assume that people's engagement with their health data is also regularly a social activity. The main point that we want to make here is a different one, namely that people could use the raw data that they obtain in this manner to donate it to causes with public benefit, and thus to help others: they could, for example, deposit it in a non-profit repository that is established as an information common (e.g. Openhumans.org; openSNP.org). They could donate their data to projects that are personal – i.e. valuable and meaningful – to them in other ways, for example, because these projects are dedicated to an area of research that people can identify with. In addition, being able to access their own health data is likely to increase awareness for what *others* can do with their health information, and may thus contribute to greater pressures on institutions to collect and use health data in a responsible manner (Casilli 2014; Pasquale 2015).

In sum, solidarity becomes pertinent in the context of raw data in at least one and potentially two ways: first, people enact solidarity if they access their raw data and donate it to purposes that support others with whom they share a goal or characteristic in common ('similarity in a relevant respect', as we call it in our definition of solidarity; this could be e.g. the joint fight against a particular disease, or the goal of supporting health research more generally; or even 'only' the goal of breaking the data monopoly of large organisations and corporations). Making personal health data available to projects or institutions that seek to serve the public good, depositing data in 'data commons' (e.g. openhumans.org; opensnp.org), or discussing information with friends and families, and making decisions or arrangements together would be manifestations of this. A second case in which solidarity could express itself would be people engaging in data generation, collection or contribution in a solidaristic way in the first place. This could be the case if they signed up to a biobank, a research project, or allowed for their clinical data or medical health records to be used by institutions (i.e. by the hospital in which they are treated; see e.g. Mooser and

Currat 2014) for purposes that are likely to generate public benefit; and if they did so on the basis of recognising similarity in a relevant respect with other people. As personalised medicine will be supported and driven by health data, and include the integration of data from the clinical, personal and research domains (ESF 2013; Global Alliance for Genomics and Health 2014; NAS 2011; NHS Blood and Transplant 2015), the question of who makes decisions on what data and information are collected, by whom, and how, and to what purposes they can be used and shared will have a central impact on the field of medicine and healthcare.

6.3.3   Public Healthcare as an Enabler for Solidaristic Personalised Medicine

Rising expenses are a notorious problem in healthcare systems. Personalised medicine, with its promise to make healthcare more effective and thus even saving costs, is frequently seen as a solution to this problem (ESF 2013; Weber et al. 2014). The reasons for the 'cost explosion' (Anders and Cassidy 2014) in healthcare are manifold. They include the development and proliferation of new and expensive technologies, and increasing longevity and other demographic changes, with the growing prevalence of chronic diseases. In some parts of the world, such as the United States, healthcare system designs that fragment the demand side and thus let suppliers dictate prices also contribute to the cost crisis. It is apparent that we cannot afford to pay for the best treatment and care for every patient.

Particularly in regions without publicly funded universal healthcare, there are deep divisions between wealthy people on the one hand whose health insurance covers even expensive interventions and services, and under- or uninsured people with little or no access to healthcare on the other. In countries with publicly funded universal healthcare, discussions are under way about how healthcare provision can be made more financially sustainable while retaining the coverage of basic services for every citizen or resident. Sometimes the proposed solution 'includes even greater use of market mechanisms to reduce cost' (McGoey 2014: 112). In other instances, groups that are considered less deserving, such as the obese, the poor or those 'choosing' unhealthy lifestyles, are singled out for exclusion from certain services (Buyx and Prainsack 2012). The latter scenario is particularly worrisome in connection with personalised medicine, because personalisation could be used as a justification for the exclusion of certain groups from interventions or services they could benefit from. Exclusion is, of course, inherent in the idea of stratification, and is not problematic in all cases. For example, if a patient whose genetic makeup clearly indicates that she would not benefit from a particular drug is not given this drug, this does not disadvantage her. On the contrary, the patient would be spared unnecessary side effects in the absence of any benefit – the treatment would not be medically indicated. Similarly, if a person in the final stages of cancer did not receive life-prolonging treatment because she clearly stated – personally, or in a living will – that she does not wish such treatment in her situation, then excluding her from such treatment is in the interest of the patient and corresponds with her explicit wishes.

But references to individual characteristics are also sometimes used to justify cost-saving measures that are *against* both the benefit and the interest of the patient. Arguing that smokers, or obese people, should pay more for healthcare or that they should have limited access to certain healthcare interventions are examples for this type of reasoning (exceptions are cases where there is clear evidence that a higher BMI or smoking makes the treatment impossible or renders the prognosis, directly, very negative). As we argued elsewhere, discriminating against people on the basis of supposed lifestyle 'choices' is ethically problematic for well-known reasons of victim-blaming, problems to determine causal responsibility for multi-factorial illnesses and the ignorance of social and other determinants of health and health behaviour (Buyx and Prainsack 2012). Such an approach would also be impossible to operationalise effectively because 'responsibility' in the domain of health is a moving target: people who are morbidly obese could be genetically predisposed to overeating, have hormonal imbalances, live in extremely 'obesogenic' environments or suffer so much adversity in life that eating is one of their only available coping mechanisms.

One could contend here that in criminal law, for example, we regularly hold people responsible for behaviours that we cannot be sure they are fully responsible for. It is widely accepted that social and family-related problems, deprivation or psychological or mental health issues play a role in shaping people's actions. In criminal law, however, there is a pressure to ensure that people who harm others are prevented from continuing to do so, and that others are deterred from engaging in similar action. In the domain of healthcare, in contrast, there is no compelling reason to do the same. A political community aspiring to be anything more than a corporation seeking to increase profits has an obligation to support its members also when they do not or cannot contribute. The extent of this support will depend on many things, including available resources, and factors such as why a citizen does not contribute. A certain basic level of support, however, should always be provided, and this basic support must include shelter, food and a level of healthcare that enables the person to lead a dignified life (we leave aside here the complex issue of how such a minimum could be determined).

Many healthcare systems, including most European ones, were designed in a solidaristic spirit. Public healthcare, where the wealthier and healthier shoulder some of the costs of caring for the poorer and sicker, is in itself a solidaristic system – we assume costs to assist others with whom we recognise similarities in a relevant respect, namely the fact that we are all vulnerable and that, at some point in our lives, we will all need healthcare. Notwithstanding this reasoning, it has been suggested that in countries with universal healthcare, individuals should shoulder more of the 'real' costs that their healthcare incurs. Following this reasoning, the more personalised medicine progresses and the more we know about the individual risks of specific people, the more – so the argument goes – we can determine the 'real costs' that individual patients incur (Prainsack 2015a). Such suggestions assume that a reduction of solidaristic arrangements and the use of ever more personalised health stratification could be a solution to the cost crisis (by way of a 'technical fix'). The other interpretation is that through the growing use of mostly high-tech, expensive tools and methods of personalised medicine, costs in the public systems will further escalate and more people will have to be excluded based on their personalised profiles.

We believe that both these interpretations miss the mark. The idea that escalating costs in the healthcare system can be addressed with a technical fix has been haunting us for a few decades and keeps reappearing in different guises; so far, the technical fixes suggested throughout the last 30 years have not made any significant dent into the costs of healthcare, nor slowed down the cost increase. The scenario that a high-tech version of personalised medicine will exacerbate the cost problem is more plausible as healthcare costs are on the rise in general. It is unclear how greater consideration of individual characteristics in the process of prevention, diagnosis and treatment would bring them down.

In addition, in both scenarios, personalised medicine is seen to serve as a potential mechanism for exclusion (Clayton 2003; Dickenson 2013; Vollmann 2013; Vollmann et al. 2015). This can and should be avoided. We argue that the best way to introduce personalised medicine more broadly into healthcare requires that we *increase*, not decrease, solidarity in our healthcare institutions and practices. Although the relation between solidarity and the trend towards personalised healthcare may not be immediately apparent to those readers who are used to associating personalisation with genomic markers, it is very powerful. Providing universal healthcare within a solidaristic arrangement that excludes as few people as possible, and includes as many services as possible, is the most effective way to pre-empt potential negative consequences of personalisation – in particular, that the increasing use of expensive tools of personalised medicine will lead to escalating healthcare costs, even faster than in the past. Indeed, if personalised medicine gives us the means to determine more precisely who is likely to benefit from prevention and certain treatments and to render prognosis more patient-specific, then not only the targeted solutions offered, but also the mechanisms by which we stratify and personalise will incur costs. If the results of these efforts are put to work in an individualistic spirit, and without considering more strongly aspects that are meaningful to specific patients, it is not hard to envisage that this could put enormous pressure on public healthcare systems and render them unsustainable in the long run.

An important condition for us to be able to avoid the scenario of introducing personalised medicine into a background of rising healthcare costs is thus to strive for an alternative vision of a healthcare system. Such a vision would emphasise and put into practice the solidaristic understanding that we *all* are different in our health risks, and that is exactly what unites us all and makes us similar. Unless there is clear evidence that (a) a particular diagnostic or treatment measure would not benefit a specific patient, or (b) the person wishes to forego this measure, individual characteristics of patients should therefore not be used to exclude people from healthcare services. A universal healthcare system organised in a solidaristic spirit would be the best safeguard against the scenario that personalisation would be used to justify undue exclusion, or distributed according to people's ability to pay, rather than their need.

We hasten to add that this does not, of course, provide in itself the solution for the complex challenge of creating sustainable healthcare systems against the cost-driving factors we have described earlier. Such a solution will lie somewhere between more rationalisation, transparent priority setting against several layers of criteria and a pronounced turn towards preventive medicine and public health (Prainsack and Buyx 2011; Buyx et al. 2011). Here, however, we make the point that a solidarity-based perspective enables us to see that personalised medicine can be harnessed and understood in a different way to the more individualistic interpretation that emerges when it is mainly considered in the context of genetic and other biomarkers (Hamburg and Collins 2010). And solidarity also gives us the tools to start harnessing this potential.

6.3.4   Redefining 'Nudges': What Solidarity Says about Incentives to Promote Healthy Lifestyles

One of the key features of the drive towards personalised healthcare in the twenty-first century is its emphasis on prevention; this emphasis is based on the assumption that preventing diseases is in most cases cheaper than treating them (Hood and Flores 2012; Topol 2015). Moreover, in the context of ageing societies, where growing numbers of people live with chronic health conditions that are typically multifactorial – such as cardiovascular disease or diabetes – the promotion of healthy lifestyles moves up higher and higher on the public health agenda. This development has received additional impetus by a discursive shift towards portraying the most pressing public health threats as being caused by individual behaviour choices. Even in the National Health Service (NHS), a paradigmatic example of a public healthcare system organised according to solidaristic principles, the focus is shifting towards tackling current 'epidemics' such as diabetes, obesity or hypertension by preventing supposedly unhealthy behaviours of individuals, as opposed to addressing societal factors, social determinants of health or health inequalities (NHS England 2014).

We sketched earlier that increasing abilities to use personalised medicine in order to stratify people according to their alleged health risks could support this trend. In this section, we look at another way personal information about specific patients could be, and sometimes already is, used, in healthcare: incentives for healthy behaviour (see also Prainsack and Buyx 2014). We conclude that while such 'nudges' that are aimed at the general population are, in principle, compatible with solidarity, in the context of personalised medicine, many nudges take on a very problematic role.

Incentives for healthy behaviour are not new and have been used for a long time. Since the publication of Richard Thaler and Cass Sunstein's book *Nudge* in 2008, they have received increasing attention (Thaler and Sunstein 2008, see also Saghai 2013). Thaler and Sunstein define nudges as 'any aspect of the choice architecture that alters people's behavior in a predictable way without forbidding any options or significantly changing their economic incentives' (Thaler and Sunstein 2008: 6). Using insights and methods from behavioural economics and psychology, these authors distinguish nudging from coercive or binding measures such as laws or contracts. Smoking bans, for example, are not nudges because they represent a legally enforceable rule – even if they may make some people stop smoking voluntarily. Thaler and Sunstein describe and suggest nudges in various areas of public policy-making – ranging from changing pension policies from opt-in to opt-out models, to nudging students to drink less alcohol. Public health has taken up the idea of nudges quite enthusiastically. Since the publication of their book, studies into incentives for healthy behaviour have increased, including work on improving eating behaviour, avoiding deaths from cold, supporting smoking cessation and lowering cardiovascular risk (see e.g. Allmark and Tod 2013; Blumenthal-Barby and Burroughs 2013; Marteau et al. 2013; Wansink and Hanks 2013). Nudging continues to gain currency also in light of the increasing emphasis on prevention in the context of precision medicine and personalised healthcare.

At the same time, criticism of the very idea of nudging has been mounting (Bonell et al. 2011). One important emphasis following from a solidarity-based perspective in this context lies on collective responsibility. Because solidarity foregrounds similarities between people, it is not so much concerned with 'chasing the offender' – i.e. punishing those who allegedly chose unhealthy lifestyles (Buyx and Prainsack 2012). Instead, it seeks to ensure that all of us live in conditions that enable healthy lives. Providing secure pavements and reliable public transportation that enable people to leave their cars at home, or even sell them, are illustrations of this; other examples include providing healthy food in schools and work places. All these are typical nudges, aimed at giving an incentive for healthy living to everyone. What distinguishes such measures from other kinds of incentives, namely those that target only subsets of the population, therefore, is that they are targeted at the entire population. With the exception of people rich enough to afford private chefs and drivers, these incentives are directed at everybody and stigmatise no one.

Nudges that target only one specific subgroup in the whole population, in contrast, seem problematic from a solidarity-based perspective, because they emphasise what sets these people apart from others. This is particularly troubling in cases where the nudge is targeted at a group whose defining characteristic carries stigma, such as being overweight, smoking, being frail or ill. Table 6.1 provides an overview of different types of nudges, separated along the lines of whom they target, and how likely the criteria used for stratification are to stigmatise the target group.

We posit that nudging is compatible with a solidarity-based perspective *in principle* when nudges are aimed at everyone, when they foreground similarities between people, and when they are designed to create societal benefits. Within these nudges, those from which vulnerable groups are most likely to benefit – such as the improvement of healthy and affordable housing, good pavements and pollution and noise reduction – are to be given priority over nudges that are formally aimed at everybody but likely to help mostly those people who are already privileged (e.g. tax credits for fitness club memberships). A solidarity-based perspective enjoins policy-makers to be very careful about how they define target groups, and particularly so, when they make use of the knowledge and tools of personalised medicine. Nudges that are based specifically on differences between people can actually work *against* the sense of shared vulnerability in the face of illness and death within healthcare systems. They would thus run

Table 6.1 *What forms of nudging are compatible with solidarity?*

Target of Nudge	Example of Nudge	Compatible with Solidarity?
Everyone	Tax breaks for investments in health; investments in clean air, reducing pollution and noise from road and air traffic; investments in 'walkable cities'	Yes. Measures that benefit vulnerable populations most (e.g. reduction of noise and pollution) should be prioritised over measures that benefit privileged populations most (e.g. tax breaks)
People with certain objectively measurable biomarkers that *do not* carry social stigma	'Freedom pass' enabling residents from 60 years of age to use local public transportation without payment (important for public health reasons as it can maintain mobility)	Yes, but measures that are targeted at everyone and that vulnerable people are most likely to benefit from are to be prioritised over nudges in this category
People with certain objectively measurable biomarkers that *do* carry social stigma	Vouchers for weight loss programmes for people above a certain BMI	No
People with characteristics that are ascribed to them by others	Incentives for sex workers to give up custody of their children based on the assumption that the children's mental and physical health and development would otherwise suffer	No

Source: Authors.

counter to the overall aim of protecting the broad and inclusive solidarity (still) underlying our embattled healthcare systems.

This problem is even more pronounced in the case of nudges where the distinguishing features used for defining the target group carry the risk of stigma, or if the nudge itself is likely to increase existing stigmas. Examples of this would be nudges aimed at groups whose members are treated as deficient in some sense (e.g. smoking pregnant women, Marteau et al. 2013). In such a case, the nudge itself can increase stigma (examples are financial incentives such as vouchers or small cash payments to nudge such women to stop smoking, Wolff 2015). This is not to say that policy planners should not strive to reduce smoking in pregnant women, but to be in line with an idea of solidarity, nudges would have to be devised in such a way that they avoid setting these women apart from mainstream society. In consequence, such nudges would possibly address a bigger and less specified target group, or use an incentive focusing on shared characteristics or behaviours – instead of being based on personalisation. For example, public investments in affordable housing and secure jobs would be incentives for healthier living to pregnant women, without focusing narrowly only on smoking.

6.4   Conclusion

In this chapter, we argued that the notion of personalised medicine is currently broadening from the aim of tailoring drugs to the genetic makeup of people to using a much wider range of information to personalise people's healthcare. We posited that a vision of personalised medicine that takes into consideration individual differences in as many domains as possible operates with a notion of 'radical' difference. Such a notion of radical difference means that every person is to be seen as her own unique case of health or illness, implying that we can no longer lump people together in groups (Prainsack 2015b). We also argued that despite this seeming radicalisation of individual difference, clinical medicine still mostly relies on stratifying patients in traditional ways, using population averages and 'normal ranges' as benchmarks. Health platforms where people receive 'personalised' advice or disease risk calculations also compare individual results to those of others. We cannot escape comparing ourselves to others, because personal health and disease only unfold their full meaning when we set ourselves in relation to others. Personalised medicine in particular involves the constant going back-and-forth between personal- and population-level data and interpretations. Most importantly, however, the very notions that we

all have 'personalised profiles' and that we are *all* different, which personalised medicine brings into stark relief, contribute to an understanding
of similarity in a relevant respect: the more we learn about the many differences between us, the more we see that we are alike in this sense – that
we are all different. Thus, the claim that personalised medicine *inevitably*
entails or fosters radical individualisation and the exclusion of some individuals or groups from healthcare rests upon a narrow understanding of
how personalised medicine can be utilised and applied in modern public healthcare systems, or on the assumption that we cannot do anything
against the economic and political circumstances and ideas that underpin
our healthcare systems.

In the second part of this chapter, we gave four examples of how the
idea of personalisation can be employed to work towards a kind of healthcare that seeks to foster solidarity, understood as enacted commitments
to accept costs to assist others with whom a person or persons recognise
similarity in a relevant respect: in our first example, we argued that the
potential of personalisation to bring the personal and collective levels
closer together needs to be harnessed by giving more importance in medical decision-making to aspects of their bodies and lives that are important
to patients. Our second example posited that patients' access to medical
data has the potential to help patients make meaningful decisions about
their own healthcare, to relate to others or even to practice solidarity –
e.g. by donating their data to research projects that aim to create public
benefits. Although our argument focused on raw data, it is applicable to
wider contexts of patient access to medical data and information. Our
third example brought out that the necessity to maintain (or create) public healthcare systems that exclude as few people as possible is one of the
most important lessons that emerge from current visions of personalised
medicine. The more fine-grained the stratification of patients according to
individual characteristics will be, the more important it is that such stratification does not lead to undue exclusion and is instead guided by criteria
that are based upon considerations of benefit to the person (and not by
the ability of the person to pay for treatments). We trust that some, if not
many, people will be willing to forego expensive treatments with only marginal expected benefits when we have a broader and more open discussion
about waste in the medical domain (see Buyx et al. 2011). Recognising that
greater emphasis on prevention is a key step on the way to lowering healthcare costs within personalised medicine, our fourth example in this chapter looked at incentives for lifestyle changes. We argued that 'nudges' are
compatible with a solidarity-based perspective if they are targeted at the

general population and avoid stigmatising particular groups. We choose these four examples to illustrate the impact of a solidaristic perspective at different levels: at the level of individual people, at the levels of institutions such as hospitals or governmental bodies and at the level of society as a whole committing to the widest sense of solidarity possible. Practices at these different levels are most effective when they support and mutually reinforce each other.

Conceptually, a solidarity-based perspective has several implications for how we think and act personalised healthcare into being. A solidarity-based perspective rejects the false dichotomy between self- and other-regarding actions and utilises many people's willingness to accept costs to support others. This can lead to the creation of systems that harness the willingness of many people to support others – such as people's willingness to contribute data, time and effort to disease research that they know will not yield direct benefits to themselves; or their willingness to forego expensive treatments that have only minimal expected benefit for the sake of saving costs for society (Buyx et al. 2011). These aspects have not received enough attention so far. Equally important is the maintenance or creation of mechanisms that ensure that those who suffer harm as a result of the contributions they made will be supported. We argued that the most basic, and yet the most important, of such mechanisms is public healthcare. Although these aspects are often not directly associated with personalised medicine and personalised healthcare, we argue that they are important conditions to harness the positive potential of the idea of personalisation and to avoid socially undesirable consequences.

Another reason why solidarity is such an important notion in connection with personalised medicine is that it foregrounds what people share in common and not what sets them apart. This does not mean, as emphasised in several places in this book, that solidarity glosses over differences between people or pretends they do not exist. What it does, instead, is to formulate a preference to foreground similarities between people insofar as action or policy is concerned. In practical terms this could mean that instead of singling out smokers as 'high-risk' individuals who should pay higher contributions, or receive fewer services, within a publicly funded healthcare system, we should consider that all of us have higher risks in some respects and lower risks in others, and that all of us have some weaknesses and strengths in character; the difference between us is that they manifest themselves in different ways and areas.

7

Solidarity and Organ Donation

7.1 Introduction

From their very beginnings, organ donation and transplantation have been subjects of intense scrutiny and debate (Kirk et al. 2014: chapter 1; Loewy 1989: chapter 9). Over the last three decades, organ transplantations have become standard medical procedures in all developed countries, following advances in intensive care medicine, immunosuppression and surgical technology (Kirk et al. 2014). Organ donation and transplantation have always been considered as a class of their own within medicine: they represent a practice that does not aim at healing a patient's failing organ, or to improve its function with the help of a drug or a medical intervention, but that replaces it fully by an organ from another person. Organs are special also because unlike blood, cells or tissue, they cannot be fully regenerated in the donor. Hence donor organs are available only from deceased donors (like the heart, or lungs), or as part of paired or partly regenerative organs (such as kidney, liver). Anyone who has witnessed the radical change in health of the patient after a successful organ transplantation has seen how a new lease on life, literally, is given by transferring an organ from one person to another. At the same time, and partly due to the uniqueness of this type of intervention, it comes with many complex ethical and social issues – it is one of the 'classic topics' in medical ethics. From the very early days of transplantation medicine, almost every element of it has been controversial (for an early overview, see Fox and Swazey 1974, 1992). Initially, concerns revolved around the risks patients were subjected to. These took a back seat when the procedure changed status from a highly experimental treatment to becoming standard medical practice, mainly due to the revolution in immunosuppressant agents in the early 1980s. There were also early critics for whom the transfer of an organ from a deceased person to a living one constituted medical hubris[1] or an instance

---

[1] Interestingly, an early pioneer of deceased liver transplantation, Thomas Starzl, was highly critical of *living* organ donations and regarded them as unethical (see Starzl 1992).

of playing God.[2] Worries were expressed that recipients might find it difficult to live with another person's organ inside them, which some indeed did, particularly with heart transplantations.[3] And from the very early days of organ donation, some were reluctant – for spiritual or religious reasons – to accept the concept of brain death, which is one of the central requirements for transplanting an organ (Truog and Robinson 2003; Veatch and Ross 2015).

At the same time, increasing numbers of suffering and dying patients needed organs, and this trend continues to this day. In 2013, in the United Kingdom alone, 7,064 patients were registered as waiting for an organ. In the same year, a total of only 2,829 organs from 1,066 deceased and 828 living donors were transplanted. This means that on average, three patients died every day because they could not get an organ (National Health Service Blood and Transplant).[4] Similar shortages exist in many other developed countries. Nationally and globally we are experiencing the so-called absolute organ scarcity, meaning that there will inevitably be fewer organs available than needed (in contrast to so-called relative scarcity, which is typically due to technical or organisational problems with supply or distribution). Most of the time, when an organ fails, a patient either receives an organ or dies. Patients on long-term kidney dialysis, the currently only standardly available organ-replacement treatment, still wait for a transplant. Both health and quality of life on dialysis are poor compared to after transplantation (Tomasz and Piotr 2003; Witzke et al. 1997; Wolfe et al. 1999). For these reasons, the gold standard for treating kidney failure is transplantation.[5]

Patients and relatives of those waiting for organs are often desperate and some are willing to do almost anything to get an organ. It is well documented that across the globe, a black market in organs from live donors exists (predominantly kidneys, Goodwin 2013; Territo and Matteson 2012; Veatch and Ross 2015: chapter 11; see also pioneering work by Scheper-Hughes 2000, 2003, 2006). On top of that, transplantation medicine in many countries has had its share of scandals around those trying to bend the rules – for patients,

[2] Objecting to 'playing God' can be framed as both an ethical and a religious concern. Over the years, most of the bigger monotheistic religious denominations included organ transplantation as an acceptable and even commendable practice in line with their particular religious teachings (Oliver et al. 2010).
[3] This phenomenon has been described as a complicated reaction of guilt due to the 'unrequitable magnitude of the gift received' and named the 'tyranny of the gift' (Fox and Swazey 1974: ix, see also McCann 1999).
[4] NHS Blood and Transplant 2015: *Organ Donation and Transplantation - Activity figures for the UK as at 26 June 2015*.
[5] For failing hearts and livers, replacement therapy is either still at the experimental stage, or only available for some patients for short periods of time (weeks).

for personal gain or for both (e.g. recent scandals in Germany, Siegmund-Schultze 2012). Consequently, these days, many ethical debates focus on how scarce organs are allocated and how the allocation of organs is monitored and regulated, as well as on the many strategies to increase organ donation and transplantation. Suggestions for the latter range from fostering more live donations, to increasing the numbers of those who register to become a donor after death, to proposals for regulated organ markets (IOM 2006; Matas et al. 2012; NCOB 2011; Veatch and Ross 2015). In this chapter, we examine several proposals to increase the number of donors from a perspective of solidarity, which we understand as enacted commitments to accept costs to assist others with whom a person or persons recognise similarity in a relevant respect (the full definition is given in Chapter 2).

7.2   Solidarity and Organ Donation

The special situation of a person making 'the gift of life' to another whilst still alive, or after her death,[6] has prompted many people to understand organ donation as a paradigmatic example of gift giving. As such and following classic works on gift giving by sociologist Marcel Mauss and social policy theorist Richard Titmuss, it is most often associated with the concepts of altruism and reciprocity, which are taken as the foundational motivations and attitudes of gift giving (Fox and Swazey 1974; Komter 2005; Mauss 1925; Titmuss 1970; see also Chapters 2 and 3).[7] Consequently, there is a body of conceptual and empirical scholarship on the attitudes and the motivations of organ donors that focuses heavily on researching altruism[8] (and, to a much lesser degree, reciprocity; see e.g. Corly et al. 2000; Fortin et al. 2010; Mazaris et al. 2012; Moorlock et al 2013; Simmons et al. 1987; NCOB 2011).

Compared to the almost ubiquitous references to altruism in the organ donation literature, references to solidarity are relatively rare (exceptions

---

[6] In keeping with established usage of the terms, we call these two types of donation, 'live/living organ donation' and 'post-mortem/cadaveric or deceased organ donation'.

[7] Note that Titmuss wrote about blood donation; yet still, his work is also very influential in the context of organ donation.

[8] For some authors, in order to satisfy a (Titmussian) definition of altruism, motives of an act must be purely other-regarding and selfless, and may not have any element of self-interest or self-regard. Others allow for some self-regarding motivations when defining altruistic acts, such as increased feelings of self-worth, or pleasure at social recognition (for accounts of altruism, see Moorlock et al. 2013). However, to the best of our knowledge, in most definitions of altruism, other-directedness is a central element and self-directed motivations can only be secondary; certainly, any form of reciprocity expectation usually disqualifies an act or a practice as altruistic.

are e.g. Aurenque 2015; Saunders 2012; Quigley 2012, although the latter does not focus on solid organs but instead on cells and tissues). Interestingly, references to solidarity in the context of organ donation are far more frequently found in public, political and regulatory discussions than in the academic literature. Some lawmakers have recently referred to solidarity when explaining and arguing for particular policies and regulation of organ donation, including the laws underlying its practical organisation (see e.g. current German Foreign Secretary Frank-Walter Steinmeier (2012)).[9] In the public sphere in German-speaking countries, for example, the expression of organ donation systems as 'lived solidarity' is prevalent in public discourse (see DSO 2012; BzGA w.y.).

Because of the heavy-duty infrastructure needed for organ donation, and because of the requirement of a big enough pool of donors (at least for post-mortem donation[10]), the organisation of donation and transplantation play out at regional or national levels. In most countries, organ donation is tied into national healthcare systems. Where healthcare systems take the form of private, or partly private, local institutions, such as in the United States, organ donation is organised within such structures (UNOS 2015). Legally, organ donation is almost always regulated at the level of national/federal law. As such, the overall organisation of organ donation and transplantation could be regarded as a national concern, and is therefore sometimes described – and, rarely, promoted – as an expression or enactment of population-wide or community solidarity (e.g. Childress and Liverman 2006: 240; Siegal and Bonnie 2006).

As stated earlier, sweeping descriptions of a whole field of organ donation as 'solidaristic' are problematic. Instead of such – mostly aspirational – rhetoric, we believe it is important to examine actual practices and policies against and within their particular context. In the following sections, we analyse a number of policies and practices in the field of organ donation to examine whether and how they correspond to our understanding of solidarity. In the space available here, it is not possible to test *all* practices associated with organ donation and transplantation that could potentially

---

[9] Such references are more prevalent in continental European countries, which have a stronger tradition of solidarity within their political and legal systems (for an overview see Prainsack and Buyx 2011, and Chapter 2 in this volume).

[10] A pool of organ donors – the bigger, the better – is necessary for successful transplantation because not all organs match all donors, and the better the match, the better the outcomes. Organs are matched through algorithms to the best donors. Criteria change from organ to organ, and can include blood type, matching of size and age, antigen levels and tissue-type matching (see www.organdonation.nhs.uk).

qualify against our solidarity framework. In order to cover as many relevant aspects as possible, we chose one illustrative example for each of the solidarity levels we describe. We also selected policies and practices that are already relatively well-known. The three examples we consider in detail are live organ donation between strangers (tier 1, inter-personal solidarity); priority allocation of organs to members of a club of registered donors (tier 2, group-based solidarity); and switching from an opt-in system of post-mortem organ donation to an opt-out system (tier 3, legal norms).

7.3 Live Organ Donation between Strangers: Inter-personal Practice of Solidarity?

7.3.1 Background Information on Live Organ Donation

Live organ donation is currently suitable only for kidneys and livers. Kidneys are paired organs and it is possible to live a healthy life with just one functioning kidney. Livers, which are transplanted in part, regenerate in the donor. Live kidney donations have become part of standard healthcare in developed medical systems. From its very inception, however, live organ donation has been one of the ethically most contested issues in transplantation, due to the fact that it meant exposing a perfectly healthy person (the donor) to significant risk[11] to help another, gravely ill, person (the recipient) (see Fox and Swazey 1992; Starzl 1992). Several healthcare systems still include rules of subsidiarity for living organ donation, which means that a live organ donation may only be attempted if no cadaveric organ is available.[12] Because the latter is often the given situation, healthcare systems need to make increasing use of organ donations from living donors. Moreover, live donations have been shown to provide significantly better outcomes to recipients than organs from deceased donors.[13] The practice is therefore steadily growing in most developed healthcare systems.

---

[11] Risks have become smaller over time, with growing experience and the introduction of keyhole surgery. But still, explanting an organ is a major operation and comes with risks of infection, risks from anaesthesia etc. Donating an organ does not, however, elevate the risk for the donor to need an organ later on. For more information, see, for example, UNOS (2015).

[12] See, for example, the German Transplantation Law (Transplantationsgesetz), §8, 1(3).

[13] For data on success rates from living versus cadaveric donation see, for example, www .nhs.uk/Conditions/Organ-donation/Pages/Recommendations.aspx. There are several reasons for these better clinical outcomes: transplantation can be better planned; donors are usually young and definitely healthy (otherwise, live organ donation is prohibited) and cold ischemia time is minimised, since explantation and transplantation can be

In most countries, only one type of live organ donation is allowed by law, namely donation between people with very close relationships. Usually, live donation may only occur within families and people with an 'established emotional relationship'[14] (the latter includes non-married couples and close friends). The reason for this specification is the aforementioned risk to the donor. There is wide consensus that the special gift of an organ should only be given voluntarily and out of genuine affection, kinship and love; in particular, any financial motivation, or any undue pressure on donors, should be avoided. With the exception of Iran, paid live organ donations are prohibited in all healthcare systems with an organ donation program (Ghods and Savaj 2006). Most healthcare systems have monitoring systems in place to ensure that donors qualify for donation in terms of their relationship with recipients and that they decide to donate freely and voluntarily. In the United Kingdom, for example, potential donors undergo extensive medical, surgical and psychological screening, and each individual case is reviewed by an independent assessor trained by the Human Tissue Authority (HTA), which oversees live organ donations. Other countries have similar systems in place, such as live organ donation committees that evaluate each case, on top of the detailed screening process (DSO 2015; Rudge et al. 2012).

Typically, the practice of live organ donation is considered an altruistic, selfless act of love; references to solidarity are rare in public discourse. In also the ethical and related literature, live organ donation to relatives is not often framed as solidaristic (an exception is Saunders 2012). Altruism is usually seen as the main motivation of donors; and when evaluating donors for donation, selflessness and lack of self-interest and particularly financial interest are amongst the most important qualifying criteria. At first sight, this may be seen to correspond with empirical findings on the actual motives of live organ donors who donate within their own family: more than 90 per cent of such donors report that they donated voluntarily and out of selfless motives such as love, kinship and the need to help a mortally ill person (Wiedebusch et al. 2009, cf. Scheper-Hughes 2007). Almost all say that they would do it again. The small percentage of people (around 5 per cent, depending on the study) who say they would not donate an organ if they could go back in time, mention feelings of guilt, obligation, jealousy etc. as reasons for their regrets (Wiedebusch et al. 2009). Screening processes are continuously improved to minimise donations where such mixed feelings are prominently involved.

---

performed literally in the same operating theatre, leading to the best possible organ function rates.

[14] Cited from FAQ organdonation.nhs.uk.

7.3.2   'Altruistic' Live Organ Donation to a Stranger

Some countries, such as the United Kingdom and the United States, allow an additional type of donation, namely live organ donation to a stranger. This practice, which overall is rare, has been referred to by many names, including non-directed live donation, unspecified live donation, unrelated live donation, Samaritan live donation or similar (the National Health Service website refers to the practice consistently as 'non-directed altruistic donation'[15]). Depending on the country, donors willing to donate an organ while alive – which is typically a kidney – can donate to a local stranger, for example someone who needs a kidney in their local transplant centre (US). They can also donate to the recipient of another donor, who can then donate to yet another recipient, whose donor can donate to another recipient and so on (so-called donor chains or domino donations, which are possible in the United Kingdom). Finally, they can also donate into the overall organ pool (e.g. in the United Kingdom). There have been several thousand such 'altruistic' donations so far in the United States. In the United Kingdom, where the practice has been legal since 2006, there were several hundred such donations between the year of legalisation and 2014 (Maple et al. 2014; NKF 2015).

As is implied by the moniker, this particular type of donation is considered even more altruistic than 'regular' live organ donation where people donate to somebody close (Boas 2011). In the absence of feelings of love and kinship towards a specific relative, partner or close personal friend, donating an organ to a stranger is considered as an act of supreme altruism, and described as such in much of the (overall scarce) literature on this phenomenon (Henderson et al. 2003). In fact, when the practice was first debated within the medical community, many thought that such a high level of altruism was not realistically possible and that those wanting to expose themselves to the risk of having a healthy organ explanted for the sake of helping a stranger had to have some psychiatric or psychological condition. This stance has been proven incorrect; the donor population willing to donate to strangers does not exhibit higher rates of mental health issues (e.g. Henderson et al. 2003; Jendrisak et al. 2005; Maple et al. 2014). Ethical debates of the practice, not surprisingly, also prominently revolved around whether such a donation could be considered truly voluntary (e.g. Baskin 2009; Epstein and Danovitch 2009; Glannon 2011; Henderson et al. 2003). Again, empirical data show that most of such live donations do indeed take place without any evidence of undue pressures.

---

[15] www.organdonation.nhs.uk/faq/living-organ-donation/.

Yet, notwithstanding these empirical findings, many countries prohibit the practice, presumably for fears of lack of true voluntariness either due to psychological reasons or because pressure on donors is suspected. And when donors are evaluated in countries where the practice is legal, they have to go through extensive assessment of their capacity to consent and of the degree of selflessness and voluntariness motivating them.[16] In particular, any financial benefits, or any other kind of direct reciprocity, are seen as inappropriate, and the screening process is geared towards preventing such donations.

7.3.3   'Regular' Live Organ Donation and Solidarity

While 'regular' live organ donation between family members or close friends has sometimes been called an act of solidarity, donating to a stranger is, as the name indicates, often considered the ultimate act of selfless altruism. We believe that there is some confusion in these ascriptions.

'Regular' live organ donation within families or between very close friends is indeed correctly understood as a primarily other-directed practice typically motivated by love or kinship.[17] When examined against our understanding of solidarity, it becomes obvious that it would indeed be mistaken to call live donation within close emotional relationships a practice of inter-personal solidarity. As we argued in Chapter 3, the bonds that underlie donations to those whom we love and/or share kinship with – family members, partners, close friends – are stronger than bonds of solidarity, and the accompanying emotions are more immediately motivating for live donors within such relationships. Solidarity and its motivating force, the recognition of similarity in a relevant respect, are *always* subsidiary to the stronger emotions and motives of love, kinship, possibly family obligation etc. Similarity in a relevant respect may be recognised within a family or with friends, of course, but this will merely be one of the many bonds that bind families or friends together. In other words: if you love someone, you act because you love them, not because you recognise similarity in a relevant respect with them – particularly not in a situation of desperate need (Box 7.1).[18]

[16] See guidelines for evaluation, e.g. Dew et al. (2007) and The British Transplantation Society and The Renal Association (2011).
[17] This does not mean that the practice has to be wholly selfless; indeed, familial donors also report 'self-interested' reasons of pride, self-fulfilment, etc. for donating, next to love, responsibility etc. (see Boas et al. unpublished).
[18] Indeed, most live organ donors describe their decision as instant and intuitive. It is well documented that most donors make an instant, emotional, largely unreflected decision to

---

BOX 7.1   A NOTE ON SOLIDARITY WITHIN FAMILIES

The concept of solidarity within families, put forward by social scientists, is problematic. The kinds of bonds, motives, emotions that bind family members or lovers together are much stronger than solidarity. For us, solidarity arises on the basis of people recognising similarity in a relevant respect with others. There might be solidarity in extended families amongst those with overall weaker bonds (that is, where distant family members are more akin to acquaintances, or in some cases of inter-generational, inter-family solidarity). However, to describe family relationships as relationships of solidarity adds no analytic value. Instead, it overstretches the concept and clouds the analysis of a cluster of relationships – namely, different kinds of family relationships – for which there is already a full arsenal of descriptors and categories available (see e.g. Komter 2005: 151). A focus on solidarity is redundant where love and all the other, often complicated emotions at play within families determine what people are willing to do to and for each other. Rather than calling every instance of mutual assistance, even between parents and children, between lovers or between close friends, solidarity, these stronger bonds of kinship, love and friendship should be recognised and analysed as such.

7.3.4   Non-related Organ Donation: A Solidaristic Practice

However, in contrast to 'regular' live organ donation, what is currently called 'altruistic' non-directed, or non-related, donation could justifiably be described as a solidaristic practice between individuals (tier 1 solidarity). When Nadya donates an organ to Jill although she barely knows Jill, Nadya is by definition not bound to Jill through bonds of love or friendship that are, as we argued, 'thicker' than solidarity.[19] Much of the literature sees such donations to strangers as an expression of 'true altruism' – but is altruism really the right term?

Altruism reflects the idea that somebody's action is *either* self-serving or other-regarding, with altruism being solely other-regarding.[20] Such a

---

donate, which is examined later in the screening process and for which motivations are later described, as part of self-analysis (love, want or need to help, parental responsibility etc.; see Ummel et al. 2011; Zeiler et al. 2010).

[19] In some systems, such as in Israel, living donations are not organised through a state or healthcare facility. A recipient and their donor have to 'find' each other outside the healthcare system. The ways donors and recipients meet are thus dependent on the social and cultural context and always involve the donor-recipient couple meeting before the donation takes place. In most other countries that allow altruistic donation, donors can receive information on the recipient after transplantation, and some donor-recipient couples meet.

[20] For a helpful discussion of definitions of altruism in the context of organ donation, see Saunders (2012).

dichotomous understanding between self- and other-regarding practice is incompatible with the relational understanding of personhood that underpins our concept of solidarity, and we have rejected it in several places in this book. If our concern for others is always also part of who we are, how can we neatly distinguish between actions that serve ourselves and actions that serve others? Most of our actions are not purely selfish or not purely 'altruistic' (for an overview of empirical studies reporting on 'mixed' – i.e. both self- and other-regarding – motives in the donation context, see Buyx 2009). A study by Simon Cohn on blood donors in the United Kingdom also illustrates the simultaneity of self-interested and other-regarding motivations (Cohn 2015).[21]

We thus argue that the notion of 'altruistic' organ donation to strangers is mistaken altogether. Framing it as such has tangible negative consequences in medical practice where, for example, potential donors are tested for being motivated by 'genuine' altruism rather than self-serving motives (see Prainsack in preparation). It is of course necessary to have safeguards in place to prevent clear cases of coercion or exploitation. But the idea that everybody who does not donate either out of love or friendship or out of entirely selfless motives is not a worthy donor does not correspond to the realities of the lives of most people. Moreover, it stands in a tension with an understanding of personhood that treats concerns for others – may they be close relatives or friends, or more generally fellow humans, or even animals (Rock and Degeling 2015) – as integral to the person instead of something external to her. The notion of solidarity allows us to capture practices that contain both self-regarding and other-regarding elements, assuming that they are typically intertwined.

If in a case of organ donation love and kinship and other bonds thicker than solidarity are absent, this does not mean that the donation is *automatically* solidaristic. A person's willingness to donate an organ could be motivated by the expectation of a direct benefit (such as in the case of payment) or even by a person's urge to harm herself. For an organ donation to qualify as solidaristic, the donor's willingness to help another human being needs to be related to a recognition of similarity in a relevant respect with this other person. This similarity in a relevant respect

---

[21] Participants in Cohn's study explicitly referred to reciprocity as a motivation for their donation; however, this 'self-regarding' thought was connected to the desire to help fellow human beings, as in the words of a 63-year-old woman: 'I just think that being able to give is important, it's doing your bit. And anyway, what goes around comes around, as they say' (cf. Cohn 2015). A 'mix' between self-regarding and other-regarding motivations was very frequent, if not typical, among Cohn's respondents.

could be something generic – such as a common human vulnerability – or something very specific, such as personal experience with organ failure, transplantation or life-threatening disease.[22] And indeed, empirical data support this: in an Israeli study on living donor motivation (Boas et al. not published), the unrelated donors who were donating to strangers or distant acquaintances reported markedly different reasons for donation than related donors. Instead of love, parental or spousal responsibility or other familial motives, they referred to 'a sense of community, of a shared collectivity and of mutualism, as the incentives to donate' (Boas et al. not published). Importantly, the authors of this study emphasise, altruism did not play a role as incentive to donate. The authors conclude that in these donors, 'senses of solidarity precede altruism' (ibid). In the United Kingdom, findings from the entire cohort of non-related organ donors from 2006 until 2014 show that next to so-called altruistic motives, around 40 per cent of unrelated donors mention similarity in a relevant respect as an important motivation to donate. Either they have (had) relatives with organ failure, another experience with organ donation and transplantation, or they have experienced serious and life-threatening diseases themselves or in loved ones. They name the recognition of such experience in those needing an organ as reason for their decision to donate on organ (Maple et al. 2014).

Unfortunately, however, the fact that unrelated live organ donation is often an act of solidarity is not currently reflected in regulation. All monitoring and screening policies for unrelated organ donation that we are aware of focus on other-directed motivations for donation, on selflessness and, above all, on voluntariness and the absence of pressure and any forms of dependency. Screening tests do not reflect that many donors, when asked, cite a feeling of connectedness or a recognition of similarity with others as important reasons for their willingness to donate. It is likely that because of the mislabelling of such donations as 'altruistic', donors who are more strongly motivated by solidarity could fall out of the system by being prevented from donating. This is problematic both for conceptual and practical reasons. The assumption that unrelated organ donations are always or mainly altruistic is likely wrong, because the very term altruism includes a false dichotomy between other- and self-regarding action that does not correspond with empirical reality. Moreover, not

---

[22] Such recognition of similarity does not require that the donor experienced this on her own body; she could have experienced this as a parent, child, sibling, spouse or friend of a person suffering from it.

recognising solidarity as an acceptable motivation for organ donation exacerbates the shortage of organs. Thus, policies assessing whether non-related donations are 'truly' altruistic should be changed. Policies should promote non-directed live donations explicitly as also acts of solidarity.[23] This would also mean that psychological and social screening processes would explicitly recognise that motivations to donate can be complex and do not need to be 'purely' other-regarding.

7.4   Donor Clubs and Priority to Donors: Group-based Solidarity?

7.4.1   LifeSharers: 'Clubs' of Organ Donors

As mentioned earlier, because of increasing organ shortage, proposals to increase donation have been discussed for decades. What has also been debated in this context is whether a person's own willingness to donate should affect if or when she herself should receive an organ if she ever needed one. Some authors think that such a system would in fact increase donation and alleviate organ shortage; they also describe it as a solidarity-based model of donation (Gubernatis 1997).

Giving priority to people who are willing to donate organs them-selves over those who are not willing is currently illegal in most coun-tries. However, it continues to be discussed, and in some cases variants of this practice have been realised. Here, we focus on two versions – donor clubs and other modes of giving donors preferential treatment over non-donors when organs are allocated. In the following section, we will exam-ine whether these can be described as solidaristic practices in accordance with our understanding of solidarity. We examine this at the group level, because the most famous example – LifeSharers[24] – started out as an infor-mal group practice and remains a local phenomenon.[25]

---

[23] Note that unlike some authors who discuss directed donation under a solidarity label (although there is some confusion with reciprocity, Saunders 2012), we do not have the problem of worrying about the practice being hijacked by those who would donate only to white, or non-Jewish, or male etc. recipients (e.g. see Boas et al. unpublished). Because donation would remain *non-directed* and *anonymous*, only solidarity-based reasons of a recognition of similarity in a *relevant* sense (that is, the donation/severe illness context), and not personal characteristics such as race, gender, which are irrelevant in the donation context, would and could play a role. Note also that in our understanding of solidarity, paid donations that donors engage in because of the payment would not qualify as solidaristic.

[24] www.lifesharers.org.

[25] There is a contractual element to clubs such as LifeSharers, as those becoming members sign a particular organ donor card. Moreover, the second proposal we discuss later in this

LifeSharers is a non-profit national network that brings together registered organ donors in the United States. (Note that we are now examining practices in donation after death, not live organ donation as in the previous section.) Prospective donors specify that by becoming members of the organisation, they want to give special preference to other members of LifeSharers, that is, to other registered organ donors in the LifeSharers network. This could, at first glance, indicate a solidaristic practice: members would join because they are willing to donate and this willingness is a strong part of their identity; moreover, they would sign up to the club upon a recognition of similarity with others who do the same. Such coming together in a group of organ donors could qualify as a group-based solidaristic practice (tier 2 solidarity).

Surprisingly, this is not how the idea of LifeSharers is framed by the organisation itself. The organisation does not use the term solidarity at all; on the contrary, the organisation states clearly that they expect members to be motivated by self-interest (www.lifesharers.org). The rationale underlying this is that members of LifeSharers can improve their odds of getting an organ by joining the club (indeed, the website's taglines are 'improve the odds' and 'it could save your life'). Membership in the network serves the goal of participants giving 'fellow members first access to their organs' and receiving such access in return.[26] There is no focus in any of the materials on other-regarding motives or benefits, at least not in those that are publicly available (Undis 2005). The idea behind the network is instead to address the perceived unfairness of a significant number

---

chapter is an instance of contractual (tier 3) solidarity. Because of the heavy-duty infrastructure of organ donation, even group level (tier 2) practices need to tie into the overall organisational (contractual) structure of regional or national transplantation programmes. It is thus not surprising that group practices are rare in donation and transplantation; and we are not aware of any other practices at group level that could qualify as solidaristic practices. As a bottom-up, non-profit and explicitly non-governmental structure, LifeSharers comes as close to group-based solidarity as is probably possible in the context of organ donation and transplantation.

[26] The first three paragraphs of the landing site text read as follows: 'If you ever need an organ for a transplant operation, chances are you will die before you get one. You can improve your odds by joining LifeSharers. Membership is free. LifeSharers is a non-profit national network of organ donors. LifeSharers members promise to donate upon their death, and they give fellow members first access to their organs. As a LifeSharers member, you will have access to organs that otherwise may not be available to you. As the LifeSharers network grows, more and more organs may become available to you - if you are a member. Even if you are already a registered organ donor, you should join the LifeSharers network. By doing so, you will have access to organs that otherwise may not be available to you.'

of organs in the national pool going towards those who are not registered. Alleviating this unfairness, and improving one's own chances of getting an organ if one needs one,[27] underpins the notion of reciprocity that the organisation promotes.[28] Without a better and empirically informed understanding of the *actual* motives of those joining LifeSharers, we do not know whether donors sign up out of the motives emphasised by the organisation – self-interest and reciprocity – or whether they sign up out of a recognition of similarity in a relevant respect. What is clear is that at least those running the organisation disregard any possibility of the practice being solidaristic – despite there being the potential that it could, in fact, qualify as a solidaristic model of donation.

7.4.2   The Israeli Organ Transplantation Act 2008

The first – and so far, only – country to have implemented a 'club model' at the level of national law is Israel. The Israeli Organ Transplantation Act, which came into effect in 2010, gives those who have live-donated, or family members whose first-degree relative has donated after death, 'maximum priority'. As such, this is a different kind of priority-giving system – not at the informal level of clubs such as LifeSharers, but at national level. So-called 'regular' priority is given to those who hold a donor card; and 'second priority' to first-degree relatives of registered donors, even if they do not hold a card themselves (Cronin 2014; Lavee et al. 2010). Priority for children, and priority for patients in situations of emergency, both of which are common priority rules in most transplant systems, remain in place.[29]

Israel's organ donation law has been surrounded by ethical debates around brain death, and it has also revolved around potential injustices

---

[27] 'Our promise - the next life you save may be your own, or someone dear to you.' (LifeSharers landing page)

[28] The organisation's Q&A page reads: 'By joining LifeSharers you take an additional step – you indicate that you want to donate your organs to other registered organ donors. You also increase your chances of getting a transplant if you ever need one, because you'll get first access to the organs of other LifeSharers members.' (LifeSharers Q&A page) 'LifeSharers rewards the generosity of organ donors by giving them fair access to organs. This reward becomes more meaningful every time someone joins LifeSharers. [. . .]By offering your organs first to other organ donors you create an incentive for non-donors to become donors. As more people register as organ donors, fewer people will die waiting for transplants.' (LifeSharers landing page).

[29] National Transplant Center (2015).

between donor 'classes' depending on family size: people who have many children or siblings, for example, have a greater chance of a close relative holding a donor card or having donated an organ and thus have a higher chance of receiving preferential treatment than people with few first-degree relatives (see e.g. Cronin 2014; Lavee and Brock 2012; Quigley et al. 2012). Here, we do not seek to provide a comprehensive ethical assessment of the 'priority' model employed in Israel, but we focus on whether or not this practice can be understood as a solidaristic practice (Kliemt and Gubernatis 2000; Saunders 2012), or at least, as the Israeli physician and lawyer Gil Siegal called it, 'a signal of solidarity' (Siegal 2014).

The idea of reciprocity seems to have been a guiding principle behind the Israeli Organ Transplantation Act. As nephrologist Antonia Cronin put it:

> The system is consistent with the view that since the supply of donor organs has been outstripped by demand, and they may be considered a scarce societal resource, a fair concept of justice demands that those who are willing to receive an organ should also be willing to donate one. It also redresses the perceived unfairness of "free riders" willing to receive an organ but unwilling to donate.

(Cronin 2014: 8)

At the same time, individual autonomy remains an important value in the regulation of organ donation in Israel. Siegal notes that '[a]llowing individuals to designate their estate (use my money for X or Y) or to some extent their organs (to other registered donors) seems to be an act that extends individual autonomy in yet another regard' (Siegal 2014: 5). Despite the allusions to 'communitarian' ideas behind the Act (Cronin 2014; Siegal 2014), solidarity is not discussed with any prominence in connection with the Israeli Act, except when it is mentioned in a programmatic capacity. We argue that authors who insist that such a model is solidaristic (Gubernatis 1997; Saunders 2012) conflate solidarity and reciprocity (see the note on reciprocity below). Although reciprocity will, as we argued in Chapter 3, regularly be a feature of institutionalised practices of solidarity, it is not identical with solidarity (Box 7.2). Paid organ donations, for example, could be seen as a realisation of direct reciprocity – something is given for something else. At the same time, few people would claim this to be an instance of solidarity. Within our own model, a sole or decisive expectation of a reciprocal benefit disqualifies the practice as solidaristic (see Chapter 3).

BOX 7.2   RECIPROCITY, SOLIDARITY AND ORGAN DONATION

Reciprocity in the three tiers of solidarity – what does it mean for organ donation frameworks?[30]

Reciprocity is an important feature of organ donation systems on the contractual – usually national – level. On this higher level of institutionalisation, that is, on the societal level, reciprocity ensures that systems of helping or giving behaviour are perceived as fair, and stable (too many 'free riders' would undermine and ultimately destroy the system). As we explained earlier and in Chapter 3, reciprocity is not the same as solidarity; reciprocity merely describes a situation of symmetry between two actors, and not why this symmetry of any particular exchange between the actors exists. On higher levels of institutionalisation, reciprocity can be seen to assume a 'solidarity-stabilising' function (e.g. as part of consent systems for organ donation, see the following text). That said, we believe that with careful analysis, it is possible to distinguish ideal-type cases of the relationship between solidarity and reciprocity. A motivation such as the one put forward on LifeSharers – I sign up to give my organ to members within a specific group, so that I get an organ from this specific group if I need one – obviously carries little in the way of a recognition of similarity beyond this particular, mutual expectation based on self-interest. At the level of individual people, it seems to be possible to distinguish such reasons and motives quite clearly. On the higher levels of institutionalisation, and in particular, at the highest, contractual level, reciprocity and solidarity 'move closer' conceptually, because at that level, some types of indirect reciprocity do not represent an expectation of a reward or 'earned' gain. Instead, they are more akin to the appropriate attitude within particular social agreements. In other words: the higher the level of institutionalisation – that is, the less these concepts are enacted in a general instead of an individual way, the more overlap between solidarity and reciprocity.[31]

Another way to specify the role reciprocity plays in our model, particularly on the higher levels of institutionalisation, has been described by Albert Weale as 'the conversational implicature of contractual relations'.[32] When people enter into contractual relations, the presupposition of the parties is that circumstances will be such that each of the parties can deliver on their side of the deal. Events can happen that make the contract unprofitable for one of the parties, but these would not normally

---

[30] We are very grateful to Albert Weale, whose comments on reciprocity have informed our understanding and have helped us to further develop it.

[31] This is true for many state-level practices that could be understood as solidaristic practices at tier 3; for example, vaccinations.

[32] These remarks are taken from correspondence with Albert Weale. We are very grateful for his insights, and for this particularly fitting expression. We are also grateful to participants in a UCL/KCL bioethics workshop for their comments that have informed our thinking on reciprocity, in particular Lorenzo Del Savio, Benedict Rumboldt and Annette Rid.

SOLIDARITY AND ORGAN DONATION

overturn the contract; the losses just lie where they fall. However, there might be exceptional circumstances when unpredictable events occur, or the presuppositions of the contract turn out to have been wildly wrong, where it would be right for the beneficiary from performance of the contract not to insist on that performance. This could be seen to apply also to the EU's fiscal contract, where the reason for writing down struggling countries' debts is often expressed in terms of European solidarity.

It is very likely that some or even most people who register as organ donors in Israel do so upon recognising similarity in a relevant respect with others whom they want to help, thus rendering their action solidaristic practice. The particular similarity that they recognise with others could, again, be a general human vulnerability, or a more specific feature such as experience with a particular illness. The priority that the Israeli system gives to donors or their first-degree relatives, however, has nothing to do with solidarity as put forward in this book. There is no indication that prioritising donors and their relatives over non-donors enjoins people to register as donors because they see a shared commonality with others whom they would like to help. On the contrary, if somebody registers as a donor or donates an organ *merely* because she expects to be rewarded by being given priority over others if she ever needed an organ herself, this is clearly not a solidaristic practice. Thus, the Israeli Organ Transplantation Act embodies, in the absence of concrete evidence to the contrary, not more but potentially even *less* solidarity than organ transplantation frameworks that do not offer rewards to individuals or families to incentivise donation. It does give focus to a particular similarity in a relevant respect – being related – and at first glance could thus qualify as solidaristic. However, as we have argued earlier, familial bonds are thicker than those of solidarity. Moreover, promising personal or familial rewards to those opting into 'donation club' systems gives prominent attention to a feature setting people *apart* from others by stressing their status as a 'relative of a donor'. A focus on differences instead of similarities runs against a practice serving as an enactment of solidarity, just as a payment with the intention of providing an incentive does.[33]

---

[33] It is important to note that while we hold that the Israeli donor 'club model' detracts from solidaristic motivations, this does not mean that it does not work. Indeed, there are signs that

7.5   Opt-Out Consent to Deceased Organ Donation: An Instance of Contractual Solidarity?

We have touched upon national policies for organ donations in the previous section, and will explore these some more in this one. Because organ donation requires complex infrastructures and considerable organisational and monitoring effort, and because it is a matter of life or death, it is typically considered a matter of national priority and is regulated at national levels (see e.g. Bendorf et al. 2013; Rudge et al. 2012; Shepherd et al. 2014). Most national laws determine that organs can only be taken from those who have been pronounced dead according to a set of standard criteria (dead donor rule).[34] Other elements in organ donation and transplantation are rules about how organs are allocated, and the organisational and oversight structure. Usually, there is a central governmental agency or authority, or a quasi-governmental or non-profit organisation, to oversee the donation and transplantation context. Rules for patients to get listed are part of national policies, as are, importantly, forms of consent for prospective post-mortem donors.

7.5.1   Opt-In and Opt-Out Consent Systems

In the realm of cadaveric organ donation, there are two main types of consent systems in place worldwide.[35] The first is opt-in consent, where a prospective donor has to consent explicitly to donate their organs after death, by filling in a donor card, or by specifying their wishes in a registry or in some other formal way. Most countries with opt-in systems, including the United States, the United Kingdom and Germany, allow relatives to give proxy consent in the absence of explicit consent from a donor (Gevers et al. 2004). The main argument for opt-in consent is personal autonomy; a donor should

---

the Act has led to an increase in the number of people obtaining donor cards (see Boas et al. 2015; it is not possible however to determine how much of that increase is due to the priority system). If this trend is confirmed, we have an instance where a 'reward-based' system is more effective than a 'solidaristic' system. This is not surprising. While we build an argument broadly in favour of solidaristic practices and policies over non-solidaristic ones (see Chapters 3 and 4), because donations save lives, this could be an exception to this rule.

[34] There are differences between countries in this respect, which indicates the philosophical, ethical and religious or spiritual complexity of this issue; and indeed, debates around the acceptability and validity of brain death and the permissibility of donors after cardiac death have not abated these last few decades.

[35] For an overview, see Bendorf et al. (2013); Rudge et al. (2012) and Shepherd et al. (2014). No consent/involuntary donation is unequivocally considered unethical for obvious reasons.

decide herself, so this view holds, what she wants to happen to her organs after death. Proxy consent after somebody's death has the explicit aim to mimic what the deceased person would have likely decided for herself. This means that proxies – often family members – are not supposed to decide what they themselves would want to happen to the organs of the deceased.

The other type is opt-out consent (often also called presumed consent), where it is assumed that a person agrees to her organs being taken for transplantation after her death unless she recorded her dissent. Among the few nations or regions that use opt-out systems for organ donations – which include Austria, Belgium, Spain and Wales – there is considerable variation in how the model is implemented, ranging from 'hard' opt-out (i.e. it is not due process to ask relatives of the deceased before taking organs from the deceased) to systems where it is common practice to get the close relatives' consent as well.

What kind of consent is prevalent in a country often has historical reasons. In nations that use opt-out systems, the main argument in favour of this solution has been that populations have been shown many times to generally support donation and transplantation, with stable majorities willing to donate after death (Eurobarometer 2010[36]; also see recent vote in Wales[37]). The proportion of people registering as organ donors is usually lower than the percentages of those willing to donate if they were asked. Analysts have argued that this is because of reasons of inertia or avoidance; many people who would be happy to become donors in principle do not go through the trouble of registering, or shy away from engaging with a depressing topic such as illness and death. In this light, presumed consent (opt-out) systems could be seen as rectifying this problem by opting people in by default, whilst assuming that those who have religious, spiritual or other important reasons for not wanting to donate organs will find these sufficiently grave to register their dissent.

7.5.2 Solidarity and Forms of Consent

Which consent system – opt-in or opt-out – is preferable, has long been a subject of ethical debate.[38] We do not want to enter into this debate along the lines that have been discussed for a long time. Instead, by

---

[36] Der Europäische Datenschutzbeauftragte (2015).

[37] BBC News (2013): *Organ donation*.

[38] The literature on the ethical aspects of opt-in and opt-out is too large to reference here. As a stand-in for many other interesting works, we point to the debates that have happened in the *Journal of Medical Ethics* between 2010 and 2012, between lawyers, physicians and

examining the two systems from a solidarity perspective, we hope to add a new perspective on this debate. In particular, we hope that our perspective will inform discussions in countries operating opt-in systems that are currently debating moving to an opt-out system (e.g. the United States, the United Kingdom and Germany).

Both models, the opt-in and the opt-out system, could be understood as solidaristic practices at the individual level: a person is willing to assume the cost of becoming an organ donor (having to think about death, maybe overcoming some unease, taking the action of registering and renewing that registration). She decides that she wants to donate her organs because she feels she shares something relevant in common with other people (e.g. she recognises that she might need an organ someday, or because she already has had experiences with donation, or with life-threatening illness, in her family, etc.). She enacts solidarity by registering her explicit consent in an opt-in system. The same applies to a person within an opt-out system who makes a decision based on these reasons not to register dissent.

At the collective level, things look more complex. As mentioned, many people who would in fact be willing to donate an organ do not go through the effort of registering. A policy that allows for such a gap between motivation and actual practice is not only a faulty policy as such, but it also harms the opportunity to implement solidarity within society. This, in our view, is an important reason to reconsider and improve upon opt-in consent systems for organ donation. Existing opt-out systems, on the contrary, face the issue that they only embody and foster solidarity if people are truly aware of consent being presumed in their country (and donate on the basis of recognising similarities with other people whom they are thus willing to help). This, as we know, is not a given; the aforementioned EU-wide Eurobarometer survey in 2010 showed that in Austria, for example, only 19 per cent of respondents were aware that they were presumed to have agreed to becoming an organ donor after their death.

Switching from the current opt-in to an opt-out system could be considered as solidaristic practice. However, this would depend firstly on this legal change being based on research into the motives of the population for donating, and into actual donation rates including of marginalised groups. People's motivations to donate would need to meet the criteria of solidarity (recognition of similarity in a relevant respect, willingness to accept 'costs' to help others). Such a shift from opt-out to opt-in would

---

philosophers such as Ben Saunders, Martin Wilkinson, Jurgen de Wispelaere, Govert den Hartogh, James Stacy Taylor, John Harris and Antonia Cronin.

also require that the population is adequately informed of the shift, so that those who have an important personal, spiritual, religious or other reason not to donate can register their dissent. Moreover, if a switch from opt-in to opt-out happened without information, education and participation of the population in that process, and if this happened in a country where people did not trust their state organisations and maybe even feared for their safety (e.g. an authoritarian or totalitarian regime), this would not only violate individual autonomy requirements, but would also not correspond to any form of contractual solidarity. If, however, the same law was implemented in a process of several steps, including consultation and information of and by the people, and if this happened within a state system where overall people trusted that state institutions would keep their word and protect their interests, then this could indeed be seen as an enactment of solidaristic practice at the level of legal norms (tier 3). This goes to show that in addition to the motivational core of a practice or policy, the context in which it is enacted and implemented is vital for it to be considered a true enactment of solidarity.

7.6   Conclusions

Organ donation and transplantation are long-standing issues in bioethical debates. In this chapter, we did not foreground the well-known ethical arguments in these debates, but instead we analysed a number of policies from a solidaristic perspective. We showed that beyond vague solidarity rhetoric, solidarity as a clear concept can help to illuminate where current policies ignore/fail to recognise important other-oriented motivations which cannot be fully captured with the label of altruism. This is the case in non-related live organ donation, which, based on current empirical research, is often a solidaristic practice. Yet notwithstanding these findings, policy rhetoric strongly focuses on altruism in non-related live donation and this could 'crowd out' some donors who do not have 'purely' altruistic, but in fact solidaristic, motivations. We believe that where policies are in place to allow for non-related live donation, they should be changed to reflect, and indeed, encourage, that this type of donation can regularly be a solidaristic practice. Moreover, the evidence of solidaristic motivations gives weight to calls for lifting the existing bans of this practice in other countries. Pure altruism might indeed be rare and this leads some to worry about the decision-making of such donors. The mixed self- and other-regarding considerations at work in solidaristic motivations, however, are likely to be more frequent and less prone to exploitation or misunderstandings.

We found that models such as priority-clubs for donors do not correspond to solidarity criteria. This conclusion is surprising at least insofar as that these models were introduced into academic literature explicitly under the solidarity label in the first place. However, this ascription appears to rest on a confusion of solidarity with reciprocity.

Finally, a solidarity-based perspective, with its in-built necessity to consider the concrete context of each case, has been shown to be helpful in the analysis of whether and how a switch from opt-out to opt-in could be managed. This case shows the importance of context of a switch from one policy to another – the same law can qualify as an enactment of contractual solidarity within a particular society, and as a top-down state imposition, hollowed out by lack of trust.

PART III

Conclusions

Solidarity with Whom? Conclusions and Ways Forward

8.1 Introduction

In this chapter, reflecting on what we have developed and discussed so far in this book, we present some of the broader implications of our work on solidarity in biomedicine and beyond. To recapitulate what we have done so far: in Chapter 1, we gave a brief overview of uses of the concept of solidarity throughout history and a summary of (English language) scholarship on this topic in bioethics and social and political theory in the last two decades. In Chapters 2–4, we developed our understanding of solidarity and situated it within pertinent theoretical debates. We then applied it to three policy contexts in Chapters 5–7, drawing out a number of implications for specific policies and practices. In this concluding chapter, we bring together some overarching conclusions from our study regarding the analytical value and the practical utility of solidarity as we understand it: as enacted commitments of people to accept costs to assist others with whom a person or persons recognise similarity in a relevant respect. Such commitments manifest themselves in practices and policies at various levels, from the inter-personal (tier 1) and group-based (tier 2) levels to the level of contractual, administrative and legal norms (tier 3). In previous chapters, we have been careful not to overstretch what our definition of solidarity can do. In this final chapter, we paint with a slightly broader brush. We want to draw out some wider claims from our work, as well as sketch out some ideas of how we envisage a solidarity-based perspective to inform conceptualisation, policy and practice beyond the cases we have analysed in this book.

We start in the opposite direction from how we have moved in our book so far. First we draw out some broader implications for the practical application of our understanding of solidarity from the case studies in this book (Chapters 5–7). We then follow up with a number of ideas for policy-making, illustrating what kinds of innovative strategies could be based on solidarity in biomedicine. The later parts of this chapter are devoted to presenting some overarching conceptual conclusions, and demonstrating how our understanding of solidarity can be fruitfully applied to broader fields than biomedicine. We close with a few suggestions for future work.

8.2   Solidarity in Biomedical Practice and Policy

8.2.1   Conclusion 1: Unlocking and Shaping Debates

Three overarching conclusions follow from the three case studies in this book (health databases, personalised medicine and healthcare and organ donation). First, our understanding of solidarity has the potential to change the point of gravity within scholarly and policy debates. It can unlock or reframe debates exactly where they need doing so. Introducing solidarity-based governance of health databases, for example, helps to understand – and overcome – the significant disconnect between a practice that is very often prosocial and oriented towards societal benefit,[1] yet is governed through policies that are overwhelmingly geared towards protecting individual autonomy (Chapter 5). This disconnect has undesirable effects on research participants who are confronted with bureaucracy and legalese that does not capture what really matters to them, and that is often designed to protect institutions rather than participants. Such policies also regularly prevent people and institutions from creating personal and social value – by accessing their own data, or by making data more widely available for research, etc. A solidarity-based perspective mandates the creation of governance frameworks that acknowledge that many people are willing to accept certain costs to support others, and that, at the same time, ensure that people are not left alone when they suffer actual harm.

A focus on our understanding of solidarity can also help when contributing to the debates around defining a still emerging field, and engaging in some early agenda setting. In Chapter 6, we showed that thinking about personalised medicine and healthcare from a solidarity-based perspective directs our attention away from technical modalities concerned with stratification. Instead, a solidarity-based perspective demands that we find ways to give more room to aspects and practices that are meaningful to patients even if these conflict with technical rationalities. Most importantly, it also requires that we ensure that everybody has access to healthcare. These measures will help to avoid that greater stratification of patients into more

---

[1]   At least in research databanks, participants usually donate samples, tissue and information without any expectation of personal benefits; empirical research shows that their motivation is to help others they feel a connection with, or help medicine overall. See Chapter 5.

specific criteria impacting preventive and clinical trajectories will lead to undue exclusion of people from services. We also expect that when patients have more agency in making subjectively meaningful decisions regarding their own healthcare, they will be in a better position to opt out of interventions that are not useful to them, thereby making resources available for others.

Finally, our solidarity approach is helpful in reframing longstanding debates that have become stuck. Introducing solidarity into the discussions about which practices and policies we should allow, and foster, in organ transplantation, which we do in Chapter 7, helps to avoid the 'argumentative deadlock' of the rigid (and often incorrect) dichotomy of 'altruism vs. self-interest'. It can also unlock potentials for recognising motives for organ donation that have so far remained below the radar of regulatory frameworks. Bringing a solidarity-based perspective to the regulation of organ donation may even lead to new types of donors.

8.2.2   Conclusion 2: Practical Utility

If the application of solidarity is based on a clearly stated understanding, such as the one we have presented in this book, it is indeed possible to apply it with significant and direct practical utility to complex and challenging contexts of policy-making in biomedicine (and, we will sketch later, also to areas beyond the field of biomedicine). This may sound very obvious to those with sympathy towards the concept. It is worth emphasising nevertheless, because there is still a widespread assumption that solidarity is too vague to be usefully applied to a specific situation of policy-making. It is also important because several of the current practices of 'application' of solidarity to policy are indeed mislabelled, or utilise an under-determined conception of solidarity. They thus give credence to the concern that introducing solidarity as a consideration or even a basis for policy-making cannot work.

We have responded to the concern about the conceptual vagueness of solidarity by developing a definition that establishes specific requirements for solidarity and sets it apart from related terms such as charity, altruism or reciprocity. We believe that such a definition of solidarity has significant analytic value. It allows us to assess whether a particular practice or policy is solidaristic, or whether it is an instance of something else. Clearly defined, solidarity can guide policy development just like other concepts have been doing for a long time (e.g. patient autonomy, beneficence, etc.). These latter concepts have received far more attention from theorists and policy-makers alike, and have been further specified and operationalised for various contexts and situations. Those who seek to apply solidarity to practice and policy-making, in contrast, have had very little material to fall back on. We hope that together with others who also work on solidarity we can change this situation for the better, and provide policy-makers and practitioners with more case studies, more context analyses and more policy guidance and recommendations. This book is a step in this direction.

One of the key tasks ahead, and one in which we have engaged in the case study chapters in this book, is to 'debunk' practices and policies that are labelled as solidaristic that do not, according to our understanding, deserve to be called such. An inflationary association of solidarity with everything that a particular author or politician deems positive or desirable has led to the aforementioned concern about the practical value of solidarity. Most likely, such misapplications of the term solidarity stem from the fact that solidarity has for a long time had very strong political and sometimes religious connotations, and has often served as a political, religious or moral ideal. While it is not surprising that this patterned history colours uses of the term until this day, if solidarity is to be useful for policy-making on a societal scale, then it should be acknowledged as a political concept, yet one that is not wedded to any particular camp in party politics (see also Scholz 2015). This is one important overarching recommendation that we make for future work on and with solidarity: if employed in a public context for guiding practice and policy, an understanding of solidarity should be applied that fulfils the criteria of conceptual clarity, firmness and specificity that we apply to other such concepts as well. It should also, as far as possible, avoid presupposing any strong political, religious or moral connotation.

8.2.3 Conclusion 3: Importance of Background Conditions

The third overarching conclusion we can draw from our work on the three case studies is the importance of background conditions for solidaristic practice and policy to function and to flourish. As we set out in Chapter 4, we do not regard solidarity as one of the concepts that help determine the minimum conditions for decent human lives. This is the realm of universal concepts such as justice and human rights, or approaches such as the capabilities approach (in whichever accepted and institutionalised form; see e.g. Venkatapuram 2011). From these concepts or approaches, enforceable obligations and duties of conduct can be derived. Neither, however, should solidarity be regarded as a 'luxurious' principle for guiding life in society, in the manner of e.g. principles of pure aesthetics. As a mid-level concept, solidarity sits between the more formal principles and rules of justice, mostly in forms of law, and those practices and norms that 'thicken' justice. Most of us agree that we do not want a society that is merely minimally decent and just. We want a society that is good. Solidarity is one of the concepts that can provide guidance in the area beyond the decent minimum, where we address issues that prevent people from truly flourishing, and our societies from being as liveable as possible. As such, solidarity is very important to many areas of practice and policy-making, particularly those where we deal with prosocial practices and institutions that make up a lot of the social 'glue'.

Our case studies have shown the importance of both the specific situation of a solidaristic practice or policy, and of the background conditions against which a solidaristic practice plays out, or into which a new solidaristic policy is to be implemented. What a 'similarity in a relevant respect' is that people recognise and then base their solidaristic practices upon depends to a large extent on the specifics of a concrete situation. The bonds that people see as connecting them to others – may it be a shared experience, a shared religion or a shared group affiliation – are not naturally given; they are a matter of the person seeing a particular characteristic as something that is part of herself and of somebody else. If similarities between people were something that could be ascertained in an 'objective' way, then all women, all people living in the same postcode or people in the same socio-economic group would be solidaristic with each other, which is clearly not the case. Thus, when we speak of people recognising similarities with others, then such recognition in turn creates and reinforces bonds between people; it is not the recognition of something that exists 'naturally'.

This is where the background conditions come in. Economic, social, environmental and institutional background factors have the potential to make it less or more likely that people will see similarities with others and support others even if this incurs 'costs' for them. In societies where people can trust public and corporate institutions, and where there are arrangements in place that ensure that people will not be left alone if they need help, they can take greater risks (in our terminology, 'costs') to support others. The question of whether or not a specific practice is an instance of solidarity depends on whether or not it meets the requirements of the acceptance of costs to support others on the basis of a recognition of similarity in a relevant respect (Chapter 3). The existence of good background conditions, including a certain level of economic and political stability, trustworthy institutions and a value system that promotes concern for others makes it more *likely* that such solidaristic practices emerge in the first place.

All our case studies demonstrated the importance of background conditions for the existence and flourishing of solidaristic practice. To mention just one example from each of them: whether a health database is suitable for a solidarity-based governance framework depends on whether or not people know what they are contributing to a database and how their data will be used; whether the database aims at the creation of social value and whether or not the expectation of direct benefit is the main motivator for people to participate (Chapter 5). All of these features are more likely to be present in societies that are democratic, relatively transparent, and provide a certain level of social security. In Chapter 6, the link between background conditions and solidaristic practice was most obvious when we argued that the provision of public healthcare is an important requirement for avoiding unintended consequences of personalisation in medicine and healthcare. In Chapter 7, we argued that the switch from an opt-in law for cadaveric organ donation to a solidaristic opt-out model needs to be embedded in a well-functioning and reliable medical system (Chapter 7). In sum, we believe that any solidaristic practice or policy will be more successful when the overall circumstances are more conducive to solidarity. In contexts and situations where the importance of e.g. relationality for human flourishing is already recognised and enacted in various ways, in societies where each individual finds at least decent economic, social, etc. conditions to live a meaningful human life and in societies where public institutions are built on transparency, accountability and trust, solidaristic practices and policies will thrive, and solidaristic laws will face little danger of being 'empty shells', solidaristic in name only.

Another significant implication of the importance of background conditions and context is that any *change* in these potentially affects solidaristic practices or policies. If recognition of similarity or relevant background circumstances change significantly, this will have implications for the emergence or continuation of solidaristic practices and norms at all three levels. Of course, *any* policy, whether solidaristic or not, should be regularly revisited and monitored, so it can be adapted if circumstances change. However, going further, we would argue that such revisiting should be a mandatory, built-in part of any solidaristic policy. This, therefore, is our second larger recommendation for practice and policy development: those seeking to develop and implement solidarity-driven policies should not only evaluate that their policy corresponds with solidarity on lower levels of institutionalisation but also build into their policy a way to monitor change; ideally, a mandatory, regular update of context analysis.[2] This is obviously a tall order, but we believe it is doable and will contribute to good, sustainable practice and policy-making.

8.2.4 Ways Forward in Practice and Policy: A Quick Sketch

Solidarity can indeed be fruitfully applied to different fields of practice and policy-making in biomedicine and beyond. We are currently sketching out a research agenda for the following years. We will continue our conceptual work on the concept, as discussed further later. But in addition, we look forward to applying our understanding to many more policy areas, and hope that others might be inspired to follow suit. There are some obvious 'low-hanging' fruits for this application. That is, there are policy contexts that are particularly suited to an assessment whether and how solidarity could underpin policy and practice. Criteria include that there are collective practices involved (ideally, these already take the form of practices that support others); that at least part of the motives at play are prosocial and that potential costs that would have to be carried are small. This is not to say that these are necessary or sufficient criteria to determine whether solidarity can be applied. But if these criteria are fulfilled, it is very likely that solidarity can be helpful in the ways described earlier – by unlocking and reframing debates that have become stuck, and by providing specific guidance for policy change or policy development.

In Chapters 5 and 6, we looked into solidaristic practices that take place also in research contexts (in biobanking and health databases, and in personalised medicine). Indeed, we believe that a systematic exploration of what types of medical research correspond with our understanding of solidarity is the most obvious place to start looking for future policy application. However, since we have addressed biomedical research already in this book, here we want to expand briefly on an alternative idea. One interesting example would be to explore the growing role of exchange we see in many areas of our lives, exemplified by trends towards both not-for-profit

---

[2] The idea of regular policy evaluation that includes context and background conditions is not something new. Ideally, it should be performed for all policy. We stress the point here specifically because it is of particular importance in solidarity-based practice and policy, for the reasons we have described.

and commercial exchange of goods and services, and including for example 'couchsurfing'[3] and temporary flatsharing, or online skill- and goods-based exchange networks. This could be adopted in other areas, and in line with our understanding of solidarity.

Many forms of support for e.g. elderly people and those living with chronic illnesses do not require a clinical setting or even medical professionals. Neither do they require that those who assist each other are health professionals, nor that they are already patients, themselves. A system could be created which enables people to provide care to others outside of the healthcare system and get 'points' in return. Tasks would range from those that require no special skills, such as shopping for somebody who is too ill to do so themselves, to tasks for which some level of training will be necessary. People could provide these services when they can, e.g. if they are students, unemployed, on leave, or even at weekends if they choose to do so. The points received for these services would go into a personal account (or, if that is the preference of everybody involved, into a family or group account). People could use these 'health points' later on to pay for their own care, or for medical procedures that their own insurance does not cover. In order to avoid a situation in which the points themselves become a traded commodity, they could not be sold or transferred to anybody outside of the immediate group with which the person has chosen to share.

Rendering 'social tasks', such as shopping for an ill or frail person part of a solidaristic exchange system is likely to have further positive knock-on effects: it could enable some people to live at home for longer, rather than in a hospital or care home, and it could mitigate the level of social isolation for some. We believe that such a model of 'health points' could be a promising example of solidaristic practice. Many particulars would have to be explored and assessed, particularly safeguards, and obstacles to potential exploitation of the model, before it could be considered. Careful analysis of context and background conditions would have to be performed. However, we believe that it could provide many benefits, ranging again from avoiding social isolation to helping people stay out of institutionalised care for longer. London-based social enterprise Participle has trialled a similar model they call Circle (www.participle.net/circle). Initial results are promising enough to give these kinds of ideas more attention.

---

[3] Offering a place to sleep, via online platforms, in one's flat or house, often in exchange for being able to do the same elsewhere.

8.3 Beyond Biomedicine: Theoretical Upshots and Conclusions

8.3.1 Solidarity as a Point of Intersection of Many Debates

We now turn to the insights and overarching conclusions we draw from our work in the theoretical part of this book (Chapters 1–4). The first chapter offered an overview of the history of the concept of solidarity more generally and its use in bioethics and social and political theory more specifically. Solidarity has a patterned history in several areas of scholarship and politics, ranging from sociology to theology, and from welfare state politics to feminist movements. It has so far played an only marginal role in bioethics and related areas compared to other concepts, such as e.g. autonomy or justice, but this is currently changing. While there are, and have been, many different understandings of solidarity, throughout its history it has been often understood to capture a particular type of bond that ties individuals, groups and communities together beyond personal relationships and feelings (such as love, or kinship).

We have shown in this book that it is indeed possible to develop a definition of solidarity that captures its unique aspects and features, and that at the same time allows for the concept to be applied to practical questions of practice and policy-making. Another important motive to work on solidarity was our initially mostly intuitive assumption that solidarity was a hitherto unrecognised focal point for a number of important scholarly debates of the last 50 years. This role had not been brought out sufficiently in the literature. In the second chapter of this book, we therefore presented the intellectual background and several key themes in debates of the last century that have influenced our understanding of solidarity. We believe that the issues and theories covered in these debates bring out a number of elements that are central to solidarity and that in fact, solidarity is the point of intersection where these debates interlock. A number of important strands of thinking overlap in the concept of solidarity.

8.3.2 Importance of Relationality

One of the key themes that sits at the heart of large debates and at the same time is also essential to solidarity is an understanding of the person and of the self as embedded, and partly shaped by her social, natural and artefactual environments. Critical discussions of the tendency towards the increasing individualisation in modern societies and the accompanying view of an atomistic self have catalysed the creation of alternative visions of society. This includes an emphasis on the importance of relationships and community for people to develop, be and flourish. Such relational understandings of persons and their autonomy and ways of decision-making – obviously in the many shades that academic debates tend to produce – have been put forward by communitarian and feminist scholarship, by ethicists of care, anthropologists, social biologists, neuroscientists and post-modernist thinkers. Accounts differ in specifics of course, but what connects many of them is the acknowledgement of a person's social and relational nature and the need to de-emphasise the boundaries that set apart 'me' from 'you'. Allowing for such fluidity and weakening the dualism between individuals and their environments resonate with other strands of thinking that enjoin us to reflect on what connects people, as opposed to what sets them apart – be it vulnerability and a need for care, as emphasised in feminist and ethics of care literature, or the ability to overcome conflict and develop consensus, important ideas for many agonist thinkers. These key themes are reflected centrally in our understanding of solidarity, which builds both on a relational conception of the person, as well as on the recognition of similarity between people. Because we are relational beings – our identities, lives, relationships and behaviours all socially shaped and embedded – we turn to others, and are able to see what connects us with them. Because we are relational beings, we have an ability to see similarities in others despite many important differences (and despite often being in situations of conflict in our world).

We believe it is in the spirit of the debates we reviewed in the earlier chapters of this book to go even further and argue that we, as individuals, have strong interests – in fact, we have a need – to exercise this ability to see similarities with others. In order to flourish, people have to exercise their 'solidarity muscles' and enact – practise – their relationality on a regular basis. This argument is not pulled from thin air; empirical studies provide evidence on the beneficial effects of recognising similarities in others and help, for example on mental health. Medical advice on tackling milder forms of depression includes suggestions to devote time and effort to assist others to improve well-being and satisfaction. And public, non-scholarly publications (which we take to reflect some common beliefs) from self-help books to glossy magazines regularly emphasise that it simply 'feels good' to help others one feels connected to.[4] In addition, the societies

---

[4] That it 'feels good' to the person doing it is true for any helping behaviour (which can also be of a more asymmetrical, charitable kind). It would be interesting to examine whether the more symmetrical helping relationships that occur in solidaristic practices have a more, less or comparably positive effect on people's well-being.

in which prosocial, solidarity-based practices occur often and are well-institutionalised usually also score well on indices of overall well-being and equality. Broadly speaking, humans benefit and prosper when solidaristic practices are frequent.

8.3.3   Importance of Inter-Individual Solidarity

These considerations are mainly grounded in and focused on our interpersonal level of solidarity, as described in Chapter 3, which flows from a relational concept of the person. It is one of the novel aspects of our approach to solidarity that it takes this level very seriously. In most of the literature on solidarity, the main, if not exclusive, focus is on the group level; solidaristic practices are often understood as being tied into, part of or emerging from group identity. As we argued in Chapter 4, such narrow and static interpretations of solidarity as necessarily tied to a pre-existing group identity can run the danger of being inherently conservative, affirming a sometimes problematic status quo. (Such interpretations could even deteriorate, as some critics have stated, into a caricature of solidarity as autocratic group rule.) Without the personal level to explain the motivation for informal, spontaneous or newly emerging solidaristic practices, solidarity would be tied to a fixed understanding of pre-existing groups, and novel and enormous outpourings of voluntary help and support, such as the ones that could be observed during the refugee crisis in Europe in the second half of 2015, could not be framed as solidarity at all. Many of the practices that were seen as part of the civil society response to the refugee crisis of 2015 – on an unprecedented scale in recent decades – were obviously solidarity-based and at the same time *not* tied to any kind of clearly delineated pre-existing group. Volunteers of all ages and walks of life expressed as their motives to help that they saw themselves in the mothers, fathers, children, etc. arriving from war-torn countries, and the press and social media used solidarity to frame what was happening far more often than e.g. charity.[5] Social media were flooded with narratives from volunteers, in which they very explicitly talked about the fact that it was sudden recognitions of the kind 'in another life, this would be me', or 'she seems so similar to me, and yet she suffers so much and I am so comfortable – how can I not help?' that prompted them to get up and help.

---

[5] There is, as of now, no scholarly literature available on this phenomenon we could cite. However, Google shows that, e.g. in German-speaking press and social media, solidarity with refugees has become a key expression.

It is such newly emerging phenomena of assistance and support that are based on recognising similarity in relevant respects with others at the personal level that we are very interested in, and which we want to see rightly recognised as solidaristic practices.

8.3.4   Importance of Community

Our emphasis on solidarity on the inter-personal level is meant to give more visibility to this type of axiological solidarity, which enacts who a person feels she is and what she believes in. We also want to stress how new solidaristic practices emerge, and thus also to show where 'traditional' group solidarity stems from in the first place. But this should not be misunderstood as ignoring that many – if not most – solidaristic practices in our societies come in the shape of group solidarity. On the contrary, underlining the relational nature of ourselves and our choices and practices ties in directly with several long-standing debates on how important communities and how central participation in groups are, not only to individuals, but also to societies overall. Scholars and researchers from diverse fields – communitarians, social scientists, psychologists, behavioural economists, philosophers, etc. – have stressed this repeatedly over the last decades.

At this group level, as we described in Chapter 3, the inter-personal practices have been solidified into more widely shared practices. To stay with the example of the refugee crisis of 2015, some of the spontaneous voluntary help was quickly organised and solidified, in a bottom-up way, without any state intervention, sometimes with the help of civil society organisations that have experience with humanitarian help, such as the Red Cross, Voluntary Fire Brigade, etc. People at train stations and in refugee camps came together into – initially loose – groups that quickly established shift rotas, what kinds of duties had to be carried out by whom, how resources were to be divided, how more volunteers could be recruited and incorporated in the existing support structure, etc. And in many cases, refugees themselves took active parts in these activities, after having overcome initial exhaustion; for example, medically trained refugees in camps started treating fellow refugees together with local European health professionals. Such phenomena that emerge out of inter-personal solidarity and are based on mutual recognition of similarity are examples of new and productive group-based solidaristic practice. At this level, solidaristic practices are still transient, but they become more stable, and, if the groups establish rules that are to be followed, more enforceable. And if at the national political level novel legislation responds to these emerging practices, for example by allowing refugees to work, or by making some healthcare services accessible to them, these are institutionalised norms that can be enforced just like other legal rules. This level of national, supranational or international law is highly important for solidarity to flourish; solidarity is never an excuse for the withdrawal of the state from responsibilities for and duties towards people.

As we emphasised in Chapter 4, for legal and administrative norms in the spirit of solidarity to be stable and widely effective, they need to be aligned with actual solidaristic practices at inter-personal and group levels. If they were simply developed at the drawing board and imposed top-down on a population that did not engage in solidaristic practices, such policies would amount to 'empty shells' of supposedly binding, deontic rules of solidarity. They would be little more than a pretence of solidarity, using the term as an empty label for a law or regulation that does not have the kind of support in the population truly solidaristic policies need.

8.3.5   Limits of Solidarity

Many solidaristic practices, and particularly those at group and contractual, administrative and legal levels, have existed for a long time and have become part of the social, political and economic fabric of our societies. The longstanding debates that examine the welfare state and the role solidarity plays in it (which we reference frequently throughout this book) usually focus on such long established practices. Indeed, we follow those who argue that the welfare state is one of the best examples – and arguably also one of the most successful – of institutionalised solidarity. In many countries, including the United Kingdom, the Netherlands or Germany, each particular version of the welfare state still has broad and stable public support (if dwindling political backing).[6] Put into solidarity language, welfare arrangements can be understood as systems that assume that people are willing to accept costs to support others with whom they recognise similarity in a relevant respect. This similarity could be a shared national identity, or the shared risks to face hardship. It is jeopardised when people within that community stop feeling that the bonds that connect them to each other are weaker than the factors that separate them.

---

[6] Despite frequent portrayals of the British National Health Service (NHS) as embattled or endangered, polls show high levels of support for the NHS and for the welfare state more broadly (Ipsos MORI 2011; Lord Ashcroft Polls 2015; YouGovReports 2013).

However, the welfare state, and, of course even more so, assistance to refugees are also good examples of the 'flip side' of our understanding of solidarity, to which we now turn. We have described in Chapter 4 that our definition of solidarity – namely that solidarity comprises manifestations of people's willingness to accept costs to support others with whom they recognise similarity in a relevant respect – cannot prevent that those outside of the group will be harmed as a result. We gave the example of members of a terrorist group whose aim is to kill those who refuse to subscribe to their beliefs. Although practices of members within the group may meet all requirements of solidarity, their mutual support would make the group stronger and more effective in killing people outside. We argued that two important characteristics of solidarity become apparent here: first, that solidarity in itself is not always positive, and second, that in order to assess whether a concrete instance of solidarity is desirable, we need to take a look at the context of the practice.

We have stressed in Chapter 3 that every practice of solidarity includes processes of 'othering' to some extent – group solidarity most significantly. Whether or not this is problematic depends on the context. Solidarity cannot be seen in separation from the role that we want a particular solidaristic practice to play in society. And again here, it can be argued that societies with trustworthy institutions, political stability and where people have reasonable safety nets in case something goes wrong (i.e. high levels of institutionalised solidarity) are those where the effects of exclusion from group-based practice of informal solidarity are less harsh than in other societies. To stick with our example of a terrorist group that is solidaristic internally and cruel to the outside, such groups would be a subject of effective criminal prosecution in such societies.

Another limitation of our understanding of solidarity is that we cannot escape the fact that our approach depends on the recognition of similarity, and on how far this recognition goes. In a country where no volunteers show up at the train stations and in the refugee camps, where there is no civic movement of support and help for refugees and where the population is deeply opposed to accepting refugees, there is a chance that this is not only due to bias and fear, but also due to a lack of recognition of similarity with refugees. In such cases, it would be very difficult for the government of that country to impose any laws on populations that would support refugees and require some sacrifice from residents and call these 'solidaristic'. They could of course still be imposed, but would have to be justified in a different way; solidarity would be a wrong label for them. And going further – it would also be difficult to 'force' such a country to be solidaristic and help with a refugee crisis situation within, say, the larger context of Europe. Instead, here, any pressure applied to such a country to open itself to helping refugees would have to appeal to concepts such as justice (as fairness) between European countries and utilise instruments such as European law. In other words, this would be a discussion about minimums and enforceable policies, and not about solidarity.

This is sobering, because it is reflected, to some degree, in what we can currently observe in Europe. Populations and countries exhibit very different levels of prosocial support for refugees – yet the discussion with and about those countries that are opposed to taking and helping more refugees is, at the EU level, nonetheless couched in terms of solidarity. This is misleading; referring to concepts such as fairness and justice, and to whatever legal instruments are available, would be more honest.

8.4   Solidarity with Whom? Conclusions and Recommendations

Here, then, is where the rubber hits the road regarding solidarity. To very crudely evoke the name of a famous discussion in political philosophy, the 'equality of what?' debate that focussed on the 'currency' of equality: in order to develop and implement solidarity-based practice and policy, we need to ask: 'Solidarity with whom?' In other words, with whom, and how far, do we recognise similarity in a relevant respect? We cannot simply assume that such recognition and solidarity exists; we have to actually find out if it does. At the highest level of institutionalisation of solidarity (tier 3), our account therefore emphasises the need for evidence-based, context-sensitive and particularistic approaches to justifying, developing and implementing solidaristic norms and policies. Overall, it is unlikely that broadly idealistic or universal solidaristic norms correspond with the reality of people's actual recognition of similarity. Each context we want to apply a solidarity-based approach to, and each solidaristic policy we want to implement, requires careful analysis of the particulars at play – any social practices already in existence, prevalent values and motives of those involved and the degree of willingness to recognise similarity (as well as, described earlier, analysis of background conditions).

This does not mean that we suggest taking the status quo as it is and, if sufficient levels of recognition of similarity or practices that enact it cannot be found, turn away and give up on striving towards solidaristic policy and practice. On the contrary, contextual analysis of similarity can help to uncover 'blinders', biases or vested interests at play within a particular context. It can help us devise strategies to overcome such obstacles to similarity recognition. For example, as we briefly discussed in Chapter 6, it is a relatively prevalent misunderstanding that within the healthcare system there are some who intentionally live in ways that pose particularly grave risks to their health – smoking, eating too much, drinking too much, etc. – and that their illnesses are therefore unnecessary. A careful contextual analysis around such arguments includes a comprehensive assessment of all health risks and broad lines of causation of ill health. It will – and indeed, has – led to the realisation that arbitrarily singling out particular risks for health, but completely ignoring others that are also intimately connected to the way we now live, is not appropriate. Such analysis can encourage the realisation that denying similarity based on health risks is misguided – and the 'blinders' in this respect should fall away.

We firmly believe that most people have a need and greatly benefit from helping and supporting others and from seeing what connects us instead of what sets us apart. However, particularly where the costs of a solidaristic practice or policy are high, this also has its limits. The higher the costs and the bigger the likelihood that people's recognition of similarity with others starts fading, or gets overwhelmed by other motives, the more efforts there should be to support and foster this recognition. This is another central, overarching conclusion of our work overall: as we have laid out in previous chapters, we do not believe that solidarity as such is an intrinsically good thing, or that all solidaristic practices are good. But we do believe that societies that allow for a high degree of solidaristic practices to flourish are, overall, better for both individuals and societies. From this follows a broad normative recommendation – namely that if we want to have more solidarity, and if we want to keep the level of institutionalised solidarity that we already have, then we need to foster social practices that emphasise similarity. In other words, people's recognition of similarity with others can be fragile, and it does not come out of nowhere. It needs to be supported and conditions need to be established that allow for it to flourish and grow. This entails attention at two levels: broad, general encouragement in public debates of a sense of interconnectedness between people is important; and reminders of what we share, and how much we all depend on each other. At the more concrete level, fostering solidarity, however, must be done carefully and with a sense of proportion. Calling a practice or policy solidaristic when it is not is confusing at best and offensive and dangerous at worst. In the worst case it can be truly harmful to its implementation, as we have shown in various parts of this book. Public policy debates in relevant contexts, wherever possible and wherever applicable, should be framed around relevant and concrete similarities, and around mutuality and the things that connect us. Based on good analysis of each context, they should also try to bring into the open potential misunderstandings regarding differences, and thus work towards reducing unconscious biases and fears, and towards stripping away the aforementioned 'blinders'. This does not only hold within societies, but also beyond any national or regional borders: with whom we recognise similarity is not determined by who we are or where we live; it is also partly shaped by what we see. In a situation of violent conflict, say, people who assist those on their own side can be assumed to do so because they see the common threat, the common enemy and the other commonalities that define their being on one side of the conflict. Other people, however, also help those on the other side. These situations are instances of solidarity if in the suffering of those on the other side, people still recognise their own suffering, and this recognition of similarity is the motivation to provide assistance. Here it becomes apparent again why the notion of practice is so important for our understanding of solidarity: it is the concrete situation of a practice including the discursive, political and economic structures that it is embedded in that influences the similarities and differences between us and others that we see, be it in a national context, or in cases that transcend borders. A further normative conclusion that we draw is therefore that politicians, writers and everybody else influencing public discourse has an obligation to help foreground connections between people – and we recommend making this explicit for example in training programmes.

Whether we will have more solidaristic practices, then, and whether we will be able to maintain the ones we already have, will depend on all of us. This is a fitting note on which to end a book on solidarity. Concretely, we call upon more of our colleagues in biomedicine and beyond to further explore the potential to develop and implement solidarity in policy and practice. Solidarity is a rich, yet firm enough, concept that can be applied fruitfully in many areas, and there is still much to do. But beyond this, it takes us all to make solidarity happen.

AFTERWORD

Graeme Laurie

School of Law, University of Edinburgh

Reading this book reminded me very powerfully of the experience of writing my own Cambridge University Press monograph, *Genetic Privacy*,[1] which was set against the myriad contributions from a wealth of disciplines on the very notion of *privacy* itself. The particular phrase that sprung to mind (unattributed and misquoted) was: 'Privacy, like an elephant, is more easily recognised than described.' Barbara Prainsack and Alena Buyx have demonstrated admirably that much the same can be said about solidarity, although we owe them a considerable debt not only for leading us skilfully through the relevant literatures, but also for offering a very rich and workable definition of solidarity that takes us well beyond the merely descriptive aspects of the concept. They have consummately delivered on their overarching objective '... to improve the analytical value of solidarity'. Indeed, I believe that there are numerous ways in which they have achieved this even beyond their own account of their contribution.

Beyond Description

The essentially human experiences that are captured by appeals to concepts such as solidarity (and privacy) can lead us all too quickly to imagine, and assume, that we can *only* provide accounts in descriptive, experiential terms. While establishing their contribution determinedly in the prosocial sphere, Prainsack and Buyx have argued convincingly that we can, and must, transcend these purely descriptive accounts of solidarity as something that simply 'is' or 'is not'. It is trite that empirical studies can offer evidence of the sentiment-based aspects of solidarity, but this is not the basis of the claims in this work. The authors reject a definition that is solely about a 'value', an 'obligation' or a 'feeling', while embracing both the descriptive

---

[1] Laurie (2002) – an early contribution when this series was in its nascent stages.

187

and prescriptive potential of solidarity. They are able to do so by not losing sight of the essentially human experiential aspect of solidarity by grounding their contribution in *enacted practices*. Thus, something must be 'done' by humans, not merely prescribed or felt. In this sense, I would suggest that we can further assist Prainsack and Buyx in their analysis by contrasting solidarity with the anthropological notion of *communitas*. The Scots-born anthropologist, Victor Turner, is renowned as the modern father of accounts of liminality, that is, moments in space and time when individuals are in transition from one status or phase of life to another, and often liminality is experienced collectively. In particular, Turner suggested that in such moments a sense of what he called 'communitas' springs up among persons in a liminal state (Turner 1969: 116):

> [A]t certain life crises such as adolescence, the attainment of elderhood, and death, varying in significance from culture to culture, the passage from one structural status to another may be accompanied by a strong sense of 'human-kindness', a sense of the generic bond between all members of society – even in some case transcending tribal or national boundaries – regardless of their subgroup affiliations or incumbency of structural positions.

At first blush, this might appear as if Turner is merely identifying solidarity, but his wife Edith Turner, herself an accomplished authority, has made a set of all-important and differentiating observations (Turner 2012: 4):

> Communitas is exciting; it makes people able to organize and work together. With this power, they will eventually develop organizational habits, structures, and rules of behavior, and ranks and positions. These often work well if they remain on the human level; yet if they become overly law-bound, communitas will bubble up again from below and question the old system.

For her, communitas is characterised by '. . . its shyness and untouchability by commercialization and institutionalization' (Turner 2012: xii). Most importantly, for present purposes (ibid: 5):

> Communitas should be distinguished from Emile Durkheim's 'solidarity', which is a bond between individuals who are collectively in opposition to some other group . . . This is the 'in-group versus out-group' opposition. But in the way communitas unfolds, people's sense is that it is for everybody – humanity, bar none.

Thus, while communitas is inclusive, it is not amenable to design. It cannot be manufactured or prescribed. Communitas, simply, 'is' or it 'is not'.[2]

---

[2] I discuss communitas and liminality further in the biomedical context in: G Laurie, 'Liminality and the Limits of Law in Health Research Regulation: What Are We Missing in

I posit that this is an important further analytical distinction that helps us to understand the nature and the extent of the contribution by Prainsack and Buyx in several respects. First, communitas provides us with an example of a concept that is *only* explicable by description alone. This is in contra-distinction to the authors' descriptive–prescriptive claims in this work. Second, communitas and solidarity can co-exist around the same experiences but not necessarily for the same groups or with the same effects. Consider, for example, an illustration of communitas provided by Edith Turner, the Olympic Games:

> Communitas is sought in the Olympic Games, where the possibility of a finely tuned human body is the one truly common factor among all humankind, open to all, whatever one's rank and class. The communitas spirit, or sporting spirit, is not limited to any one institution. It does not take sides; it does not rush to 'in-group–out-group' competitiveness. Nevertheless, it can be woefully prostituted to produce prejudice against an 'enemy' (Turner 2012: 5).

The concern about abuse apart, we can see the global spectator experience of feeling 'the Spirit of the Games' as an instance of communitas, is however fleeting. It can be contrasted with the sense of solidarity experienced by national team members, sportsmen and women, managers, physiotherapists, assistants and administrators joined together in the common objective of doing what is best for one's country, at considerable personal and professional cost. It 'costs' the global audience nothing to participate in the passive experience of watching the Games. It costs the teams considerable sacrifice and collective commitment to participate – as *acts* of solidarity. These enactments of solidarity go beyond what the actors themselves might feel towards others. On this basis, we have good reasons to believe that Prainsack and Buyx's account of solidarity has a plausible and valuable basis as something grounded in human practices and not merely in human sentiments.

Beyond Conflict

Emile Durkheim's central influence in so many contributions to sociology and sociological concepts is often acknowledged, and Prainsack and Buyx have also duly recognised this in the literatures on solidarity. Yet,

the Spaces In-between?', forthcoming, the product of a Wellcome Trust Senior Investigator Award entitled 'Confronting the Liminal Spaces of Health Research Regulation' (Award No: WT103360MA).

as illustrated by the quote from Edith Turner earlier, Durkheim's view of
solidarity has tended to set up the concept and its social role as essentially
oppositional or even necessarily confrontational. This book suggests that
this is not an inevitable consequence of engaging with solidarity, nor is
it a prerequisite to giving solidarity a prescriptive punch by 'othering'.
Indeed, a particularly powerful contribution of Prainsack and Buyx's
account of solidarity is the way in which it allows us to move beyond
conflictual understandings of what is at stake. As the authors say: it can
help us to 'overcome the unproductive dichotomy between personal and
common benefit'. This turns on the centrality of the authors' view that
solidarity is about 'reflecting commitments to accept costs to help others
with whom we recognise similarity in a relevant respect'. They point out,
rightly, that this can occur even with respect to those outside of a particular group or beyond one's own self-interest. Indeed, from a legal and
policy perspective, this account greatly helps us to reconceptualise what
is at stake in the protection and promotion of private *and* public interests. Arguably, the lamentable, albeit unlooked-for consequence of law's
increased recognition of the value of arguments about the need to give
effect to autonomy-based claims has been to 'other' the value of arguments
based in the – apparently – oppositional public interests also in play. There
has been something of a feel of inevitability about this slide towards polarisation and opposition. This book quietly, but nonetheless boldly, throws
down a challenge to the autonomy-focused perspective, particularly as to
how this is so often expressed in practice. It provides us with a conceptual framework that can assist in overcoming the paradigm of polarisation
between private and public interests, and also with a solid intellectual
and practical basis to challenge oppositional assumptions, such as altruism vs. self-interest. Prainsack and Buyx offer us a way to see – and to
operationalise – self- and other-regarding considerations at the same time.
This is because their solidarity perspective can recognise that autonomous individuals are, indeed, often willing to assume costs to help others,
while at the same time not abandoning the same individuals to the vagar-
ies of their own choices. The potential value of this should not be under-
estimated. While many disciplines have contributed to the analytical
critique of the rise and rise of autonomy, this has not necessarily resulted
in much impact on the way in which laws and policies continue to promote a highly individualistic, impoverished view of what it means to be a
rights bearer and autonomous chooser in modern Western societies. This
book offers a viable way out of such an impasse.

Towards Humility

The reach and significance of this work is well demonstrated by Chapter 8 for the consideration therein of applications beyond biomedicine and also for the further theoretical insights that the authors' concept of solidarity can offer. It is claimed, legitimately, that these include deeper understandings of relationality and community. But the authors are also open in recognising the limits of their contribution. This is redolent of the necessary humility that must accompany any work of this kind, but it is also illustrative of the virtue so characteristic of the authors themselves. I would suggest that this virtue is also reflected in the prescriptive dimension of this work, and most notably the extent to which the authors suggest that solidarity can be reflected in, and serve as an objective for, law. As they recognise:

> [S]olidaristic laws and regulations, in order to become durable, need to be based on actual practices that people engage in voluntarily and not merely to avoid social or legal repercussions: When there are no actual axiological practices to support these norms, such laws and regulations would amount to little more than 'deontic shells' (80).

I take this to be a call to law- and policy-makers to be humble in their aspirations to embody solidaristic values and objectives in their social projects. This is not to suggest that this is not a valid or viable enterprise, but rather that it is a reminder that we must recognise solidarity for its central feature as a human *concern*: a concern for others as demonstrated by what people actually do, or are willing to do. We cannot mandate *concern* any more than we can mandate *communitas*. Prainsack and Buyx suggest, however, that we can recognise that such concern can and does exist in myriad features of our social worlds. It is the task of law- and policy-makers to design and deliver social structures that support and give effect to this where possible, and to accept that – thankfully – willingness to act with solidarity probably occurs far more frequently than we currently acknowledge. We should be grateful to Prainsack and Buyx for making this so clear to us in this important contribution to our Cambridge University Press series.

BIBLIOGRAPHY

Aarden, Erik, Hoyweghen, Ine Van, and Horstman, Klasien 2010. 'Solidarity in Practices of Provision: Distributing Access to Genetic Technologies in Health Care in Germany, the Netherlands and the United Kingdom', *New Genetics & Society* 29(4): 369–388.

Academy of Medical Sciences 2011. *A New Pathway for the Regulation and Governance of Health Research*. Available at: www.acmedsci.ac.uk/viewFile/publicationDownloads/newpathw.pdf (Accessed: 16 October 2015).

Alexander, Jeffrey C. 2006. *The Civil Sphere*. Oxford University Press.

Allmark, Peter and Tod, Angela M. 2013. 'Can a Nudge Keep You Warm? Using Nudges to Reduce Excess Winter Deaths: Insight from the Keeping Warm in Later Life Project (KWILLT)', *Journal of Public Health* 36(1): 111–116.

Althusser, Louis Pierre 2006. 'Ideology and Ideological State Apparatus (Notes Towards an Investigation)', in Sharma, Aradhana and Gupta, Akhil (eds), *The Anthropology of the State: A Reader*. Wiley-Blackwell, Oxford. pp. 86–111.

Anand, Sudhir, Peter, Fabienne, and Sen, Amartya 2004. *Public Health, Ethics, and Equity*. Oxford: Oxford University Press.

Anders, Corina and Cassidy, Andrea 2014. 'Effective Organizational Change in Healthcare: Exploring the Contribution of Empowered Users and Workers', *International Journal of Healthcare Management* 7(2): 132–151.

Anderson, Elizabeth S. 2000. 'What is the Point of Equality?', *Ethics* 109(2): 287–337.

Anderson, Benedict 1991. *Imagined Communities: Reflections on the Origin and Spread of Nationalism*. London: Verso.

Anderson, Charles M. 2007. 'What We Talk about When We Talk about Goals', *AMA Journal of Ethics* 9(6): 407–409.

Angrist, Misha 2015. 'Start Me Up: Ways to Encourage Sharing of Genomic Information with Research Participants', *Nature Reviews Genetics* 16(8): 435–436.

Arendt, Hannah 1978. *The Life of the Mind*. San Diego, CA: Harcourt.

2005. *The Promise of Politics*. New York, NY: Schoken.

Aristoteles; Irwin, Terence 2006. *Nicomachean Ethics*. (2nd edn). Indianapolis, IN: Hackett.

Arts, Wil and Verburg, Rudi 2001. 'Modernisation, Solidarity and Care in Europe: The Sociologist's Tale', in Ter Meulen, Ruud, Arts, Wil, and Muffels, Ruud (eds), *Solidarity in Health and Social Care in Europe*. Dordrecht: Kluwer Academic Publishers.

Ashcroft, Richard E., Campbell, Alastair V., and Jones, Susan 2000. 'Solidarity, Society and the Welfare State in the United Kingdom', *Health Care Analysis* 8: 377–394.

Aulisio, Mark P. 2006. 'Bioethics in a Global Village', *American Journal of Bioethics* 6: 1–4.

Aurenque, Diana 2015. 'Why Altruism is not a Convincing Argument for Promoting Post-Mortem Organ Donation: Responsibility and Solidarity as Key Concepts', in Jox, Ralf, Assadi, Galia, and Marckmann, Georg (eds), *Organ Transplantation in Times of Donor Shortage. Challenges and Solutions.* Switzerland: Springer International Publishing AG.

Ausiello, Dennis and Shaw, Stanley 2014. 'Quantitative Human Phenotyping: The Next Frontier in Medicine', *Transactions of the American Clinical and Climatological Association* 125: 219–228.

Aylesworth, Gary 2013. 'Postmodernism', in Zalta, Edward N. (ed.), *The Stanford Encyclopedia of Philosophy*. (Fall 2013 edn). Available at: www.plato.stanford .edu/archives/sum2013/entries/postmodernism/ (Accessed: 16 October 2015).

Baldwin, Peter 1990. *The Politics of Social Solidarity: Class Bases of the European Welfare State, 1875–1975.* Cambridge: Cambridge University Press.

de la Ballacasa, Maria P. 2011. 'Matters of Care in Technoscience: Assembling Neglected Things', *Social Studies of Science* 41(1): 85–106.

Barry, Andrew 2001. *Political Machines. Governing a Technological Society.* London: The Athlone Press.

Baskin, Joseph H. 2009. 'Giving Until it Hurts?: Altruistic Donation of Solid Organs', *Journal of American Academy of Psychiatry and the Law* 37(3): 377–379.

Bastow, Ruth and Leonelli, Sabina 2010. Sustainable Digital Infrastructure. *EMBO Reports* 11(11): 730–734.

Baurmann, Michael 1999. 'Solidarity as a Social Norm and as a Constitutional Norm', in Bayertz, Kurt (ed.), *Solidarity.* Dordrecht: Kluwer, pp. 243–269.

Bayer, Ronald and Galea, Sandro 2015. 'Public Health in the Precision-Medicine Era', *New England Journal of Medicine* 373(6): 499–501.

Bayertz, Kurt 1998. *Solidarität. Begriff und Problem.* Stuttgart: Suhrkamp.
    1999. *Solidarity.* Dodrecht: Kluwer.
    1999. 'Four Uses of Solidarity', in Bayertz, Kurt (ed.), *Solidarity.* Dordrecht: Kluwer, pp. 3–28.

Baylis, Francoise, Kenny, Nuala P., and Sherwin, Susan 2008. 'A Relational Account of Public Health Care Ethics', *Public Health Ethics* 1(3): 196–209.

BBC News 2013. *Organ Donation: Presumed Cosent to Start in December 2015.* Available at: www.bbc.co.uk/news/uk-wales-24032031 (Accessed: 16 October 2015).

Beauchamp, Tom L. and Childress, James F. 2008. *Principles of Biomedical Ethics.* (6th edn). Oxford: Oxford University Press.
    2012. *Principles of Biomedical Ethics.* (7th edn). Oxford: Oxford University Press.

Beck, Ulrich, Giddens, Anthony, and Lasch, Scott 1993. *Reflexive Modernization. Politics, Tradition and Aesthetics in the Modern Social Order*. Cambridge, MA: Polity Press.

Bell, Daniel 1993. *Communitarianism and Ist Critics*. Oxford: Clarendon Press.

   2013. 'Communitarianism', in Zalta, Edward N. (ed.), *The Stanford Encyclopedia of Philosophy*. (Fall 2013 edn). Available at: www.plato.stanford.edu/archives/fall2013/entries/communitarianism/ (Accessed: 16 October 2015).

Bellah, Robert N., Madsen, Richard, Sullivan, William M., Swidler, Ann, and Tipton, Steven M. 1985. *Habits of the Heart: Individualism and Commitment in American Life*. Berkeley, CA: University of California Press.

Benatar, Solomon R., Daar, Abdallah S., and Singer, Peter 2003. 'Global Health Ethics. "The Rationale for Mutual Caring"', *International Affairs* 79(1): 107–138.

Bendorf, Aric, Pussell, Bruce A., Kelly, Patrick J., and Kerridge, Ian H. 2013. 'Socioeconomic, Demographic and Policy Comparisons of Living and Deceased Kidney Transplantation Rates Across 53 Countries', *Nephrology (Carlton)* 18(9): 633–640.

Bengtsson, Linus, Lu, Xin, Thorson, Anna, Garfield, Richard, and von, Schreeb, Johan 2011. 'Improved Response to Disasters and Outbreaks by Tracking Population Movements with Mobile Phone Network Data: A Post-Earthquake Geospatial Study in Haiti', *PLoS Medicine* 8/8: e1001083.

Benhabib, Seyla 1985. 'The Generalized and the Concrete Other: The Kohlberg-Gilligan Controversy and Feminist Theory', *Praxis International* 4: 402–424.

   1992. *Situating the Self: Gender, Community and Postmodernism in Contemporary Ethics*. Cambridge: Cambridge University Press.

Berman, Eli and Laitin, David D. 2008. 'Religion, Terrorism and Public Goods: Testing the Club Model', *Journal of Public Economics* 92(10): 1942–1967.

Bertelsmann-Stiftung 2012. 'Solidarity: For Sale? The Social Dimension of the New European Economic Governance', in Bajnai, Gordon, Nicolaïdis, Kalypso, Rossi, Vanessa, and Watt, Andrew (eds), *Europe in Dialogue 2012(1)*. Gütersloh: Bertelsmann-Stiftung. Available at: www.bertelsmann-stiftung.de/de/publika tionen/publikation/did/solidarity-for-sale/ (Accessed: 16 October 2015).

Bierhoff, Hans-Werner and Küpper, Beate 1997. 'Sozialpsychologie der Solidarität', in Bayertz Kurt (ed.), *Solidarität. Begriff und Problem*. Stuttgart: Suhrkamp, pp. 263–296.

Blumenthal-Barby, Jennifer S. and Burroughs, Hadley 2013. 'Seeking Better Health Care Outcomes: The Ethics of Using the "Nudge"', *American Journal of Bioethics* 12(2): 1–10.

Boas, Hagai 2011. 'Where Do Human Organs Come From? Trends of Generalized and Restricted Altruism in Organ Donations', *Social, Science & Medicine* 73(9): 1378–1385.

Boas, Hagai, Mor, Eytan, Michowitz, Rachel, Rozen-Zvi, B., and Rahamimov, Richard 2015. 'The Impact of the Israeli Transplantation Law on the Socio-Demographic

Profile of Living Kidney Donors', *American Journal of Transplantation* 15(4): 1076–1080.

Boas, Hagai, Michowitz, Richard, and Rahamimov, Ruth. *Family, Gender, Social Solidarity and the Ethics of Relatedness: How Do Living Kidney Donors Conceptualize their Donation.* Unpublished.

Bonell, Chris, McKee, Martin, Fletcher, Adam, Wilkinson, Paul, and Haines, Andy 2011. 'One Nudge Forward, Two Steps Back', *British Medical Journal* 342: d401.

Bonnie, Linda H.A., Akker, Marjan van den, Steenkiste, Ben van, and Vos, Rein 2010. 'Degree of Solidarity with Lifestyle and Old Age among Citizens in the Netherlands: Cross-Sectional Results from the Longitudinal SMILE Study', *Journal of Medical Ethics* 36: 784–790.

Boshammer, Susanne and Kayß, Matthias 1998. 'Review Essay: The Philosopher's Guide to the Galaxy of Welfare Theory: Recent English and German Literature on Solidarity and the Welfare State', *Ethical Theory and Moral Practice* 1: 375–385.

British Medical Association 2012. *Medical Ethics Today.* (3rd edn). Chichester: Wiley-Blackwell.

Brock, Gilian 2015. 'Global Justice', in Zalta, Edward N. (ed.), *The Stanford Encyclopedia of Philosophy.* (Spring 2015 edn). Available at: www.plato .stanford.edu/archives/spr2015/entries/justice-global (Accessed: 16 October 2015).

Brunkhorst, Hauke 2005. *Solidarity: From Civic Friendship to a Global Legal Community.* Cambridge, MA: MIT Press.

Bukatman, Scott 1993. *Terminal Identity. The Virtual Subject in Postmodern Science Fiction.* Durham, NC: Duke University Press.

Bundeszentrale für gesundheitliche Aufklärung (BZgA) 2012. *Pressemitteilung des Bundesministerium für Gesundheit zu den Vorfällen an den Transplantationszentren in Göttingen und Regensburg.* Press release. Available at: www .organspende-info.de/presse-portal/pressemitteilungen/archiv/pm-060812 (Accessed: 16 October 2015).

Busch, Lawrence 2014. 'A Dozen Ways to Get Lost in Translation: Inherent Challenges in Large Scale Datasets', *International Journal of Communication* 8(18): 1727–1744.

Butler, Judith 1990. 'Gender Trouble, Feminist Theory, and Psychological Discourse', in Nicholson, Linda (ed.), *Feminism/Postmodernism.* New York, NY: Routledge.

Buyx, Alena 2008a. 'Personal Responsibility for Health as a Rationing Criterion: Why We Don't Like It and Why Maybe We Should', *Journal of Medical Ethics* 34: 871–874.

2008b. 'Be Careful What You Wish For? Theoretical and Ethical Aspects of Wish-Fulfilling Medicine', *Medicine, Healthcare and Philosophy* 11: 133–43.

2009 'Blood Donation, Payment, and Non-Cash Incentives – Old Problems Gathering Renewed Interest', *Transfusion Medicine and Hemotherapy* 36(5): 329–39.

Buyx, Alena and Prainsack, Barbara 2012. 'Lifestyle-Related Diseases and Individual Responsibility Through the Prism of Solidarity', *Clinical Ethics* 7: 79–85.

Buyx, Alena, Friedrich, Daniel, and Schöne-Seifert, Bettina 2011. 'Ethics and Effectiveness. Rationing Healthcare by Thresholds of Minimum Effectiveness', *British Medical Journal* 342: 531–3.

Buzek, Jerzey and Surdej, Aleksander 2012. 'Paradigm Lost, Paradigm Rediscovered? Prospects for the Development of Solidarity-Oriented Economy in Post-Communist Poland', *International Journal of Sociology and Social Policy* 32(1/2): 56–69.

Calhoun, Craig 2002. 'Imagining Solidarity: Cosmopolitanism, Constitutional Patriotism, and the Public Sphere', *Public Culture* 14(1): 147–171.

Callahan, Daniel 1998. *False Hopes. Overcoming the Obstacles to a Sustainable, Affordable Medicine.* New Brunswick, NJ: Rutgers University Press.

2003. 'Individual Good and Common Good: A Communitarian Approach to Bioethics', *Perspectives in Biology and Medicine* 46(4): 496–507.

Callahan, Daniel and Jennings, Bruce 2002. 'Ethics and Public Health: Forging a Strong Relationship', *American Journal of Public Health* 92(2): 169–176.

Caney, Simon 1992. 'Liberalism and Communitarianism: A Misconceived Debate', *Political Studies* 40(2): 273–290.

Capaldi, Nicholas 1999. 'What's Wrong with Solidarity?', in Bayertz, Kurt (ed.), *Solidarity.* Dordrecht: Kluwer, pp. 39–56.

Casilli, Antonio A. 2014. 'Four Theses on Mass Surveillance and Privacy Negotiation', *Medium* (26 October). Available at: https://medium.com/@AntonioCasilli/four-theses-on-digital-mass-surveillance-and-the-negotiation-of-privacy-7254cd3cdee6 (Accessed: 14 November 2014).

Cassel, Eric J. 1982. 'The Nature of Suffering and the Goals of Medicine', *New England Journal of Medicine* 306(11): 639–645.

Castells, Manuel 1996. *The Rise of the Network Society.* Vol. 1. Wiley: Wiley-Blackwell.

Chadwick, Ruth 1999. 'Genetics, Choice and Responsibility', *Health, Risk & Society* 1: 293–300.

Childress, James F. and Liverman, Catharyn T. 2006. *Organ Donation: Opportunities for Action.* Washington, DC: National Academies Press.

Childress, James F., Faden, Ruth R., Gaare, Ruth D., Gostin, Lawrence O., Kahn, Jeffrey, Bonnie, Richard J., Kass, Nancy E., Mastroianni, Anna C., Moreno, Jonathan D., and Nieburg, Philipp 2002. 'Public Health Ethics: Mapping the Terrain', *Journal of Law, Medicine & Ethics* 30: 170–178.

Chodorow, Nancy 1980. 'Gender, Relation, and Difference in Pyschoanalytical Perspective', in Eistenstein, Hester and Jardine, Alice (eds), *The Future of Difference.* Boston, MA: G.K. Hall.

Churchill, Larry R. 2002. 'What Ethics Can Contribute to Health Policy', in Daniels, Marion, Clancy, C., Carolyn, M., and Churchill, Larry R. (eds), *Ethical Dimensions of Health Policy*. Oxford: Oxford University Press, pp. 51–64.

Cesuroglu, Tomris, Ommen, Ben van, Malats, Núria, Sudbrak, Ralf, Lehrbach, Hans, and Brand, Angela 2012. 'Public Health Perspective: From Personalized Medicine to Personal Health', *Personalized Medicine* 2(9): 115–119.

Clayton, Ellen W. 2003. 'Ethical, Legal, and Social Implications of Genomic Medicine', *New England Journal of Medicine* 349(6): 562–569.

Coggon, John 2010. 'Does Public Health Have a Personality (and If So, Does It Matter If You Don't Like It)?', *Cambridge Quarterly of Healthcare Ethics* 19: 235–248.

Coleman, James S. 1990. *Foundations of Social Theory*. Cambridge, MA: Belknap Press of Harvard University Press.

Comte, Auguste 1875 [1851]. *System of Positive Policy*. Vol. I. London: Longmans Green.

Cohen, Julie E. 2012. *Configuring the Networked Self: Law, Code, and the Play of Everyday Practice*. New Haven, CT: Yale University Press.

Cohen, Glenn I., Amarasingham, Ruben, Shah, Anand, Xie, Bin, and Lo, Bernard 2014. 'The Legal and Ethical Concerns that Arise from Using Complex Predictive Analytics in Health Care', *Health Affairs* 33(7): 1139–1147.

Cohn, Simon 2015. 'Blood and the Public Body: A Study of UK Blood Donation and Research Participation', *Critical Public Health* 26(1): 1–12.

Cook, Noam S.D. 2008. 'Design and Responsibility: The Interdependence of Natural, Artifactual, and Human Systems?', in Vermaas, Pieter E., Kroes, Peter, Light, Andrew, and Moore, Steven A. (eds), *Philosophy and Design: From Engineering to Architecture*. Dordrecht: Springer, pp. 259–269.

Cook, Noam and Wagenaar, Hendrik 2012. 'Navigating the Eternally Unfolding Present: Toward an Epistemology of Practice', *The American Review of Public Administration* 42(1): 3–38.

Cordell, Sean 2011. 'The Biobank as an Ethical Subject', *Health Care Analysis* 19: 282–294.

Corly, Mary C., Elswick, R.K., Sargeant, Carol C., and Scott, Susan 2000. 'Attitude, Self-Image and Quality of Life of Living Kidney Donors', *Nephrology Nursing Journal* 27(1): 43–50.

Craig, Jeff 2011. 'Economist Speaks to Student Researchers', *The Optimist* (30 March). Available at: www.acuoptimist.com/2011/03/economist-speaks-to-student-researchers/ (Accessed: 16 October 2015).

Critchley, Christine R., Nicol, Dianne, Otlowski, Margaret F., and Stranger, Mark J.A. 2012. 'Predicting Intention to Biobank: A National Survey', *European Journal of Public Health* 22(1): 139–144.

Cronin, Antonia J. 2014. 'Points Mean Prizes: Priority Points, Preferential Status and Directed Organ Donation in Israel', *Israel Journal of Health Policy Research* 3(1): 8.

Davies, Gail, Frow, Emma, and Leonelli, Sabrina 2012. 'Bigger, Faster, Better? Rhetorics and Practices of Large-Scale Research in Contemporary Bioscience', *BioSocieties* 8(4): 386–396.

Dawson, Angus and Jennings, Bruce 2012. 'The Place of Solidarity in Public Health Ethics', *Public Health Reviews* 34: 65–79.

Dawson, Angus and Verweij, Marcel 2012. 'Solidarity: A Moral Concept in Need of Clarification', *Public Health Ethics* 5(1): 1–5.

Dancy, Jonathan 2013. 'Moral Particularism', in Zalta, Edward N. (ed.), *The Stanford Encyclopedia of Philosophy*. (Fall 2013 edn). Available at: www.plato.stanford .edu/archives/fall2013/entries/moral-particularism/ (Accessed: 16 October 2015).

Daniels, Norman 2006. 'Equity and Population Health. Towards a Broader Bioethics Agenda', *Hastings Center Report* 36(4): 22–35.

2008. *Just Health*. Cambridge: Cambridge University Press.

Dean, Jodi 1996. *Solidarity of Strangers: Feminism after Identity Politics*. Berkeley, CA: University of California Press.

De Craemer, Willy A. 1983. 'A Cross-Cultural Perspective on Personhood', *The Milbank Memorial Fund Quarterly. Health and Society* 61(1): 19–34.

Deleuze, Gilles and Guattari, Félix 1977 [1972]. *Anti-Oedipus. Capitalism and Schizophrenia*. Translated by Huxley, Robert, Seem, and Lane, Helen R. New York, NY: Viking Press.

Dennis, Carina 2012. 'The Rise of the Narciss-Ome', *Nature* News; 10.1038/ nature.2012.10240 (16 March). Available at: www.nature.com/news/the-rise-of-the-narciss-ome-1.10240 (Accessed: 16 October 2015).

Der Europäische Datenschutzbeauftragte 2015. *Glossar*. Available at: https:// secure.edps.europa.eu/EDPSWEB/edps/site/mySite/pid/74 (Accessed: 16 October 2015).

Derpmann, Simon 2009. 'Solidarity and Cosmopolitanism', *Ethical Theory and Moral Practice* 12: 303–315.

2013. *Gründe der Solidarität*. Münster: Mentis.

Desmond-Hellmann, Susan 2012. 'Toward Precision Medicine: A New Social Contract?', *Science Translational Medicine* 4(129): 129ed3.

Deutsche Stiftung Organspende (DSO) 2012. *Ministerin Steffens: Vorbildlicher Einsatz bei Organspende hilft schwerkranken Menschen - Auszeichnung für acht Krankenhäuser*. Press release. Available at: www.dso.de/dso-pressemitteilungen/einzelansicht/article/ministerin-steffens-vorbildlicher-einsatz-bei-organspende-hilft-schwerkranken-menschen-auszeichnu.html (Accessed: 16 October 2015).

2015. *Orgaspende- und Transplantation: Lebendspende*. Available at: www .dso.de/organspende-und-transplantation/lebendspende.html (Accessed: 16 October 2015).

Dew, Mary A., Jacobs, Cheryl L., Jowsey, Sheila G., Hanto, R., Miller, C., and Delmonico, Francis L. 2007. 'Guidelines for the Psychological Evaluation of

Living Unrelated Kidney Donors in the United States', *American Journal of Transplation* 7(5): 1047–1054.

De Wachter, Maurice A.M. 1998. 'How Useful is Leuven Personalism in the World of Bioethics? The Test Case of Artificial Insemination', *European Journal of Obstetrics Gynecology and Reproductive Biology* 81(2): 227–233.

Dickenson, Donna 2013. *Me Medicine vs. We Medicine: Reclaiming Biotechnology for the Common Good*. New York, NY: Columbia University Press.

Die Welt 2015. *Krankenhaus-Team mit Flüchtlingen für Flüchtlinge*. Available at: www.welt.de/regionales/hamburg/article145755292/Krankenhaus-Team-mit-Fluechtlingen-fuer-Fluechtlinge.html (Accessed: 16 October 2015).

Dixon, Pam and Gellman, Robert 2014. 'The Scoring of America: How Secret Consumer Scores Threaten Your Privacy and Your Future', *World Privacy Forum* (2 April). Available at: www.pogowasright.org/the-scoring-of-america-how-secret-consumer-scores-threaten-your-privacy-and-your-future/ (Accessed: 22 February 2015).

Di Martino, Adriana, Yan, C.G., Li, G., Denio, E., Castellanos, F.X., Alaerts, K., Anderson, J.S., Assaf, M., Bookheimer, S.Y., Dapretto, M., Deen, B., Delmonte, S., Dinstein, I., Ertl-Wagner, B., Fair, D.A., Gallagher, L., Kennedy, D.P., Keown, C.L., Keysers, C., Lainhart, J.E., Lord, C., Luna, B., Menon, V., Minshew, N.J., Monk, C.S. Mueller, S., Müller, R.A., Nebel, M.B., Nigg, J.T., O'Hearn, K., Tyszka, J.M., Uddin, L.Q., Verhoeven, J.S., Wenderoth, N., Wiggins, J.L., Mostofsky, S.H., and Milham, M.P. 2014. 'The Autism Brain Imaging Data Exchange: Towards a Large-Scale Evaluation of the Intrinsic Brain Architecture in Autism', *Molecular psychiatry* 19(6): 659–667.

Doz, François, Marvanne, Patrice, and Fagot-Largeault, Anne 2013. 'The Person in Personalised Medicine', *European Journal of Cancer* 49(5): 1159–1160.

Durkheim, Emile 1893. *The Division of Labour in Society*. London: Macmillan.

Dworkin, Ronald 1989. 'Liberal Community', *California Law Review* 77: 479–504.

Eagle, Nathan and Greene, Kate 2014. *Reality Mining: Using Big Data to Engineer a Better World*. Cambridge, MA: MIT Press.

Eckenwiler, Lisa, Straehle, Christine, and Chung, Ryoa 2012. 'Global Solidarity, Migration, and Global Health Inequity', *Bioethics* 26(7): 382–390.

Elster, Jon 1989. *The Cement of Society*. Cambridge University Press.

Epstein, Charlotte 2013. 'Theorizing Agency in Hobbes's Wake: The Rational Actor, the Self, or the Speaking Subject?', *International Organization* 67(2): 287–316.

Epstein, Miran and Danovitch, Gabriel 2009. 'Is Altruistic-Directed Living Unrelated Organ Donation a Legal Fiction?', *Nephrology Dialysis Transplantation* 24(2): 357–360.

Epstein, Steven 2007. *Inclusion. The Politics of Difference in Medical Research*. Chicago, Il: University of Chicago Press.

Etzioni, Amitai 2011. 'On a Communitarian Approach to Bioethics', *Theoretical Medicine and Bioethics* 32(5): 363–374.

European Comission 2009. *Eurobarometer. Organ Donation and Transplantation*. Available at: www.ec.europa.eu/public_opinion/archives/ebs/ebs_333a_en.pdf (Accessed: 16 October 2015).

European Science Foundation (ESF) 2013. *Personalised Medicine for the European Citizen – Towards More Precise Medicine for the Diagnosis, Treatment and Prevention of Disease*. Strasbourg: ESF.

Faden, Ruth and Shebaya, Sirine 2010. 'Public Health Ethics', in Zalta, Edward N. (ed.), *The Stanford Encyclopedia of Philosophy* (Summer 2010 edn). Available at: www.plato.stanford.edu/entries/publichealth-ethics/ (Accessed: 16 October 2015).

Flam, Faye 2015. 'Duke U Cancer Fraud Scandal: A Cautionary Tale For Obama's Precision Medicine Push', *Forbes*. Available at: www.forbes.com/sites/fayeflam/2015/01/22/investigator-offers-lessons-from-precision-medicines-cancer-scandal/ (Accessed: 16 October 2015).

Fortin, Marie-Chantal, Dion-Labrie, Marianne, Hébert, Marie-Josée, and Doucet, Hubert 2010. 'The Enigmatic Nature of Altruism in Organ Transplantation: A Cross-Cultural Study of Transplant Physicians' Views on Altruism', *BMC Research Notes* 3: 216.

Foucault, Michel 1973. *The Birth of the Clinic. An Archaeology of Medical Perception*. Translated by Sheridan-Smith, A.M. London: Tavistock.

1977. *Discipline and Punish: The Birth of the Prison*. New York, NY: Vintage.

Fox, Renée C. and Swazey, Judith P. 1974. *The Courage to Fail. A Social View of Organ Transplants and Dialysis*. University of Chicago Press.

1992. *Spare Parts: Organ Replacment in American Society*. New York, NY: Oxford University Press.

Fraser, Nancy and Olson, Kevin 1999. *Adding Insult to Injury: Social Justice and the Politics of Recognition*. London: Verso.

Frazer, Elizabeth and Lacey, Nicola 1993. *The Politics of Community: A Feminist Critique of the Liberal-Communitarian Debate*. Hemel Hempstead: Harvester Wheatsheaf.

Gadamer, Hans-Georg 1967. 'The Limitations of the Expert', in Misgeld, Dieter and Nicholson, Graeme (eds), *Hans-Georg Gadamer on Education, Poetry, and History. Applied Hermeneutics*. Albany, NY: State University of New York Press.

Gamlund, Espen 2010. 'Supererogatory Forgiveness', *Inquiry* 53: 540–564.

Gaus, Gerald, Courtland, Shane D., and Schmidtz, David 2015. 'Liberalism', in Zalta, Edward N. (ed.), *The Stanford Encyclopedia of Philosophy*. (Spring 2015 edn). Available at: www.plato.stanford.edu/archives/spr2015/entries/liberalism/ (Accessed: 16 October 2015).

Gawanda, Atul 2014. *Being Mortal: Mecicine and What Matters in the End*. New York, NY: Metropolitan Books.

Gevers, Sjef, Janssen, Anke, and Friele, Roland 2004. 'Consent Systems for Post Mortem Organ Donation in Europe', *European Journal of Health Law* 11(2):175–186.

Ghods, Ahad J. and Savaj, Shekoufeh 2006. 'Iranian Model of Paid and Regulated Living-Unrelated Kidney Donation', *Clinic Journal of the American Society of Nephrology* 1(6): 1136–1145.

Gibbon, Sahra and Novas, Carlos (eds) 2007. *Biosocialities. Genetics and the Social Sciences*. London: Routledge.

Giddens, Anthony 1994. *Beyond Left and Right. The Future of Radical Politics*. Cambridge, MA: Polity Press.

Gilbar, Roy 2011. 'Family Involvement, Independence, and Patient Autonomy in Practice', *Medical Law Review* 19(2): 192–234.

Gilligan, Carol C. 1982. *In a Different Voice. Psychological Theory and Women's Development*. Cambridge, MA: Harvard University Press.

Gitelman, Lisa 2013. *"Raw data" is an Oxymoron*. Cambridge, MA: MIT Press.

Glannon, Walter 2011. 'Is it Unethical for Doctors to Encourage Healthy Adults to Donate a Kidney to a Stranger? Yes', *British Medical Journal* 343: d7179.

Glasner, Peter and Rothman, Harry 2001. 'New Genetics, New Ethics? Globalisation and its Discontents', *Health Risk & Society* 3: 245–259.

Global Alliance for Genomics and Health 2014. *Framework for Responsible Sharing of Genomic and Health-Related Data*. Available at: www.genomicsandhealth .org/about-the-global-alliance/key-documents/framework-responsible-sharing-genomic-and-health-related-data (Accessed: 16 October 2015).

Goodwin, Michele 2013. *Black Markets. The Supply and Demand of Body Parts*. Cambridge: Cambridge University Press.

Gostin, Lawrence O., Heywood, Mark, Ooms, Gorik, Grover, Anand, Røttingen, John-Arne, and Chenguang, Wang 2010. 'National and Global Responsibilities for Health', *Georgetown Law Faculty Publications and Other Works*. Paper 471. Available at: www.scholarship.law.georgetown.edu/facpub/471 (Accessed: 16 April 2015).

Gould, Carol C. 2004. *Globalizing Democracy and Human Rights*. Cambridge: Cambridge University Press.

  2007. 'Transnational Solidarities', *The Journal of Social Philosophy* 38(1): 146–162.

  2010. Does Global Justice Presuppose Global Solidarity? AMINTAPHIL working paper. Available at: www.philosophy.utah.edu/AMINTAPHIL/papers/Papers 2010/Gould%20Justice%20Solidarity.pdf (Accessed: 25 October 2016).

  2014. *Interactive Democracy. The Social Roots of Global Justice*. Cambridge: Cambridge University Press.

Grabe, Hans J., Assel, Heinrich, Bahls, Thomas, Dörr, Marcus, Endlich, Karlhans, Endlich, Nicole, Erdmann, Pia, Ewert, Ralf, Felix, Stephan B., Fiene, Beate, Fischer, Tobias, Flessa, Steffen, Friedrich, Nele, Gadebusch-Bondio, Mariacarla, Salazar-Gesell, Manuela, Hammer, Elke, Haring, Robin, Havemann, Christoph, Hecker, Michael, Hoffmann, Wolfgang, Holtfreter, Birte, Kacprowski, Tim, Klein, Kathleen, Kocher, Thomas, Kock, Holger, Krafczyk, Janina, Kuhn, Jana, Langanke, Martin, Lendeckel, Uwe, Lerch, Markus M., Lieb, Wolfgang,

Lorbeer, Roberto, Mayerle, Julia, Meissner, Konrad, Meyer zu Schwabedissen, Henriette, Nauck, Matthias, Ott, Konrad, Rathmann, Wolfgang, Retting, Rainer, Richardt, Claudia, Saljé, Karen, Schminke, Ulf, Schulz, Andrea, Schwab, Matthias, Siegemund, Werner, Stracke, Sylvia, Suhre, Karsten, Ueffing, Marius, Ungerer, Saskia, Völker, Uwe, Völzke, Henry, Wallaschofski, Henri, Werner, Vivian, Zygmunt, Marek T. and Kroemer, Heyo K. 2014. 'Cohort Profile: Greifswald Approach to Individualized Medicine (GANI_MED)', *Journal of Translational Medicine* 12(1): 144.

Green, Robert C., Berg, Jonathan S., Grody, Wayne W., Kalia, Sarah S., Korf, Bruce R., Martin, Christa L., McGuire, Amy L., Nussbaum, Robert L., O'Daniel, Julianne M., Ormond, Kelly E., Rehm, Heidi L., Watson, Michael S., Williams, Marc S., and Biesecker, Leslie G. 2013. 'ACMG Recommendations for Reporting of Incidental Findings in Clinical Exome and Genome Sequencing', *Genetics in Medicine* 15(7): 565–574.

Gubernatis, Gundolf 1997. 'Solidarity Model as Nonmonetary Incentive Could Increase Organ Donation and Justice in Organ Allocation at the Same Time', *Transplantation Proceedings* 29(8): 3264–3266.

Gunson, Darryl 2009. 'Solidarity and the Universal Declaration on Bioethics and Human Rights', *Journal of Medicine and Philosophy* 34(3): 241–260.

Gunsteren, Herman R. van 1998. *A Theory of Citizenship. Organizing Plurality in Contemporary Democracies*. Boulder, CO: Westview.

Gymrek, Melissa, McGuire, Amy L., Golan, David, Halperin, Eran, and Erlich, Yaniv 2013. 'Identifying Personal Genomes by Surname Inference', *Science* 339(6117): 321–324.

Habermas, Jürgen 1984. *Theory of Communicative Action Volume One: Reason and the Rationalization of Society*. Boston, MA: Beacon Press.

1986. 'Gerechtigkeit und Solidarität', in Edelstein, W. and Nunner-Winkler, G. (eds), *Zur Bestimmung der Moral*. Frankfurt a. M.: Suhrkamp, pp. 11–64.

1994. *Justification and Application: Remarks on Discourse Ethics*. Cambridge: Policy.

1998. *The Inclusion of the Other: Studies in Political Theory*. Cambridge, MA: MIT Press.

Habermas, Jürgen, Cronin, Ciaran P., and Greiff, Pablo de (eds) 2000. *The Inclusion of the Other. Studies in Political Theory*. Cambridge, MA: MIT Press.

Haddow, Gillian, Laurie, Graeme, Cunningham-Burley, Sarah, and Hunter, Kathryn G. 2007. Tackling Community Concerns about Commercialisation and Genetic Research: A Modest Interdisciplinary Proposal. *Social Science & Medicine* 64(2): 272–282.

2004. 'Another Look at Dignity', *Cambridge Quarterly of Healthcare Ethics* 13: 7–14.

2005. 'Precaution and Solidarity', *Cambridge Quarterly of Healthcare Ethics* 14(2): 199–206.

Hafen, Ernst, Kossmann, Donald, and Brand, Angela 2014. 'Health Data Cooperatives – Citizen Empowerment', *Methods of Information in Medicine* 53(2): 82–86.

Haggerty, Kevin D., and Ericson, Richard V. 2000. 'The Surveillant Assemblage', *The British Journal of Sociology* 51(4): 605–622.

Haidt, Jonathan 2001. 'The Emotional Dog and its Rational Tail: A Social Intuitionist Approach to Moral Judgment', *Psychological Review* 108(4): 814.

Hamburg, Margaret A., and Collins, Francis S. 2010. 'The Path to Personalized Medicine', *New England Journal of Medicine* 363(4): 301–304.

Hanson, Marc J. and Callahan, Daniel 1999. *The Goals of Medicine: The Forgotten Issue in Health Care Reform*. Washington, DC: Georgetown University.

Haraway, Donna 1993. 'The Biopolitics of Postmodern Bodies: Determinations of Self in Immune System Discourse', in Kauffman, Linda (ed.), *American Feminist Thought at Century's End: A Reader*. Cambridge, MA: Blackwell, pp. 199–233.

Harford, Tim 2014. 'Big Data: Are We Making a Big Mistake?' *Financial Times Weekend Magazine* 29/30 March: 28–31.

Harmon, Amy 2010. 'Havasupai Case Highlights Risks in DNA Research', *The New York Times*. Available at: www.nytimes.com/2010/04/22/us/22dnaside.html (Accessed: 16 October 2015).

Harmon, Shawn H.E 2006. 'Solidarity: A (New) Ethic for Global Health Policy', *Health Care Analysis* 14: 215–236.

    2009. 'Semantic, Pedantic or Paradigm Shift? Recruitment, Retention and Property in Modern Population Biobanking', *European Journal of Health Law* 16: 27–43.

Harris, Katherine M., Maurer, Jürgen, and Kellermann, Arthur L. 2014. 'Influenza Vaccine – Safe, Effective, and Mistrusted', *New England Journal of Medicine* 363(23): 2183–2185.

Hawdon, James, Ryan, John, and Agnich, Laura 2010. 'Crime as a Source of Solidarity: A Research Note Testing Durkheim's Assertion', *Deviant Behavior* 31(8): 679–703.

Häyry, Matti 2003. 'European Values in Bioethics: Why, What, and How to be Used?', *Theoretical Medicine* 24: 199–214.

Heald, David 2006. 'Varieties of Transparency', in Hood, Christopher and Heald, David (eds), *Transparency. The Key to Better Governance?* Oxford: Oxford University Press, pp. 24–43.

Hechter, Michael 1987. *Principles of Group Solidarity*. Berkeley, CA: University of California Press.

    2015. 'Sociology of Solidarity', in Wright, James D. (ed.), *International Encyclopedia of Social & Behavioral Sciences*. Vol. 23, (2nd edn). Oxford: Elsevier, pp. 6–9.

Heidegger, Martin 1996 [1972]. *Sein und Zeit*. Tübingen: Niemayer.

Held, Virginia 2006. *The Ethics of Care*. New York, NY: Oxford University Press.

Hellsten, S.K. 2008. 'Global Bioethics: Utopia or Reality?', *Developing World Bioethics* 8: 70–81.

Henderson, Antonia J., Landolt, Monica A., McDonald, Michael F., Barrable, William M., Soos, John G., Gourlay, William, Allison, Colleen J., and Landsberg, David N. 2003. 'The Living Anonymous Kidney Donor: Lunatic or Saint?', *American Journal of Transplantation* 3(2): 203–213.

Hermerén, Göran 2008. 'Aesthetic Qualities, Values and Emotive Meaning', *Theoria* 39(1–3): 71–100.

Heyd, David 1982. *Supererogation: Its Status in Ethical Theory*. Cambridge: Cambridge University Press.

  2007. 'Justice and Solidarity: The Contractarian Case Against Global Justice', *Journal of Social Philosophy* 38(1): 112–130.

  2012. 'Supererogation', in Zalta, Edward N. (ed.), *The Stanford Encyclopedia of Philosophy*. (Winter 2012 edn). Available at: www.plato.stanford.edu/archives/win2012/entries/supererogation/ (Accessed: 16 October 2015).

  2015. 'Solidarity: A Local, Partial and Reflective Emotion', *Diametros* 43: 55–64.

Hickey, Shane 2015. 'Are Car Insurance Firms Prejudiced Against Older People?', *The Guardian* (26 June 2015). Available at: www.theguardian.com/money/2015/jun/26/car-insurers-older-people-sheila-hancock (Accessed: 29 June 2015).

Hildebrandt, Mireille and De Vries, Katja (eds) 2013. *Privacy, Due Process and the Computational Turn*. Abingdon: Routledge.

Hills, John, Ditch, John, and Glennerster, Howard 1994. *Beveridge and Social Security. An International Retrospective*. Oxford: Oxford University Press.

Hinrichs, Karl 1995. 'The Impact of German Health Insurance Reforms on Redistribution and the Culture of Solidarity', *Journal of Health Politics, Policy and Law* 20(3): 653–687.

Hobbs, Abbi, Starkbaum, Johannes, Gottweis, Ursula, Wichmann, H.E., and Gottweis, Herbert 2012. 'The Privacy-Reciprocity Connection in Biobanking: Comparing German with UK Strategies', *Public Health Genomics* 15(5): 272–284.

Hoelzl, Michael 2004. 'Recognizing the Sacrificial Victim: The Problem of Solidarity for Critical Social Theory', *Journal for Cultural and Religious Studies* 6(1): 45–64.

Hoffmann, Bjørn 2009. 'Broadening Consent – And Diluting Ethics?', *Journal of Medical Ethics* 35: 125–129.

Hogarth, Stuart, Hopkins, Michael, and Faulkner, Alex 2012. 'Personalized Medicine: Renewing the Social Science Research Agenda', *Personalized Medicine* 9(2): 121–126.

Holdrege, Craig and Wirz, Johannes 2001. 'Life Beyond Genes. Reflections on the Human Genome Project', *In Context #5*. Available at: www.natureinstitute.org/pub/ic/ic5/genome.htm (Accessed: 16 October 2015).

Holm, Søren 1995. 'Not Just Autonomy – The Principles of American Biomedical Ethics', *Journal of Medical Ethics* 21: 332–338.

2008. *Background Paper on Article 14 of the Bioethics Declaration from a Philosophical Perspective.*

Holm, Søren and Williams-Jones, Bryn 2006. 'Global Bioethics – Myth or Reality?', *BMC Medical Ethics* 7: 10.

Hood, Leroy and Flores, Mauricio 2012. 'A Personal View on Systems Medicine and the Emergence of Proactive P4 Medicine: Predictive, Preventive, Personalized and Participatory', *New Biotechnology* 29(6): 613–624.

Houtepen, Rob and Ter Meulen, Ruud 2000a. 'New Types of Solidarity in the European Welfare State', *Health Care Analysis* 8: 329–340.

2000b. 'The Expectation(s) of Solidarity: Matters of Justice, Responsibility and Identity in the Reconstruction of the Health Care System', *Health Care Analysis* 8: 355–376.

Howie, Lynn, Hirsch, Bradford, Locklear, Tracie, and Abernethy, Amy P. 2014. 'Assessing the Value of Patient-Generated Data to Comparative Effectiveness Research', *Health Affairs* 33(7): 1220–1228.

Hoyweghen, Ine Van 2010. 'Taming the Wild Life of Genes by Law? Genes Reconfiguring Solidarity in Private Insurance', *New Genetics & Society* 19(4): 431–455.

Hoyweghen, Ine Van and Horstman, Klasien 2010. 'Solidarity Matters: Embedding Genetic Technologies in Private and Social Insurance Arrangements', *New Genetics and Society* 29(4): 343–350.

Husted, Jürgen. 1999. 'Insurance, Genetics and Solidarity', in McGleenan, T., Wiesing, U., and Ewald, F. (eds), *Genetics and Insurance*. Oxford: BIOS, pp. 1–16.

IBM 2014. 'Putting Watson to Work', *IBM Watson website* (n.d.). Available at: www-03.ibm.com/innovation/ca/en/watson/watson_in_healthcare.shtml (Accessed: 9 December 2014).

Ingold, Tim 2011. *Being Alive: Essays on Movement, Knowledge and Description.* London: Routledge.

2012. 'Toward an Ecology of Materials', *Annual Review of Anthropology* 41(1): 427–442.

Ingold, Tim and Pálsson, Gísli (eds) 2013. *Biosocial Becomings: Integrating Social and Biological Anthropology.* New York, NY: Cambridge University Press.

Institute of Medicine (IOM) 2006. *Organ Donation: Opportunities for Action.* Available at: www.iom.edu/Reports/2006/Organ-Donation-Opportunities-for-Action.aspx (Accessed: 5 May 2015).

Institute of Medicine 1988. *The Future of Public Health.* Washington, DC: National Academy Press.

Ipsos MORI 2011. *Public Perceptions of the NHS and Social Care Survey.* Available at: www.ipsos-mori.com/researchpublications/publications/1469/

Public-Perceptions-of-the-NHS-and-Social-Care-Survey.aspx (Accessed: 16 October 2015).

Jaeggi, Rahel 2010. 'Solidarity and Indifference', in ter Meulen, Ruud, Arts, Wil, and Muffels, Ruud (eds), *Solidarity in Health and Social Care in Europe*. Dordrecht: Kluwer, pp. 287–308.

Janssens, A. and Cecile, J.W. 2014. 'Raw data: Access to Inaccuracy', *Science* 343(6174): 968.

Jarvik, Gail P., Amendola, Laura M., Berg, Jonathan S., Brothers, Kyle, Clayton, Ellen W., Chung, Wendy, Evans, Barbara J., Evans, James P., Fullerton, Stephanie M., Gallego, Carlos J., Garrison, Nanibaa A., Gray, Stacy W., Holm, Ingrid A., Hullo, Iftikhar J., Lehmann, Lisa S., McCarthy, Cathy, Prows, Cynthia A., Rehm, Heidi L., Sharp, Richard R., Salama, Joseph, Sanderson, Saskia, van Driest, Sara L., Williams, Marc S., Wolf, Susan M., Wolf, Wendy A., and Burke, Wylie 2014. 'Return of Genomic Results to Research Participants: The Floor, the Ceiling, and the Choices in Between', *The American Journal of Human Genetics* 94(6): 818–826.

Jeffries, Vincent 2014. *The Palgrave Handbook of Altruism, Morality, and Social Solidarity: Formulating a Field of Study*. Basingstoke, UK: Palgrave Macmillan.

Jendrisak, Martin D., Hong, B., Shenoy, S., Lowell, J., Desai, N., Chapman, W., Vijayan, A., Wetzel, R.D., Smith, M., Wagner, J., Brennan, S., Brockmeier, D., and Kappel, D. 2005. 'Altruistic Living Donors: Evaluation for Nondirected Kidney or Liver Donation', *American Journal of Transplantation* 6(1): 115–120.

Jennings, Bruce 2001. 'From the Urban to the Civic: The Moral Possibilities of the City', *Journal of Urban Health* 78(1): 88–102.

2007. 'Public Health and Civic Republicanism: Toward an Alternative Framework for Public Health Ethics', in Dawson, Angus and Verwij, Marcel (eds), *Ethics, Prevention, and Public Health*. Oxford: Oxford University Press, pp. 30–58.

2015. 'Relational Liberty Revisited: Membership, Solidarity and a Public Health Ethics of Place', *Public Health Ethics* 8(1): 7–17.

Jennings, Bruce and Dawson, Angus 2015. 'Solidarity in the Moral Imagination of Bioethics', *The Hastings Center Report* 54 (5): 31–38.

Kahane, David 1999. 'Diversity, Solidarity and Civic Friendship', *Journal of Political Philosophy* 7(3): 267–286.

Kahneman, Daniel 2011. *Thinking, Fast and Slow*. New York, NY: Farrar, Strauss, Giroux.

Kamm, Frances 1985. 'Supererogation and Obligation', *Journal of Philosophy* 82: 118–138.

Kant, Immanuel 1784. *Idea for a Universal History from a Cosmopolitan Point of View*. Translated by Beck, Lewis W. Indianapolis, IN: Bobbs-Merrill.

1795. *Project for a Perpetual Peace. A Philosophical Essay*. Translated by Smith, Campbell M. London: George Allen and Unwin.

Kay, Lily E. 2000. *Who Wrote the Book of Life? A History of the Genetic Code.* Stanford: Stanford University Press.

Kelsen, Hans 1967. *Pure Theory of Law.* Berkeley, CA: University of California Press.

Kerasidou, Angeliki 2015. 'Sharing the Knowledge: Sharing Aggregate Genomic Findings with Research Participants in Developing Countries', *Developing World Bioethics* 15(3): 267–274.

Kittay, Eva F. 1999. *Love's Labor: Essays on Women, Equality, and Dependency.* New York, NY: Routledge.

Kirk, Allan D., Knechtle, Stuart J., Larsen, Christian P., Madsen, Joren C., Pearson, Thomas C., and Webber, Steven A. (eds) 2014. *Texbook of Organ Transplantation.* Oxford: John Wiley & Sons.

Kliemt, Hartmut and Gubernatis, Gundolf 2000. 'A Superior Approach To Organ Donation and Allocation', *Transplantation* 70: 699–707.

Kliksberg, Bernardo 2003. *Social Justice: A Jewish Perspective.* Jerusalem: Gefen.

Knoppers, Bartha M. and Chadwick, Ruth 2005. 'Human Genetic Research: Emerging Trends in Ethics', *Nature Reviews Genetics* 6(1): 75–79.

Koenig, Barbara A. 2014. 'Have We Asked Too Much of Consent?', *Hastings Center Report* 44(4): 33–34.

Komter, Aafke 2005. *Social Solidarity and the Gift.* Cambridge: Cambridge University Press.

Koops, Bert-Jaap 2013. 'On Decision Transparency, or How to Enhance Data Protection after the Computational Turn', in Hildebrandt, Mireille and De Vries, Katja (eds), *Privacy, Due Process and the Computational Turn.* Abingdon: Routledge, pp. 196–220.

Kopf, Gereon 2004. 'Between Identity and Difference: Three Ways of Reading Nishida's Non-Dualism', *Japanese Journal of Religious Studies* 31(1): 73–103.

Krishnamurty, Meena 2013. 'Political Solidarity, Justice, and Public Health', *Public Health Ethics* 6(2): 129–141.

Kristeva, Julia 1980. *Desire in Language: A Semiotic Approach to Literature and Art.* New York, NY: Columbia University Press.

Kuhse, Helga 1997. *Nurses, Women and Ethics.* Oxford: Blackwell.

Kymlicka, Will 1989. *Liberalism, Community and Culture.* Oxford: Clarendon Press.

Lacan, Jacques and Fink, Bruce 2002. *Ecrits: A Selection.* New York, NY: W.W. Norton and Company.

Laclau, Ernesto L. and Mouffe, Chantal 2001. *Hegemony and Socialist Strategy. Towards a Radical Democratic Politics.* London: Verso.

Lamont, Julian and Favor, Christi 2014. 'Distributive Justice', in Zalta, Edward N. (ed.), *The Stanford Encyclopedia of Philosophy.* (Fall 2014 edn). Available at: www .plato.stanford.edu/archives/fall2014/entries/justice-distributive (Accessed: 16 October 2015).

Laurie, Graeme T. 2002. *Genetic Privacy: A Challenge to Medico-Legal Norms.* Cambridge: Cambridge University Press.

2004. The Right Not to Know: An Autonomy Based Approach – A Reponse to Andorno. *Journal of Medical Ethics* 30, pp. 439–440.

2011. 'Reflexive Governance in Biobanking: On the Value of Policy Led Approaches and the Need to Recognise the Limits of Law', *Human Genetics* 130: 347–56.

Lavee, Jacob, Ashkenazi, Tamar, Gurman, Gabriel, and Steinberg, David 2010. 'A New Law for Allocation of Donor Organs in Israel', *Lancet* 375: 1131–1133.

Lavee, Jacob and Brock, Dan W. 2012. 'Prioritizing Registered Donors in Organ Allocation: An Ethical Appraisal of the Israeli Organ Transplant Law', *Current Opinion in Critical Care* 18(6): 707–711.

Law, John and Mol, Annemarie 2008. 'The Actor-Enacted: Cumbrian Sheep in 2001', in Malafouris, L. and Knappett, C. (eds), *Material Agency Towards a Non-Anthropocentric Approach*. New York, NY: Springer, pp. 57–78.

2011. 'Veterinary Realities: What is Foot and Mouth Disease?', *Sociologia Ruralis* 51: 1–16.

Leff, Lisa M. 2006. *Sacred Bonds of Solidarity: The Rise of Jewish Internationalism in Nineteenth-Century France*. Stanford, CA: Stanford University Press.

Lenhart, Christian 1975. 'Anamnestic Solidarity: The Proletariat and Its Manes', *Telos* 25: 133–154.

Leonelli, Sabina 2014. Data Interpretation in the Digital Age. *Perspectives on Science* 22(3): 397–417.

Lévi-Strauss, Claude 1969. *The Elementary Structures of Kinship*. Boston, MA: Beacon.

Libert 2014. *Bundeskanzleramt Österreich: Bioethikkommission: Partizipative Medizin und Internet. Stellungnahme der Bioethikkommission*. 6 Juli 2015. Available at: www.bka.gv.at/DocView.axd?CobId=60026 (Accessed: 16 October 2015).

Life Sharers 2015. *Organs for Organ Donors*. Available at: www.lifesharers.org (Accessed: 16 October 2015).

Loewy, Erich H. 1989. *Textbook of Medical Ethics*. New York, NY: Plenum.

Loewy, Erich H. and Loewy, Roberta S. 2007. 'Framing Issues in Health Care: Do American Ideals Demand Basic Health Care and Other Social Necessities For All?', *Health Care Analysis: HCA; Journal of Health Philosophy and Policy* 15(4): 261–271.

Lord Ashcroft Polls 2015. *The People, the Parties and the NHS*. Available at: www.lordashcroftpolls.com/wp-content/uploads/2015/01/The-People-the-Parties-and-the-NHS-LORD-ASHCROFT-POLLS1.pdf (Accessed: 10 October 2015).

Lunshof, Jeantine E., Chadwick, Ruth, Vorhaus, Daniel B., and Church, George M. 2008. 'From Genetic Privacy to Open Consent', *Nature Review Genetics* 9(5): 406–411.

Lunshof, Jeantine E., Church, George M., and Prainsack, Barbara 2014. 'Raw Personal Data: Providing Access', *Science* 343(6169): 373–374.

Lyotard, Jean-François 1984. *The Postmodern Condition.* (1st edn). Minneapolis, MN: University of Minnesota Press.

MacIntyre, Alasdair C. 1981. *After Virtue. A Study in Moral Theory.* (2nd edn). Notre Dame, IN: University of Notre Dame Press.

Mack, Eric 2015. 'Robert Nozicks's Political Philosophy', in Zalta, Edward N. (ed.), *The Stanford Encyclopedia of Philosophy.* (Summer 2015 edn). Available at: www .plato.stanford.edu/archives/sum2015/entries/nozick-political/ (Accessed: 10 October 2015).

Mackenzie, Catriona and Stoljar, Nathalie, 2000. *Relational Autonomy. Feminist Perspectives on Autonomy, Agency, and the Social Self.* New York, NY: Oxford University Press.

Maclean, Alasdair 2013. *Autonomy, Informed Consent and Medical Law. A Relational Challenge.* Cambridge: Cambridge University Press.

Made, Jan van der, Ter Meulen, Ruud, and Burg, Masja van den 2010. 'Solidarity and Care in the Netherlands', in Ter Meulen, Ruud, Arts, Wil, and Muffels, Ruud (eds), *Solidarity in Health and Social Care in Europe.* Dordrecht: Kluwer, pp. 229–253.

Malhotra, Aseem, Maughan, D., Ansell, J., Lehman, R., Henderson, A., Gray, M., Stephenson, T., and Bailey, S. 2015. 'Choosing Wisely in the UK: the Academy of Medical Royal Colleges' Iniative to Reduce the Harms of Too Much Medicine', *British Medical Journal* 350.

Manson, Neil C. and O'Neill, Onora 2007. *Rethinking Informed Consent in Bioethics.* Cambridge: Cambridge University Press.

Maple, Hannah, Chilcot, Joseph, Burnapp, Lisa, Gibbs, Paul, Santhouse, Alastair, Norton, Sam, Weinman, J., and Mamode, N. 2014. 'Motivations, Outcomes, and Characteristics of Unspecified (Nondirected Altruistic) Kidney Donors in the United Kingdom', *Transplantation* 98(11): 1182–9.

Margalit, Avishai 2009. *The Decent Society.* Harvard, MA: Harvard University Press.

Marmot, Michael, Atkinson, Tony, Bell, John, Black, Carol, Broadfoot, Patricia, Cumberlege, Julia, Diamond, Ian, Gilmore, Ian, Ham, Chris, Meacher, Molly, and Mulgan, Geoff 2010. *Fair Society, Healthy Lives, Strategic Review of Health Inequalities post-2010.* London. Available at: www.instituteofhealthequity .org/projects/fair-society-healthy-lives-the-marmot-review/fair-society-healthy-lives-executive-summary.pdf (Accessed: 16. October 2015).

Marteau, Theresa M., Thorne, Josephine, Aveyard, Paul, Hirst, Julie, and Sokal, Rachel 2013. 'Financial Incentives for Smoking Cessation in Pregnancy: Protocol for a Single Arm Intervention Study', *BMC Pregnancy and Childbirth* 13: 66.

Mason, Andrew 2000. *Community, Solidarity and Belonging: Levels of Community and Their Normative Significance.* Cambridge: Cambridge University Press.

Mason, John K. and Laurie, Graeme T. 2011. *Law and Medical Ethics*. Oxford: Oxford University Press.

Matas, Arthur J., Satel, Sally, Munn, Stephen, Richards, Janet R., Tan-Alora, Angeles, Ambagtsheer, Frederike J., Asis, Micheal D.H., Baloloy, Leo, Cole, Edward, Crippin J., Cronin, David, Daar, Abdallah S., Eason, James, Fine, Richard, Florman, Sander, Freeman, Richard, Fung, John, Gaertner, Wulf, Gaston, Robert, Ghahramani, Nasrollah, Ghods, Ahad, Goodwin, Michelle, Gutmann, Thomas, Hakim, Nadey, Hippen, Benjamin, Huilgol, Ajit, Kam, Igal, Lamban, Arlene, Land, Walter, Langnas, Alan, Lesaca, Reynaldo, Levy, Gary, Liquette, Rose-Marie, Marks, William H., Miller, Charles, Ona, Enrique, Pamugas, Glenda, Paraiso, Antonio, Peters, Thomas G., Price, David, Randhawa, Gurch, Reed, Alan, Rigg, Keith, Serrano, Dennis, Sollinger, Hans, Sundar, Sankaran, Teperman, Lewis, van Dijk, Gert, Weimar, Willem, and Danguilan, Romina 2012. 'Incentives for Organ Donation: Proposed Standards for an Internationally Acceptable System', *American Journal of Transplantation* 12(2): 306–312.

Mauss, Marcel 1925. *The Gift*. London: Routledge.

Mayer-Schönberger, Victor and Cukier, Kenneth 2013. *Big Data. A Revolution that Will Transform How We Live, Work, and Think*. New York, NY: Houghton Mifflin Harcourt.

Mazaris, Evangelos M., Warrens, Anthony N., Smith, Glenn, Tekkis, Paris, Papalois, and Vassilios, Papalois E. 2012. 'Live Kidney Donation: Attitudes Towards Donor Approach, Motives and Factors Promoting Donation', *Nephrology, Dialysis, Transplantation* 27(6): 2517–2525.

McCann, Richard 1999. 'The Resurrectionist', in Fiffer, S.S. (ed.), *Body*. Avon: New York, pp. 135–147.

McGoey, Linsey 2014. 'The Philanthropic State. Market-State Hybrids in the Philanthrocapitalist Turn', *Third World Quarterly* 35(1): 109–125.

McGuire, Amy L. and Beskow, Laura M. 2010. 'Informed Consent in Genomics and Genetics Research', *Annual Review of Genomics and Human Genetics* 11: 361–381.

Mellema, Gregory 1991. *Beyond the Call of Duty: Supererogation, Obligation, and Offence*. Albany, NY: State University of New York Press.

Merchant, Brian 2015. 'Looking Up Symptoms Online? These Companies are Tracking You', *Motherboard*, 23 February. Available at: www.motherboard.vice .com/read/looking-up-symptoms-online-these-companies-are-collecting-your-data?utm_content=buffer51fbc&utm_medium=social&utm_source=twitter.com&utm_campaign=buffer (Accessed: 25 February 2015).

Meyer, Michelle N. and Chabris, Christopher F. 2015. 'Please, Corporations, Experiment on US', *The New York Times*, 21 June. Available at: www.nytimes .com/2015/06/21/opinion/sunday/please-corporations-experiment-on-us. html?_r=0 (Accessed: 8 November 2016).

Meyers, Diana 1994. *Subjection and Subjectivity*. New York, NY: Routledge.

Mirowski, Philip 2014. *Never Let a Serious Crisis Go to Waste: How Neoliberalism Survived the Financial Meltdown*. London: Verso.

Mittelstadt, Brent D. and Floridi, Luciano 2016. 'The Ethics of Big Data: Current and Foreseeable Issues in Biomedical Contexts', *Science and Engineering Ethics* 22(2): 303–341.

Mol, Annemarie 2002. *The Body Multiple: Ontology in Medical Practice*. Durham, NC: Duke University Press.

2008. *The Logic of Care: Health and the Problem of Patient Choice*. London: Routledge.

Molm, Linda, Collett, Jessica L., and Schaefer, David R. 2007. 'Building Solidarity through Generalized Exchange: A Theory of Reciprocity', *American Journal of Sociology* 113(1): 205–242.

Moorlock, Greg, Ives, Jonathan, and Draper, Heather 2013. 'Altruism in Organ Donation: An Unnecessary Requirement?', *Journal of Medical Ethics* 40(2): 134–138.

Mooser, Vincent and Currat, Christine 2014. 'The Lausanne Institutional Biobank: A New Resource to Catalyse Research in Personalised Medicine and Pharmaceutical Sciences', *Swiss Medical Weekly* 144: w14033.

Moses, Jonathon W. 2006. 'The Umma of Democracy', *Security Dialogue* 37(4): 489–508

Mouffe, Chantal 2000. *The Democratic Paradox*. London, Verso.

MRC 2015. *Stratified Medicine*. Available at: www.mrc.ac.uk/research/initiatives/stratified-medicine/ (Accessed: 16 October 2015).

Naslund, John A., Grande, Stuart W., Aschbrenner, Kelly A., and Elwyn, Glyn 2014. 'Naturally Occuring Peer Support through Social Media: The Experiences of Individuals with Severe Mental Illness Using YouTube', *PloS One* 9(10): e110171.

National Academics of Sciences (NAS) 2011. *Toward Precision Medicine. Building a Knowledge Network for Biomedical Research and a New Taxonomy of Disease*. Washington, DC: National Academies Press.

National Kidney Foundation (NKF) 2015. *Organ Donation and Transplantation Statistics*. Available at: www.kidney.org/news/newsroom/factsheets/Organ-Donation-and-Transplantation-Stats (Accessed: 20 September 2015).

National Transplant Center 2015. *Know Your Rights*. Available at: www.adi.gov.il/en/know-your-rights/ (Accessed: 8 November 2016).

NCoB 2007. *Public Health: Ethical Issues*. London. Available at: www.nuffieldbio ethics.org/public-health (Accessed: 5 May 2015).

2009. *Dementia: Ethical Issues*. London. Available at: www.nuffieldbioethics.org/project/dementia/ (Accessed: 16 October 2015).

2010. *Medical Profiling and Online Medicine: The Ethics of 'Personalised Healthcare' in a Consumer Age*. London. Available at: www.nuffieldbioethics.org/project/personalised-healthcare-0/ (Accessed: 16 October 2015).

2011. *Human Bodies: Donation for Medicine and Research*. London. Available at: www.nuffieldbioethics.org/wp-content/uploads/2014/07/Donation_full_report.pdf (Accessed: 16 October 2015).

2011. *Biofuels: Ethical Issues*. London. Available at: www.nuffieldbioethics.org/sites/default/files/Biofuels_ethical_issues_FULL%20REPORT_0.pdf (Accesssed: 16 October 2015).

2015. *The Collection, Linking and Use of Data in Biomedical Research and Health Care: Ethical Issues*. London. Available at: www.nuffieldbioethics.org/wp-content/uploads/Biological_and_health_data_web.pdf (Accessed: 16 October 2015).

Nedelsky, Jennifer 1990. 'Law, Boundaries and the Bounded Self', *Representations* 30: 162–189.

2011. *Law's Relations: A Relational Theory of Self, Autonomy, and Law*. New York, NY: Oxford University Press.

Neff, Gina 2013. 'Why Big Data Won't Cure Us', *Big Data* 1(3): 117–123.

NHS Blood and Transplant 2015. *Organ Donation and Transplantation - Activity Figures for the UK as at 26 June 2015*. Available at: www.nhsbtmedia services.blob.core.windows.net/organ-donation-assets/pdfs/weekly_stats .pdf (Accessed: 10 September 2015).

NHS England 2012. *Public Perceptions of the NHS Tracker Survey. Spring 2012 Wave Report 23.10.2012*. Available at: www.gov.uk/government/uploads/system/uploads/attachment_data/file/213052/Public-Perceptions-of-the-NHS-Tracker-Spring-2012-Report-FINAL-v1.pdf (Accessed: 10 October 2015).

2014. *Five Year Forward View*. Available at: www.england.nhs.uk/wp-content/uploads/2014/10/5yfv-web.pdf (Accessed: 16 October 2015).

2015. *Data: The Heart of Personalised Medicine*. Available at: www.genomics education.hee.nhs.uk/news/item/117-data-the-heart-of-personalised-medicine (Accessed: 16 October 2015).

Nickel, James 2014. 'Human Rights', in Zalta, Edward N. (ed.), *The Stanford Encyclopedia of Philosophy*. (Winter 2014 edn). Available at: www.plato.stan ford.edu/archives/win2014/entries/rights-human/ (Accessed: 16 October 2015).

Nietzsche, Friedrich Wilhelm 2011. *Beyond Good and Evil. Unter Mitarbeit von Steven Crossley*. Old Saybrook, CT: Tantor Media.

Nisbet, Robert A. 1974. *The Sociology of Emile Durkheim*. Oxford: Oxford University Press.

Nishida, Kitaro 1990 [1911]. *An Inquiry into the Good*. New Haven, CT: Yale University Press.

Noddings, Nel 1982. *Caring: A Feminist Approach to Ethics and Moral Education*. Berkeley, CA: University of California Press.

Notes from Nowhere 2003. *We Are Everywhere. The Irresistible Rise of Global Anti-Capitalism*. London: Verso.

Nozick, Robert 1974. *Anarchy, State and Utopia*. New York, NY: Harper.

Oliver, Kelly 1998. *Subjectivity Without Subjects: From Abject Fathers to Desiring Mothers*. Lanham, MD: Rowman & Littlefield.

Oliver, Michael, Woywodt, Alexander, Ahmed, Aimun, and Saif, Imran 2010. 'Organ Donation, Transplantation and Religion', *Nephrology, Dialysis, Transplantation* 26(2): 437–444.

O'Neill, Onora 2002. 'Public Health or Clinical Ethics: Thinking Beyond Borders', *Ethics & International Affairs* 16(2): 35–45.

2003. 'Some Limits of Informed Consent', *Journal of Medical Ethics* 29(1): 4–7.

Ould Ahmed, Pepita 2014. 'What Does "Solidarity Economy"Mean? Contours and Feasibility of a Theoretical and Political Project', *Business Ethics: A European Review* 24(4): 425–435.

Özdemir, Vural, Badr, Kamal F., Dove, Edward S., Endrenyi, Laszlo, Geraci, Christiy J., Hotez, Peter J., Milius, Djims, Neves-Pereira, Maria, Pang, Tikki, Rotimi, Charles N., Sabra, Ramzi, Sarkissian, Christineh N., Srivastava, Sanjeeva, Tims, Hesther, Zgheib, Nathalie K., and Kickbusch, Ilona 2013. 'Crowd-Funded Micro-Grants for Genomics and "Big Data": An Actionable Idea Connecting Small (Artisan) Science, Infrastructure Science, and Citizen Philanthropy', *OMICS A Journal of Integrative Biology* 17(4): 161–172.

Paczkowski, Andrzej 2015. *Revolution and Counterrevolution in Poland, 1980–1989: Solidarity, Martial Law, and the End of Communism in Europe*. Rochester, NY: University of Rochester Press.

Paras, Eric 2006. *Foucault 2.0: Beyond Power and Knowledge*. New York, NY: Other Press.

Pasquale, Frank 2015. *The Black Box Society: The Secret Algorithms that Control Money and Information*. Cambridge, MA: Harvard University Press.

Pensky, Max 2007. 'Two Cheers for Cosmopolitanism: Cosmopolitan Solidarity as Second-Order Inclusion', *Journal of Social Philosophy* 38(1): 165–184.

Pesch, Heinrich S.J. 1905–1923. *Teaching Guide to Economics*. Vol. 5. Freibourg: Herder.

Petrini, Carlo 2009. 'Ethical Issues in Preemptive Transplantation', *Transplantation Proceedings* 41(4): 1087–1089.

2010a. 'Theoretical Models and Operational Frameworks in Public Health Ethics', *International Journal of Environmental Research and Public Health* 7(1): 189–202.

2010b. 'Triage in Public Health Emergencies: Ethical Issues', *Internal and Emergency Medicine* 5(2): 137–144.

Petrini, Carlo and Gainotti, Sabrina 2008. 'A Personalist Approach to Public-Health Ethics', *Bulletin of the World Health Organization* 86(8): 624–629.

Petrini, Carlo, Gainotti, Sabrina, and Requena, Pablo 2010. 'Personalism for Public Health Ethics', *Annali Dell'Istituto Superiore Di Sanità* 46(2): 204–209.

Pickel, Andreas 1995. 'Official Ideology? The Role of Neoliberal Economic Reform Doctrines in Post-Communist Transformation', *Polish Sociological Review* 4: 361–375.

Pitkin, Hanna F. 1993. *Wittgenstein and Justice: On the Significance of Ludwig Wittgenstein for Social and Political Thought*. Berkeley, CA: University of California Press.

Poferl, Angelika 2006. 'Solidarität ohne Grenzen? Probleme sozialer Ungleichheit und Teilhabe in europäischer Perspektive. Die Europäisierung sozialer Ungleichheit. Zur transnationalen Klassen-und Sozialstrukturanalyse', in Rehberg, Karl-Siegbert (ed.), *Soziale Ungleichheit, kulturelle Unterschiede*. Frankfurt/Main: Campus, pp. 231–252.

Polanyi, Michael 1962. *Personal Knowledge. Towards a Post-Critical Philosophy*. Chicago, IL: University of Chicago Press.

Portmore, Douglas W. 2003. 'Position-Relative Consequentialism, Agent-Centered Options, and Supererogation', *Ethics* 113: 303–332.

Powers, Madison and Faden, Ruth 2006. *Social Justice: The Moral Foundations of Public Health and Health Policy*. New York, NY: Oxford University Press.

Prainsack, Barbara 2014a. 'The Powers of Participatory Medicine', *PLOS Biology* 12(4).

    2014b. 'Personhood and Solidarity: What Kind of Personalization Do We Want?', *Personalized Medicine* 11(7): 651–657.

    2015a. 'Three H's for Health – The Darker Side of Big Data', *Bioethica Forum* 8(2): 40–41.

    2015b. 'Is Personalized Medicine Different? (Reinscription: The Sequel). A Response to Troy Duster', *British Journal of Sociology* 66(1): 28–35.

Prainsack, Barbara *Personalization From Below: Participatory Medicine in the 21st Century*. New York: New York University Press. In preparation.

Prainsack, Barbara and Buyx, Alena 2011. *Solidarity. Reflections on an Emerging Concept in Bioethics*. Available at: www.nuffieldbioethics.org/sites/default/files/Solidarity_report_FOR_WEB.pdf. (Accessed: 16 October 2015).

    2012a. 'Solidarity in Contemporary Bioethics – Towards a New Approach', *Bioethics* 26(7): 343–350.

    2012b. 'Understanding Solidarity (With a Little Help From Our Friends). Response to Dawson and Verweij', *Public Health Ethics* 5(2): 206–210.

    2013. 'A Solidarity-Based Approach to the Governance of Biobanks', *Medical Law Review* 21(1): 71–91.

    2014. 'Nudging and Solidarity: Do they Go Together?', *Eurohealth* 20(2): 14–17.

Presidential Commission for the Study of Bioethical Issues 2013. *Anticipate and Communicate: Ethical Management of Incidental and Secondary Findings in the Clinical, Research, and Direct-to-Consumer Contexts*. Available at: www.bioethics.gov/node/3183 (Accessed: 16 October 2015).

Putnam, Robert D. 1993. 'The Prosperous Community: Social Capital and Public Life', *American Prospect* 13: 35–42.

    1995. 'Bowling Alone: America's Declining Social Capital', *Journal of Democracy* 6: 65–78.

    2000. *Bowling Alone: The Collapse and Revival of American Community*. New York, NY: Simon & Schuster.

Quigley, Muireann 2012. 'From Human Tissue to Human Bodies. Donation, Interventions, and Justified Distinctions?', *Clinical Ethics* 7(2): 73–78.

Quigley, Muireann, Wright, Linda, and Ravitsky, Vardit 2012. 'Organ Donation and Priority Points in Israel: An Ethical Analysis', *Transplantation* 93(10): 970–973.

Rabinow, Paul 1992. 'Artificiality and Enlightenment: From Sociobiology to Biosociality', in Crary, J. and Kwinter, S. (eds), *Zone 6: Incorporations*. New York, NY: Zone, pp. 234–253.

  1996. 'Artificiality and Enlightenment: From Sociobiology to Biosociality', in Rabinow, Paul (ed.), *Essays on the Anthropology of Reason*. Princeton, NJ: Princeton University Press, pp. 91–111.

Radin, Margaret J. 1996. *Contested Commodities. The Trouble with Trade in Sex, Children, Body Parts, and other Things*. Cambridge, MA: Harvard University Press.

Rawls, John 1971. *A Theory of Justice*. Cambridge, MA: Harvard University Press.

Raz, Joseph 1975. 'Permissions and Supererogation', *American Philosophical Quarterly* 12: 161–168.

Reitan, Ruth 2007. *Global Activism*. London: Routledge.

Renaud, Hippolyte 2010 [1842]. *Solidarité: Vue Synthétique sur la Doctrine de Charles Fourier*. Whitefish, MT: Kessinger Publishing Company.

Rieder, Bernhard 2005. 'Network Control: Search Engines and the Symmetry of Confidence', *International Review of Information Ethics* 3(1): 26–32.

Rippe, Klaus P. 1998. 'Diminishing Solidarity', *Ethical Theory and Moral Practice* 1: 355–374.

Roberts, Marc J. and Reich, Michael R. 2002. 'Ethical Analysis in Public Health', *The Lancaster* 359: 1055–1059.

Rock, Melanie J. and Degeling, Chris 2015. 'Public Health Ethics and More-than-Human Solidarity', *Social Science & Medicine* 129: 61–67.

Roemer, John E. 2009. 'Changing Social Ethos is the Key', *Economists' Voice* 6/7, Article 4. Available at: www.degruyter.com/view/j/ev.2009.6.7/ev.2009.6.7.1581/ev.2009.6.7.1581.xml?format=INT (Accessed: 16 October 2015).

Rorty, Richard 1989. *Contingency, Irony, and Solidarity*. Cambridge: Cambridge University Press.

  2000. 'Is "Cultural Recognition" a Useful Concept for Leftist Politics?', *Critical Horizons* 1(1): 7–20.

Rose, Nikolas 1996. *Inventing Our Selves. Psychology, Power, and Personhood*. Cambridge: Cambridge University Press.

  1999. *Powers of Freedom. Reframing Political Thought*. Cambridge: Cambridge University Press.

  2006. *The Politics of Life Itself: Biomedicine, Power and Subjectivity in the Twenty-First Century*. Princeton, NJ: Princeton University Press.

Rousseau, Jean-Jacques 1988 [1762]. 'On Social Contract or Principles of Political Right' in Ritter, Alan and Bondanella, Julia C. (eds), *Rousseau's Political Writings*. Vol 1, chapter 8. New York, NY: Norton.

Ruddick, Sara 1982. *Maternal Thinking. Towards a Politics of Peace.* Boston, MA: Beacon Press.

Rudge, C., Matesanz, R., Delmonico, F.L., and Chapman, J. 2012. 'International Practices of Organ Donation', *British Journal of Anaesthesia* 108(Suppl 1): 148–55.

Ruger, Jennifer P. 2006. 'Ethics and Governance of Global Health Inequalities', *Journal of Epidemiology and Community Health* 60: 998–1002.

Saghai, Yashar 2013. 'Salvaging the Concept of Nudge', *Journal of Medical Ethics* 39(8): 487–493.

Sandel, Michael J. 1981. *Liberalism and the Limits of Justice.* Cambridge: Cambridge University Press.

Santoro, Pablo 2009. 'From (Public?) Waste to (Private?) Value. The Regulation of Private Cord Blood Banking in Spain', *Science Studies* 22(1): 3–23.

Sass, Hans-Martin 1992. 'Introduction: The Principle of Solidarity in Health Care Policy', *The Journal of Medicine and Philosophy* 17: 367–370.

Saunders, Ben 2012. 'Altruism or Solidarity? The Motives for Organ Donation and Two Proposals', *Bioethics* 26(7): 376–81.

Scheler, Max 1970. *The Nature of Sympathy.* New Brunswick, NJ: Transaction Press.

Scheper-Hughes, Nancy 2000. 'The Global Traffic in Human Organs', *Current Anthropology* 41(2): 191–224.

2003. 'Keeping an Eye On the Global Traffic in Human Organs', *Lancet* 361(9369): 1645–1648.

2006. 'Organs Trafficking: The Real, the Unreal and the Uncanny', *Annals of Transplantation* 11(3): 16–30.

2007. 'The Tyranny of the Gift: Sacrificial Violence in Living Donor Transplant', *American Journal of Transplantation* 7(3): 507–511.

Schmidt, Harald 2008. 'Bonuses as Incentives and Rewards for Health Responsibility: A Good Thing?', *Journal of Medicine and Philosophy* 33: 198–220.

Scholz, Sally J. 2008. *Political Solidarity.* University Park, PA: University of Pennsylvania Press.

2009. 'Feminist Political Solidarity', in Tessman, Lisa (ed.), *Feminist Ethics and Social and Political Philosophy: Theorizing the Non-Ideal.* Dordrecht: Springer, pp. 205–220.

2015. 'Seeking Solidarity', *Philosophy Compass* 10(10): 725–735.

Schork, Nicholas J. 2015. 'Personalized Medicine: Time for One-Person Trials', *Nature* 520(7549): 609–611.

Schuyt, Kees 1995. 'The Sharing of Risks and the Risks of Sharing: Solidarity and Social Justice in the Welfare State', *Ethical Theory and Moral Practice* 1: 297–311.

Schwarz, Seth 2009. *Were the Jews a Mediterranean Society? Reciprocity and Solidarity in Ancient Judaism.* Princeton: Princeton University Press.

Scott, John 2000. 'Rational Choice Theory', in Browning, Gary, Halcli, Abigail and
    Webster, Frank (eds), *Understanding Contemporary Society: Theories of the
    Present*. London: Sage, pp. 126–138.
Scott, David 2000. 'William James and Buddhism: American Pragmatism and the
    Orient', *Religion* 30(4): 333–352.
Sen, Amartya 1999. *Development as Freedom*. New York, NY: Knopf.
Shalev, Carmel 2010. 'Reclaiming the Patient's Voice and Spirit in Dying: An Insight
    from Israel', *Bioethics* 24(3): 134–144.
Shapiro, Steven D. 2012. 'Healthcare Reform: It is Getting Personal', *Personalized
    Medicine* 9(4): 405–412.
Sharon, Tamar 2014. *Human Nature in an Age of Biotechnology. The Case for
    Mediated Posthumanism*. Dordrecht: Springer.
Shepherd, Lee, O'Carroll, Ronan E., and Ferguson, Eamonn 2014. 'An International
    Comparison of Deceased and Living Organ Donation/Transplant Rates in
    Opt-In and Opt-Out Systems: A Panel Study', *BMC Medicine* 12: 131.
Sherwin, Susan (1998). 'A Relational Approach to Autonomy in Health Care',
    in Sherwin, Susan and the Canadian Feminist Health Care Research Network
    (eds), *The Politics of Women's Health: Exploring Agency and Autonomy*.
    Philadelphia, PA: Temple University Press, p. 19–47.
Shimizu, Hirofumi 2011. 'Social Cohesion and Self-Sacrificing Behavior', *Public
    Choice* 149(3–4): 427–440.
Siegal, Gil 2014. 'Making the Case for Directed Organ Donation to Registered
    Donors in Israel', *Israel Journal of Health Policy Research* 3(1): 3–8.
Siegal, Gil and Bonnie, Richard J. 2006. 'Closing the Organ Gap', *Journal of Law,
    Medicine and Ethics* 34: 415–423.
Siegmund-Schultze, Nicola 2012. 'Transplantationsskandal an der Universität
    Göttingen: Erschütterndes Maß an Manipulation', *Deutsches Ärzteblatt*
    109(31–32): A-1534 / B-1319 / C 1299.
Sigerist, Henry E. 1943. *Civilization and Disease*. Thaka, NY: Cornell University
    Press.
Silver, Hilary 1994. 'Social Exclusion and Social Solidarity: Three Paradigms',
    International Labour Review 133: 531.
Simmons, Roberta G., Marine, S.K., and Simmons, Richard L. 1987. *Gift of Life. The
    Effect of Organ Transplantation on Individual, Family and Societal Dynamics*.
    New Brunswick: Transaction Books.
Singer, Peter A., Benatar, S.R., Bernstein, M.D., Dickens, B.M., MacRae, S.K.,
    Upshur, R.E.G., Wright, L., and Zlotnik-Shaul, R. 2003. 'Ethics and SARS:
    Lessons from Toronto', *British Medical Journal* 327: 1342–1344.
Slote, Michael 2014. 'Justice as a Virtue', in Zalta, Edward N. (ed.), *The
    Stanford Encyclopedia of Philosophy*. (Fall 2014 edn). Available at: www.plato
    .stanford.edu/archives/fall2014/entries/justice-virtue (Accessed: 16 October
    2015).

Smith, Christian and Sorrell, Katherine 2014. 'On Social Solidarity', in Jeffries, Vincent (ed.), *The Palgrave Handbook of Altruism, Morality, and Social Solidarity: Formulating a Field of Study*. Basingstoke, UK: Palgrave Macmillan, pp. 219–247.

Society of Actuaries 2014. *RP-2014 Mortality Tables February 2014*. Available at: www .soa.org/News-and-Publications/Newsroom/Emerging-Topics/Predictive-Analytics/default.aspx (Accessed: 16 October 2015).

Sommerville, Ann, Brannan, Sophie, and English, Veronica 2012. *Medical Ethics Today. The BMAs Handbook of Ethics and Law*. (3rd edn). Chichester: Wiley-Blackwell.

Spiegelhalter, David 2013. 'Are You 45% More Likely to Die in a UK Hospital Rather than a US Hospital?', *British Medical Journal* 347: 1–19.

Stark, Laura J.M. 2012. *Behind Closed Doors. IRBs and the Making of Ethical Research*. Chicago, IL: The University of Chicago Press.

Stark, Meredith and Fins, Joseph J. 2013. 'What's Not Being Shared in Shares Decision-Making?', *Hastings Center Report* 43(4): 13–16.

Starzl, Thomas E. 1992. *The Puzzle People: Memoirs of A Transplant Surgeon*. Pittsburg, PA: University of Pittsburg Press.

Steinmeier, Frank-Walter 2012. 'Organ Donation is True Solidarity', *European Journal of Cardio-Thoracic Surgery* 41(2): 240–241.

Sterckx, Sigrid, Rakic, Vojin, Cockbain, Julian, and Borry, Pascal 2015. '"You Hoped We Would Sleep Walk into Accepting the Collection of Our Data": Controversies Surrounding the UK Care. Data Scheme and their Wider Relevance for Biomedical Research', *Medicine, Health Care, and Philosophy* 19(2): 1–14.

Sternø, Steinar 2005. *Solidarity in Europe. The History of an Idea*. Cambridge: Cambridge University Press.

Stirrat, Gordon M. and Gill, R. 2005. 'Autonomy in Medical Ethics after O'Neill', *Journal of Medical Ethics* 31(3): 127–130.

Stoljar, Natalie 2011. 'Informed Consent and Relational Conceptions of Autonomy', *Journal of Medical Philosophy* 36(4): 375–384.

2014. 'Autonomy and Adaptive Preference Formation', in Veltmann, Andrea and Piper, Marc (eds), *Autonomy, Oppression and Gender*. New York, NY: Oxford University Press, pp. 227–252.

2015. 'Feminist Perspectives on Autonomy', in Zalta, Edward N. (ed.), *The Stanford Encyclopedia of Philosophy*. (Fall 2015 edn). Available at: www.plato .stanford.edu/archives/fall2015/entries/feminism-autonomy (Accessed: 16 October 2015).

Stone, Diane 2000. 'Why We Need a Care Movement', *Nation-New York*, 270(10): 13–15.

Stout, Jeffrey 1988. *Ethics After Babel: The Language of Morals and their Discontent*. Boston, MA: Beacon Press.

Strathern, Marylin 1988. *Gender of the Gift*. Berkeley, CA: University of California Press.

Streeck, Wolfgang and Schäfer, Armin (eds) 2013. *Politics in the Age of Austerity*. Cambridge, MA: Polity Press.

Streeck, Wolfgang. 2014. *Buying Time: The Delayed Crisis of Democratic Capitalism*. London: Verso.

Stresman, Gillian H., Stevenson, Jennifer C., Owaga, Chrispin, Marube, Elizabeth, Anyango, C., Drakeley, Chris, Bousema, Teun, and Cox, Jonathan 2014. 'Validation of Three Geolocation Strategies for Health-Facility Attendees for Research and Public Health Surveillance in a Rural Setting in Western Kenya', *Epidemiology and Infection* 142(9): 1978–1989.

Sutrop, Margit 2011. 'Viewpoint: How to Avoid a Dichotomy Between Autonomy and Beneficence: From Liberalism to Communitarianism and Beyond', *Journal of Internal Medicine* 269(4): 375–379.

Sutrop, Margit and Simm, Kadri (eds) 2011. 'Guest Editorial: A Call for Contextualized Bioethics: Health, Biomedical Research, and Security', *Cambridge Quarterly of Healthcare Ethics* 20(04): 511–513.

Takahashi, Nobuyuki 2000. 'The Emergence of Generalized Exchange', *American Journal of Sociology* 105: 1105–1134.

Tauber, Alfred I. 2002. 'Medicine, Public Health, and the Ethics of Rationing', *Perspectives in Biology and Medicine* 45(1): 16–30.

2003. 'Sick Autonomy', *Perspectives in Biology and Medicine* 46(4): 484–495.

Taylor, Ashley E. 2015. 'Solidarity: Obligations and Expressions', *Journal of Political Philosophy* 23(2): 128–145.

Taylor, Mark 2012. *Genetic Data and the Law: A Critical Perspective on Privacy Protections*. Vol. 16. Cambridge: Cambridge University Press.

Taylor, Charles 1985a. *Human Agency and Language: Philosophical Papers 1*. Cambridge: Cambridge University Press.

1985b. *Philosophy and the Human Sciences: Philosophical Papers*. Vol. 2. Cambridge: Cambridge University Press.

1985c. 'Atomism', *Philosophical Papers* 2: 187–210.

1989. *Sources of the Self: The Making of Modern Identity*. Cambridge: Cambridge University Press.

Ter Meulen, Ruud 2015. 'Solidarity and Justice in Health Care. A Critical Analysis of their Relationship', *Diametros* 43: 1–20.

Ter Meulen, Ruud, Arts, Wil, and Muffels, Ruud (eds) 2010. *Solidarity in Health and Social Care in Europe*. Dordrecht: Kluwer.

Territo, Leonard and Matteson, Rande (eds) 2012. *The International Trafficking of Human Organs. A Multidisciplinary Perspective*. Boca Raton, FL: Taylor & Francis.

Thaler, Richard H. and Sunstein, Cass R. 2008. *Nudge: Improving Decisions about Health, Wealth, and Happiness*. New Haven, CT: Yale University Press.

The British Transplantation Society and The Renal Association 2011. *United Kingdom Guidelines for Living Donor Kidney Transplantation.* (3rd edn). Available at: www.bts.org.uk/Documents/Guidelines/Active/UK%20Guidelines%20for%20 Living%20Donor%20Kidney%20July%202011.pdf (Accessed: 16 October 2015).

Tinghög, Gustav, Carlsson, Per, and Lyttkens, Carl H. 2010. 'Individual Responsibility for What? – A Conceptual Framework for Exploring the Suitability of Private Financing in a Publicly Funded Health-Care System', *Health Economics, Policy and Law* 5: 201–223.

Titmuss, Richard 1970. *The Gift Relationship: From Human Blood to Social Policy.* London: George Allen and Unwin.

Tönnies, Ferdinand 1957 [1887]. *Community and Society.* East Lansing, MI: Michigan State University Press.

Tomasini, Floris J. 2010. 'What Is Bioethics: Notes Toward a New Approach?', *Studies in Ethics, Law and Technology* 4(2): 1–7 (Article 7).

Tomasz, Wesolowski and Piotr, Szyber 2003. 'A Trial of Objective Comparison of Quality of Life Between Chronic Renal Failure Patients Treated with Hemodialysis and Renal Transplantation', *Annals of Transplantation* 8(2): 47–53.

Topol, Eric 2012 *The Creative Destruction of Medicine: How the Digital Revolution Will Create Better Health Care.* New York, NY: Basic Books.

2015. *The Patient Will See You Now: The Future of Medicine is in Your Hands.* New York, NY: Basic Books.

Trappenburg, Margo 2000. 'Lifestyle Solidarity in the Healthcare System', *Health Care Analysis* 8(1): 65–75.

Tronto, Joan C. 2001 'Care and Gender', in Wright, James D. (ed.), *International Encyclopedia of Social & Behavioral Sciences.* (2nd edn). Vol. 19. Oxford: Elsevier, pp. 765–770.

Truog, Robert D. and Robinson, Walter M. 2003. 'Role of Brain Death and the Dead-Donor Rule in the Ethics of Organ Transplantation', *Critical Care Medicine* 31(9): 2391–6.

Turner, Edith 2012. *Communitas: The Anthropology of Collective Joy.* Basingstoke, UK: Basingstoke Palgrave Macmillan.

Turner, Victor 1969. *The Ritual Process: Structure and Anti-Structure.* Chicago, IL: Aldine Transaction.

Turrini, Mauro and Prainsack, Barbara 2016. 'The Paradox of Consumer Genomics', *Applied & Translational Genomics* 8: 4–8.

Tutton, Richard 2012. 'Personalizing Medicine: Futures Present and Past', *Social Science & Medicine (1982)* 75(10): 1721–1728.

2014. *Genomics and the Reimagining of Personalized Medicine.* Farnham: Ashgate.

Ummel, Deborah, Achille, Marie, and Mekkelholt, Jessina 2011. 'Donors and Recipients of Living Kidney Donation: A Qualitative Metasummary of Their Experiences', *Journal of Transplantation* 2011: 626501.

Undis, David J. 2005. 'Lifesharers: Increasing Organ Supply through Directed Donation', *American Journal of Bioethics* 5: 22–24.

UNESCO 2005. *Universal Declaration on Bioethics and Human Rights*. Paris (19 October). Available at: www.portal.unesco.org/en/ev.php-URL_ID=31058&URL_DO =DO_TOPIC&URL_SECTION=201.html (Accessed: 28 July 2011).

UNOS 2015. *Donation*. Available at: www.unos.org/donation/index.php?topic=optn (Accessed: 5 May 2015).

Urmson, James O. 1958. 'Saints and Heroes', in Melden, A. (ed.), *Essays in Moral Philosophy*. Seattle, WA: University of Washington Press.

Veatch, Robert M. and Ross, Lainie M. 2015. *Transplantation Ethics*. (2nd edn). Washington, D.C.: Georgetown University Press.

Venkatapuram, Sridhar 2011. *Health Justice: An Argument from the Capabilities Approach*. London: Polity.

Venkatapuram, Sridhar and Bunn, S. 2012. *Measuring National Well-Being. Parliamentary Office for Science and Technology*. London: UK Parliament Office of Science & Technology.

Verkerk, Marian A. and Lindemann, Hilde 2010. 'Theoretical Resources for a Globalised Bioethics', *Journal of Medical Ethics* 37: 92–96.

Vessel, Jean-Paul 2010. 'Supererogation for Utilitarianism', *American Philosophical Quarterly* 47: 299–317.

Voland, Eckhart 1997. 'Die Natur der Solidarität', in Bayertz, K. (ed.), *Solidarität. Begriff und Problem*. Stuttgart: Suhrkamp, pp. 297–318.

Vollmann, Jochen 2013. 'Persönlicher–besser–kostengünstiger? Kritische medizine-thische Anfragen an die "personalisierte Medizin"', *Ethik in der Medizin* 3(25): 233–241.

Vollmann, Jochen, Sandow, Verena, Wäscher, Sebastian, and Schildmann, Jan (eds), 2015. *The Ethics of Personalised Medicine*. Farnham: Ashgate.

Wagenaar, Hendrik 2004. '"Knowing" the Rules: Administrative Work as Practice', *Public Administration Review* 64(6): 643–655.

    2014. *Meaning in Action: Interpretation and Dialogue in Policy Analysis*. New York, NY: M.E. Sharpe.

Wagner, Peter and Zimmermann, Bénédicte 2003. 'The Nation: The Constitution of a Political Organisation as a Community of Responsibility', in Lessenich, Stephan (ed.), *Foundational Concepts of the Welfare State. Historical and Current Discourses*. Frankfurt/Main: Campus, pp. 243–266.

Waldby, Catherine and Mitchell, Robert 2006. *Tissue Economies: Blood, Organs, and Cell Lines in Late Capitalism*. Durham: Duke University Press.

Waldby, Kevin and Doyle, Aaron 2009. 'Their Risks are My Risks: On Shared Risk Epidemiologies, Including Altruistic Fear for Companion Animals', *Sociological Research Online* 14(4): Article 3.

Walhof, Darren R. 2006. 'Otherness, and Gadamer's Politics of Solidarity', *Political Theory* 34(5): 569–593.

Wansink, Brian and Hanks, Andrew S. 2013. 'Slim by Design: Serving Healthy Foods First in Buffet Lines Improves Overall Meal Selection', *PLoS One* 8(10): e77055.

Weale, Albert. 1990. 'Equality, Social Solidarity, and the Welfare State', *Ethics* 100: 473–488.

2001. 'Trust and Political Constitutions', *Critical Review of International Social and Political Philosophy* 4(4): 69–83.

Weaver, Matthew 2014. 'NHS Admits it Should Have Been Clearer Over Medical Records-Sharing Scheme', *The Guardian*, 4 February. Available at: www .theguardian.com/society/2014/feb/04/nhs-admits-clearer-medical-records-sharing-scheme (Accessed: 6 February 2014).

Weber, Max 1964 [1922]. *The Theory of Social and Economic Organizations*. Translated by Henderson, A.M. and Parsons, T. (eds), New York, NY: The Free Press/Collier Macmillan.

1978 [1922]. *Economy and Society: An Outline of Interpretive Sociology*. Berkeley, CA: University of California Press.

2009 [1920]. *The Theory of Social and Economic Organization*. New York, NY: Simon and Schuster.

Weber, Griffin M., Mandl, Kenneth D., and Kohane, Isaac S. 2014. 'Finding the Missing Link for Big Biomedical Data', *The Journal of the American Medical Association* 331(24): 2479–2480.

Wesolowski, Amy, Eagle, Nathan, Tatem, Adrew J., Smith, David L., Noor, Abdisalan M., Snow, Robert W., and Buckee, Caroline O. 2012. 'Quantifying the Impact of Human Mobility on Malaria', *Science* 338(6104): 267–270.

Widdows, Heather 2011. 'Localized Past, Globalized Future: Towards an Effective Bioethical Framework Using Examples from Population Genetics and Medical Tourism', *Bioethics* 25(2): 83–91.

2013. *The Connected Self: The Ethics and Governance of the Genetic Individual*. Cambridge: Cambridge University Press.

Widegren, Örjan 1997. 'Social Solidarity and Social Exchange', *Sociology* 31(4): 755–771.

Wiedebusch, Silvia, Kreußer, Stefanie, Steinke, Cara, Muthny, Fritz A., Pavenstädt, Hermann J., Schöne-Seifert, Bettina, Senninger, N., Suwelack, B., and Buyx, Alena 2009. 'Quality of Life, Coping and Mental Health Status After Living Kidney Donation', *Transplantation Proceedings* 41(5): 1483–1488.

Wikler, Daniel 2004. 'Personal and Social Responsibility for Health', in Anand, Sudhir (ed.), *Public Health, Ethics, and Equity*. Oxford: Oxford University Press.

Williams, Thomas D. and Bengtsson, Jan O. 2009. 'Personalism', in Zalta, Edward N. (ed.), *The Stanford Encyclopedia of Philosophy*. (Spring 2014 edn). Available at: www.plato.stanford.edu/entries/personalism/ (Accessed: 16 October 2015).

Wilde, Lawrence 2013. *Global Solidarity*. Edinburgh: Edinburgh University Press.

Wildt, Andreas 1999. 'Solidarity: Its History and Contemporary Definition', in Bayertz, Kurt (ed.), *Solidarity*. Dordrecht: Kluwer, pp. 209–220.

Wilkinson, Richard G. and Pickett, Kate 2011. *The Spirit Level. Why Equality is Better for Everyone*. Old Saybrook, CT: Tantor Media.

Wilson, James 2007. 'Is Resepct for Autonomy Defensible?', *Journal of Medical Ehtics* 33(6): 353–356.

Witzke, Oliver, Becker, G., Franke, Gabriele H., Binek, M., Philipp, Thomas, and Heemann, Uwe 1997. 'Kidney Transplantation Improves Quality of Life', *Transplantation Proceedings* 29: 1569–1570.

Wolf, Susan M., Crock, Brittney N., van Ness, Brian, Lawrenz, Frances, Kahn, Jeffrey P., Beskow, Laura M., Cho, Mildred, Christman, Michael F., Green, Robert C., Hall, Ralph, Illes, Judy, Keane, Moira, Knoppers, Bartha M., Koenig, Barbara A., Kohane, Isaac S., LeRoy, Bonnie, Maschke, Karen J., McGeveran, William, Ossorio, Pilar, Parker, Lisa S., Petersen, Gloria M., Richardson, Henry S., Scott, Joan A., Terry, Sharon F., Wilfond, Benjamin S., and Wolf, Wendy A. 2012. 'Managing Incidental Findings and Research Results in Genomic Research Involving Biobanks and Archived Data Sets', *Genetics in Medicine* 14(4): 361–384.

Wolfe, Robert A., Ashby, Valarie B., Milford, Edgar L., Ojo, Akinlolu O., Ettenger, Robert E., Agodoa, Lawrence Y., Held, Philip J., and Port, Friedrich K. 1999. 'Comparison of Mortality in All Patients on Dialysis, Patients on Dialysis Awaiting Transplantation, and Recipients of a First Cadaveric Transplant', *New England Journal of Medicine* 341(23):1725–1730.

Wolff, Jonathan 2015. 'Paying People to Act in their Own Interests: Incentives Versus Rationalization in Public Health', *Public Health Ethics* 8(1): 27–30.

Wright, James D. 2015. 'Rawls, John (1921–2002)', in *International Encyclopedia of Social & Behavioral Sciences*. (2nd edn). Amsterdam: Elsevier, pp. 913–918.

YouGovReports 2013. *Healthcare Choices: NHS versus Private*. Available at: www.reports.yougov.com/sectors/insurance/insurance-uk/healthcare-choices-nhs-versus-private/ (Accessed: 16 October 2015).

Young, Iris M. 1990. *Justice and the Politics of Difference*. Princeton, NJ: Princeton University Press.

Zeiler, Kristin, Guntram, Lisa, and Lennerling, Anette 2010. 'Moral Tales of Parental Living Kidney Donation: A Parenthood Moral Imperative and its Relevance for Decision Making', *Medicine, Health Care, and Philosophy* 13(3): 225–236.

Zinsstag, J., Schelling, E., Waltner-Toews, D., and Tanner, M. 2011. 'From "One Medicine" to "One Health" and Systemic Approaches to Health and Well-Being', *Preventive Veterinary Medicine* 101(3): 148–156.

INDEX

Absolute organ scarcity, 146
Actual harm, 120
Affective affinity, 91
Affective communal and rationally
    motivated associative
    relationships in society, 21
Aggregate datasets, 117
Agonistic solidarity, 39–41
Algorithmic prediction, 130
Altruism, 5, 147, 79n10, 147n8, 150,
    151, 153, 165, 169
'Altruistic' live organ donation to a
    stranger, 151–152
Anglo Saxon countries, 24
Articulation of meaning, 45
Autism Spectrum Diagnosis, 128
Autonomy, 51, 94, 118–119, 188
    as guiding principles in health
        database governance,
        118–119
    solidarity and, 57–58
Axiomatic practices, 79

Background conditions
    importance of, 170–173
    for solidarity, 79n12
Bayertz, Kurt, 35, 73, 74n2
'Being alive', notion of, 65
Big data, power of, 99–102
'Big data' approaches, in medicine,
    128
Biobank-based research, 114–115
Biobanking, governance of, 9–10
Bioethical writing
    solidarity as an emerging concept
        in, 6–9
Biomedical ethics, 9

Biomedical practice and policy,
    solidarity in, 168
    importance of background
        conditions, 170–173
    Practical Utility, 169–170
    unlocking and shaping debates,
        168–169
    ways forward in practice and policy,
        173–174
Britain's *de facto* national ethics
    council, 5
Brunkhorst, Hauke, 22, 38
Buyx, Alena, 43n1, 50n9, 61n18, 143,
    144, 154

Callahan, Daniel, 28–29, 82
Call logs, 104
Capabilities approach, 170
Catholic notion of solidarity, 3
Charity, 5, 46, 177
    vs. solidarity, 67
Christian thought, 3
Chung, Ryoa, 91
Circle, 174
'Clubs' of organ donors, 156–158
Commonality, 54, 60
Communal solidarity, 29
Communitarianism, 24–29, 83
Communitarians, 28, 84
Community, importance of,
    178–179
Community vs. Society, 21
Comte, Auguste, 3
Concrete situation, sharing, 56
Consent, 114–115
    and solidarity-based database
        governance?, 114–115

BOOKS IN THE SERIES

Marcus Radetzki, Marian Radetzki, Niklas Juth
Genes and Insurance: Ethical, Legal and Economic Issues

Ruth Macklin
Double Standards in Medical Research in Developing Countries

Donna Dickenson
Property in the Body: Feminist Perspectives

Matti Häyry, Ruth Chadwick, Vilhjálmur Árnason, Gardar Árnason
The Ethics and Governance of Human Genetic Databases: European Perspectives

Ken Mason
The Troubled Pregnancy: Legal Wrongs and Rights in Reproduction

Daniel Sperling
Posthumous Interests: Legal and Ethical Perspectives

Keith Syrett
Law, Legitimacy and the Rationing of Health Care

Alastair Maclean
Autonomy, Informed Consent and the Law: A Relational Change

Heather Widdows, Caroline Mullen
The Governance of Genetic Information: Who Decides?

David Price
Human Tissue in Transplantation and Research

Matti Häyry
Rationality and the Genetic Challenge: Making People Better?

Mary Donnelly
Healthcare Decision-Making and the Law: Autonomy, Capacity and the Limits of Liberalism

Anne-Maree Farrell, David Price and Muireann Quigley
Organ Shortage: Ethics, Law and Pragmatism

Sara Fovargue
Xenotransplantation and Risk: Regulating a Developing Biotechnology

John Coggon
What Makes Health Public?: A Critical Evaluation of Moral, Legal, and Political Claims in Public Health

Mark Taylor
Genetic Data and the Law: A Critical Perspective on Privacy Protection

Anne-Maree Farrell
The Politics of Blood: Ethics, Innovation and the Regulation of Risk